The Guided Reader to Teaching and Learning Music

The Guided Reader to Teaching and Learning Music draws on extracts from the published work of some of the most influential education writers to provide insight, guidance and clarity about key issues affecting music teachers.

The book brings together key extracts from classic and contemporary writing and contextualises these in both theoretical and practical terms. The extracts are accompanied by a summary of the key ideas and issues raised, questions to promote discussion and reflective practice, and annotated further reading lists to extend thinking.

Taking a thematic approach and including a short introduction to each theme, the chapters cover:

- Analysing your own work as a music teacher;
- Concepts of musicality;
- Notions of musical development and progression;
- Pedagogies for teaching music musically;
- Music inside and outside the school;
- Formal, informal and non-formal approaches to music education;
- Productive methods of assessment and transition for music education;
- Creativity and music education;
- Supporting the gifted and talented in music;
- Using ICT within music education.

Aimed at trainee and newly qualified teachers including those working towards Masters-level qualifications, as well as practising teachers, this accessible but critically provocative text will be an essential resource for all teachers who wish to deepen their understanding of music education.

Jonathan Savage is Reader in Education at the Faculty of Education, Manchester Metropolitan University. He is also Managing Director of UCan Play, a company committed to supporting innovation in education.

The Guided Reader to Teaching and Learning Music

Edited by
Jonathan Savage

Routledge
Taylor & Francis Group

LONDON AND NEW YORK

First published 2013
by Routledge
2 Park Square, Milton Park, Abingdon, Oxon OX14 4RN

Simultaneously published in the USA and Canada
by Routledge
711 Third Avenue, New York, NY 10017

Routledge is an imprint of the Taylor & Francis Group, an informa business

British Library Cataloguing in Publication Data
A catalogue record for this book is available from the British Library

Library of Congress Cataloging in Publication Data
  The guided reader to teaching and learning music / edited by Jonathan Savage.
    pages cm
  1. Music—Instruction and study.   I. Savage, Jonathan, editor.
  MT1.G87 2012
  780.71—dc23

                                                             2012037241

ISBN: 978–0–415–68265–7 (hbk)
ISBN: 978–0–415–68266–4 (pbk)
ISBN: 978–0–203–56902–3 (ebk)

Typeset in Bembo and Helvetica Neue
by RefineCatch Limited, Bungay, Suffolk

Printed and bound in Great Britain by
TJ International Ltd, Padstow, Cornwall

Contents

Acknowledgements

We are grateful to all those who have granted us permission to reproduce the extracts listed below. While every effort has been made to trace and acknowledge ownership of copyright material used in this volume, the publishers will be glad to make suitable arrangements with any copyright holders whom it has not been possible to contact.

Welch, G. (2008) 'We are musical'. In Mark, M. (ed.) *Music Education: Source readings from Ancient Greece to today* (3rd edition). London, Routledge.

Swanwick, K. (1999) *Teaching Music Musically*, London, Routledge.

Lamont, A. 'Musical identity'. In Macdonald , R. *et al.* (eds) (2002) *Musical Identities*, Oxford, OUP.

MENC 'The value and quality of arts education: a statement of principles'. In Mark, M. (ed.) (2008) *Music Education: Source readings from Ancient Greece to today* (3rd edition). London, Routledge.

Goble, S. (2010) *What's So Important About Music Education?* London, Routledge.

London DfE (25 November 2011) *Music: Importance Statement*, http://www.education.gov.uk/schools/teachingandlearning/curriculum/secondary/b00199601/music.

Hallam, S. (2010) *Music Education in the 21st Century in the United Kingdom*. London, IOE.

Mills, J. (2005) *Music in the School*. Oxford, OUP.

Pineau, E. 'Teaching is performance: reconceptualising a problematic metaphor'. In Alexander, B., Anderson, G. & Gallegos, B. (eds) (2005) *Performance Theories in Education: Power, pedagogy, and the politics of identity*. Mahwah, New Jersey and London, Lawrence Erlbaum Associates.

Alexander, R. (2008) *Essays on Pedagogy*. London, Routledge.

Swanwick, K. (1988) *Music, Mind and Education*. London, Routledge.

Eisner, E. (2002) *The Arts and the Creation of Mind*. New Haven and London, Yale University Press.

Hargreaves, D. 'The social and educational context for musical learning'. In Deliege, I. and Sloboda, J. (eds) (1994) *Musical Beginnings*. Oxford, OUP.

Fautley, M. (2010) *Assessment in Music Education*. Oxford, OUP.

Eisner, E. (2005) *Reimagining Schools: The selected works of Elliot W. Eisner*. London, Routledge.

Savage, J. (2011) *Cross-Curricular Teaching and Learning in the Secondary School: The Arts*. London, Routledge.

Philpott, C. (2001) 'The body and musical literacy'. In Philpott, P. and Plummeridge, C. (eds) *Issues in Music Teaching*. London, Routledge.

Savage, J. (2011) *Cross Curricular Teaching and Learning in the Secondary School*. London, Routledge.

Green, L. 'Music as a media art: evaluation and assessment in the contemporary classroom'. In Sefton-Green, J. (ed.) (2000) *Evaluating Creativity*. London, Routledge.

Stobart, G. (2008) *Testing Times: The uses and abuses of assessment*. London, Routledge.

Adams, P. (2001) 'Resources and activities beyond the school'. In Philpott, P. and Plummeridge, C. (eds) *Issues in Music Teaching*. London, Routledge.

Somekh, B. (2007) *Pedagogy and Learning with ICT*. London, Routledge.

Hugill, A. (2008) *The Digital Musician*. London, Routledge.

Sefton-Green, J. (1999) *Young People, Creativity and New Technologies*. London, Routledge.

Armstrong, V. (2011) *Technology and the Gendering of Music Education*. Aldershot, Ashgate.

Campbell, M. *et al.* (2010) *Constructing a Personal Orientation to Music Teaching*. London, Routledge.

Phelps, R. *et al.* (2005) *A Guide to Research in Music Education*. Oxford, Scarecrow Press.

Sudnow, D. (1995) *Ways of the Hand: The organization of improvised conduct*. Cambridge, Mass., and London, MIT Press.

Phillips, D. and Carr, D. (2010) *Becoming a Teacher Through Action Research*. London, Routledge.

McIntosh, P. (2010) *Action Research and Reflective Practice*. London, Routledge.

Altricher, H. *et al.* (2008) Teachers Investigate their Work. London, Routledge.

Green, L. (2001) How Popular Musicians Learn: A way ahead for music education. Aldershot, Ashgate.

Fautley, M. and Savage, J. (2007) *Creativity in Secondary Education*. Exeter, Learning Matters (Sage).

Introduction

Welcome to this book on music education! I trust that you will find it to be an informative and enjoyable read.

The creation of a 'reader' in any subject is a highly personal matter. What I have tried to do is present a range of readings drawn from the music education literature that have inspired me over the course of my career as a music teacher and academic. To this end, the work selected here is an idiosyncratic selection but, as I hope to show, it has been compiled with due thought and diligence.

However, alongside my own personal preferences, I have also tried to include work from a range of leading researchers and teachers from around the world within the book. I have obviously not been able to include an extract of everyone's work that I wanted, but I hope that the broad selection of work herein provides a good range of perspectives and styles.

Ultimately I have to fall back on a personal defence. The extracts selected here have all either inspired me in my early career or provoked me into thinking differently about my teaching as my career has developed. If Routledge had asked you to write the book, I am sure it would have looked very different; if I get the opportunity to write it again in 20 years time, I would also hope that it would look very different. This, to me, is the essence of this type of book. It provides an introduction to the work of many writers within a framework of ideas and a structure drawn from the author's own imagination and experience.

But before I go on to introduce the various chapters, I want to reflect briefly on why it is important to develop a broad understanding of an educational literature within a specific field. Again, this will be done within a personal narrative.

In my early work as a young teacher I was curious about the role that digital technologies might play in a pupil's learning. This was in the mid 1990s, before iPods and iPads! I was fortunate to work within a Local Authority (Suffolk) that was receptive to the enthusiasm of their young teachers and, consequently, agreed to pay the fees associated with studying for a Ph.D., part-time, at the University of East Anglia (UEA).

At the UEA my work was supervised by two academics, Dr Simon Waters in the School of Music and Dr Saville Kushner in the School of Education and

Professional Development. Through the careful work of both these colleagues, I was taught how my own teaching could be infused with the ideas drawn from the world of musicology and the rich Stenhousian tradition that characterised the work of the School of Education at that time. One of the key approaches that these two supervisors adopted was to introduce me to key thinkers and writers, allowing me to thoroughly read their work and think through their ideas before beginning to apply specific ideas to my own work as a young educational researcher and teacher. As someone who has always enjoyed reading, it felt like a bit of a luxury. In those early days, I wondered whether I should be doing other research 'stuff' as well. But, for the first year at least, I did nothing but read, make notes and discuss ideas in my supervisory meetings. After swimming around in that pool of rich ideas, my own thinking about a possible research topic began to emerge.

I only mention this personal narrative because it appears to me, working within a university today, that the structure of higher degree courses has changed significantly in recent years. Looking back, the time and space that I enjoyed at that early stage in my studies seems luxurious, but it was an essential stage in my own development as a teacher-researcher.

This book is an attempt to introduce you to some of the key thinkers and writers from that period in my life, including Lawrence Stenhouse, Elliot Eisner, Keith Swanwick, Lucy Green and others. But more important than the individual authors or their ideas, it is an attempt to encourage you to find time, in what are our undoubtedly busy lives, to read and reflect on the broad literature of music education.

Someone once told me that it was always a good idea to read with a book in one hand and a pencil in the other! Despite the rise of the eBook, I suspect that this anecdote is as true today as it ever was. To help with this, every chapter includes a range of questions and some investigations for you to conduct within your teaching. Clearly, it is entirely up to you whether or not you spend any time thinking about these or completing them! However, if you are currently teaching music in any context I would encourage you to spend some time applying the ideas within the book to your own pedagogy. The questions and investigations are designed to help you begin that process. Many of them come out of my own experience of working with young teachers and helping them develop their pedagogy. In my experience, it is absolutely vital that the 'academic' work that you do never becomes separate from the 'practical' work you do as a teacher. The development of a skilful pedagogy is a blend of theory and practice which needs careful integration and constant attention.

The format of the book

Each chapter within the book follows a similar format. They contain a number of extracts, normally four, with a short introduction and summary. Following some key questions and an investigation that encourages you to apply ideas to your own work, the following text encourages you to think more deeply and more widely about those ideas. In these sections the work of other researchers is introduced, often with short extracts from research articles or other publications. Full references for these pieces of research are provided at the ends of each chapter.

The content of the book

Chapter 1 starts with music itself. It explores something of the power of music and what it means to be musical. It considers how broader processes of enculturation help develop a child's emerging musical identity before asserting the importance of a comprehensive and systematic music education for every child.

Chapter 2 provides a justification for music education. It argues that every child has the right to a music education as part of their formal school.

Chapters 3, 4 and 5 consider a range of issues centred on the development of a skilful, authentically musical pedagogy. Starting with the notion of an individual teacher's pedagogy in Chapter 3, Chapter 4 examines the relationship between this and concepts of musical development; in Chapter 5 we consider ways in which the curriculum that teachers offer their pupils can be enriched and extended in various ways.

Chapter 6 picks up the theme of assessment. It outlines some of the basic theories of assessment in music education, examining some of their inherent problems, before demonstrating how a more musical approach to assessment could be beneficial.

In Chapter 7 some of the recent ideas behind partnership ways of working are explored through a broader historical viewpoint about music inside and outside the school. Linked closely to these ideas are the uses of technology in music education, in particular what it means to be a 'digital musician'. This is the focus of Chapter 8.

Chapters 9 and 10 explore the whole area of music education research, both in general (Chapter 9) and through the selection of a particular research methodology (action research) in Chapter 10.

The concluding chapter (Chapter 11) presents a set of ideas which, it is hoped, will help you enjoy a long and meaningful career as a music educator.

1

The Power of Music

This chapter opens with an exploration of the power of music and what it means to be musical. Drawing on four key sources, it considers how broader processes of enculturation help develop a child's emerging musical identity before asserting the importance of a comprehensive and systematic music education for every child.

Extract 1.1

Source

Welch, G. (2008) 'We are musical'. In Mark, M. (ed.) (2008) *Music Education: Source readings from Ancient Greece to today* (3rd edition). London, Routledge, pp. 468–471. Reprinted with permission of the International Society for Music Education. For further information, please see www.isme.org.

Introduction

What does it mean to be musical? When does a music education actually start? This classic text from Professor Graham Welch explores both these questions. Initially published in the *International Journal of Music Education* (Welch 2005), it outlines a pathway for our musical engagement from pre-birth to formal schooling. It asserts that the influences on our musicality in our formative years are deep and profound.

Key words and phrases

musical development, musicality, early childhood, language

Extract

In one sense, it seems bizarre to be asked to be an 'advocate' for music and music education because both have a species-wide omnipresence. We are musical: it is part of our basic human design. The human brain has specialist areas whose prime functions are networked for musical processing. Also, we are musically educated, in the sense that we acquire sophisticated musical behaviors from pre-birth through enculturated experience. We do not require formalized music education in order to engage purposefully with music and to exhibit musical behaviors. Informal music education happens all the time because the experience of organized sound is a key element in our daily lives. Our basic neuropsychobiological design enables us to make sense of, and find significance in, the patterns of sound that are organized as music within our culture.

Yet, despite this human propensity for musical behavior and our desire to engage in musical activity (whether as producers or listeners), it is apparent that we are not all identical musically. As we get older, there is a continuum of engagement with music that depends, in part, on individual preference, the local context for listening or enjoying music, the availability of musical styles and genres and also on our perception and emotional 'tagging' of previous musical experiences—all of which shape the extent to which we regard ourselves as 'musical.' Indeed, there may be some rare individuals who appear to have some congenital disorder with regard to music and who find little sense or enjoyment in much musical activity.

But, for the vast majority, music is integral to our social and cultural environment and to their engagement with it. This engagement begins pre-birth. The womb is a relatively quiet environment and from the third trimester the foetus is observed to react to external sounds, especially to mother's speech and singing, as well as external musics. In particular, although speech is partially muffled and the sound spectrum is reduced for its higher frequencies, the pitch inflections of mother's speech are clearly audible. Subsequently, as newborns, we demonstrate sensitivity to our own mother's voice compared to other mothers, as well as sensitivity to the music of our maternal culture—particularly the music that mother listened to during pregnancy. Furthermore, because our developing foetal life involves a shared bloodstream, mother's emotional engagement with music (related to her neuroendocrine condition) during pregnancy is also shared. Music that she finds pleasurable, soothing, relaxing, exciting or boring to listen to is likely to produce a biased sound-associated affect in us. So we enter the world with a cognitive and emotional bias toward our mother's voice and her music.

This interweaving of language and music, speech and song from pre-birth through early childhood is further evidenced in vocal interactions between our parents (caregivers) and us as infants. The vocal sounds of these adults are intrinsically musical and encourage imitative sounds, spontaneous singing and growing vocal mastery by us during the first eighteen months of life. Mothers exaggerate critical acoustic features in speech (such as emphasizing vowels and raising vocal pitch) when addressing us as young children. Mothers also often have a special repertoire of lullabies and play songs that are characterized by relatively higher pitches, slower tempi and more emotive voice quality when compared to their usual singing style.

These common elements of vocal behavior in our upbringing as young children are key foundations for subsequent musical development and distinctive musical behaviors. However, much of these early vocal and musical interactions are other-than-conscious. Parents are rarely aware of how they are fostering, shaping and framing our musical development. Consequently, any relative lack of interaction between a parent and us, any relative paucity in our local sound environment, such as a limited encouragement to engage and explore with sound, is likely to lead to lesser musical development when compared with others who are provided with such extensive experiences and opportunities.

This diversity of pre-school musical experience needs to be understood and addressed when children enter the educational system if we are to ensure that each child's basic musicality is developed to its full potential, whatever that may be. If musical behavior is integral to human design, it should be equally integral to any educational system that professes to educate the whole person. This is not to deny that much learning in music takes place outside school, but rather to argue that such non-school experience may be haphazard and uneven at the level of the individual. Music in school, therefore, is not just a basic human and educational entitlement; it should be sensitively designed to address the diversity of our musical backgrounds, to differentiate our musical needs and to foster individual musical development.

For example, children whose mothers have sung to them during their early years and who have been encouraged to sing are highly likely to enter school at age five as relatively competent singers. Not surprisingly, children who have had fewer opportunities to sing, or to be sung to, are more likely to enter school as less developed singers. Unfortunately, this latter group are more liable to be labeled as 'unmusical' by insensitive and ill-informed adults. Negative comments from such teachers on the basis of perceived singing ability generates public humiliation in front of friends and peers and a sense of shame and inadequacy that can lead to lifelong self-perception of musical disability.

It does not need to be like this. Such negative and harmful comments arise from several false assumptions, such as people are either 'musical' or 'unmusical' and that singing is a simple activity. Because some children and adults appear to find singing easy masks its basic underlying complexity. Singing involves words and music being interwoven in a complex physical behavior that has strong cultural associations. The pre-school experiences of some young children lead them to focus on the element of the song which (for them) has the greatest significance, namely the words. The same children become much more pitch accurate when asked to focus solely on the song's musical features without the perceptual 'contamination' of its text. Furthermore, there is a highly significant school effect. Research evidence demonstrates that, whilst some schools foster song-singing development in their pupils; others do not. In some schools, children who are relatively less accurate than their peers at age five (in their pitch or word accuracy, or both) can become even more inaccurate by age seven. In contrast, in other schools children improve significantly by age seven, despite having demonstrated the same singing competency at age five, suggesting that there are important variations in the nature and quality of music teaching between schools.

It would seem that many (Western) children follow a phased-base sequence of singing development in which completely 'in-tune' song singing is preceded by simpler, less complex, singing behaviors. These phases appear to be related to the child's particular perceptual focus, which tends to progress from the song text, to melodic contour, to phrase-based accuracy and finally to an increased accuracy overall. Young children also often have a limited comfortable vocal pitch range. This range tends to expand as the children get older, with girls having wider ranges than boys for successive age groups.

As well as addressing developmental issues, school music education will be more successful if it embraces both the plurality of musical cultures within the wider community and also children's initial individual preferences for certain kinds of music (and songs). Popular music and music practices are often poorly represented in school music, leading to a mismatch between the interests and musical identities of pupils and the curricula that they experience. Young children like activity songs and often use play songs for specific purposes and individuals that link to their activities.

It is normal, therefore, for children to exhibit a range of singing behaviours and competences as part of their musical development. Because of their earliest vocal experiences with parents and caregivers, the borders between speaking and singing for young children are often blurred. 'Out-of-tune' singing behavior will likely arise from a mismatch between the child's current singing competency and the particular musical 'task' that they have been set by the teacher/adult. But children and adults who have been labelled or who have self-labeled themselves as 'non-singers' and 'tone-deaf' have been shown to improve and develop enhanced singing skills when provided with appropriate educational experiences.

We are all musical: we just need the opportunity for our musicality to be celebrated and developed. Such is the prime purpose of music education.

Summary

Welch's contention is that concepts such as 'music' and 'music education' should not initially be equated to formal education. In our early childhood, from pre-birth to the commencement of formal schooling, we are engaged in music and music education in various interrelated ways. In particular, Welch identifies the interweaving of language and music as a central ingredient in our ability to respond to sound. The extent to which these early experiences shape our emerging musicality need to be appreciated and understood more fully by parents and educators.

From this rich and varied patchwork of musical interactions in the first few years of our lives, where music is integral to our development, formal music education must be considered as a basic human and educational entitlement. Welch considers what shape or form this should take in the second half of his article. His conclusion is that all children are musical, and that the most important purpose of formal music education is to create opportunities for every child's musicality to be celebrated and developed further.

Questions to consider

1. To what extent do you understand the early musical experiences of the young child? In particular, what are the links between language and musical development that Welch refers to in the extract?

2. How can those involved in the provision of formal music education opportunities build on the natural engagement in music and music education that Welch argues all young children, quite naturally, engage in? How can we avoid the 'mismatch' between the emerging musical identities of pupils and the formal curriculum in the early years that Welch suggests may be a problem?

Investigations

What are the earliest musical experiences that you can remember? What shaped those experiences and who was involved? Whilst it may be hard to remember right back into the early years of your own childhood, if you have the opportunity why not ask those who helped nurture you in your early years about any particular musical elements or experiences within your home environment. These early musical experiences may, according to research done by Lecanuet (1994), 'contribute to shaping auditory abilities and to developing long-term preferences or general sensitivity to the type of sounds experienced' throughout our lives.

Think deeper

Anyone wanting to work in music education should have a clear understanding of the processes involved in children's natural musical development. As this extract has explored, this begins pre-birth and can be affected by the conditions that parents create for the raising of their children. The degree of musical 'enculturation' that takes place is difficult to measure, although musicologists have, over recent years, made considerable advances in this area and can provide a range of interesting research data.

For example, Trainor defines musical enculturation as 'a complex, multifaceted process that includes the development of perceptual processing specialized for the pitch and rhythmic structures of the musical system in the culture, understanding of aesthetic and expressive norms, and learning the pragmatic uses of music in different social situations' (Trainor *et al.* 2012, p.129). Their research assigned 6-month-old Western infants to six months of an active, participatory music programme or a programme in which they experienced music passively whilst playing. The infants who participated in the active music programme were shown to have enculturated the Western tonal pitch structure, had developed a larger and/or earlier brain responses to musical tones, and also exhibited a more positive social trajectory. They also found, perhaps unsurprisingly, that early exposure to the cultural norms of musical expression led to an earlier preference for those norms.

This research provides further evidence that musical enculturation begins in infancy and that active participatory music making, in a positive social setting, accelerates that process of enculturation.

Think wider

More generally, of course, a child's musical development in the early years is explicitly linked to their acquisition of motor skills and their broader psychological, physiological and emotional development. General theories of child development are beyond the scope of this book, but it will be important for beginner teachers to have a broad understanding of key theorists in this area such as Piaget, Vygotsky and others. We will be returning to these ideas in Chapter 5.

Extract 1.2

Source

'Music as metaphor' in Swanwick, K. (1999) *Teaching Music Musically.* London, Routledge, pp. 17–19.

Introduction

In this extract, Professor Keith Swanwick explores how music begins to impact our experience as a human being and, in particular, how in Susanne Langer's phrase, 'music informs the life of feeling' (Langer 1942, p. 243).

Key words and phrases

musicality, musical development, feeling, flow, metaphor

Extract

There is yet a third metaphorical shift that goes beyond hearing sound materials 'as if' they had expressive shape and these realigned gestures 'as if' they had an independent existence. This third transmutation gives rise to the strong sense of significance so often noted by those who value music. This almost magical quality of experience has attracted a variety of names, some of them problematic, including that of the 'peak experience' and 'aesthetic emotion'. Csikszentmihalyi calls it 'flow', and believes that through such optimal experiences we develop 'sensitivity to the being of other persons, to the excellence of form, to the style of distant historical periods, to the essence of unfamiliar civilizations. In so doing, it changes and expands the being of the viewer' (Csikszentmihalyi and Robinson 1990: 183).

Whilst castigating those he believes hold to the universal and unique quality of aesthetic experience, David Elliott subscribes with approval to this idea of 'flow'. 'Flow' is even thought to occur across different activities and cultures (Elliott 1995: 116–17). It is itself seen as a universal. 'Flow' is characterised by a strong sense of internal integration, by high levels of attention and concentration and – at times – complete loss of self-awareness. Similarly, aesthetic experience is seen as 'intrinsic, disinterested, distanced – involved, outgoing, responsive [. . .] absorbed by and immersed in' (Reimer 1989: 103). 'Flow' is really just one more attempt to describe and evaluate those experiences which seem to lift us out of the ruts of life and which have been variously called transcendental, spiritual, uplifting, 'epiphanies', yes, and ' *aesthetic* '. So let us not quibble over what we want to call such experiences, but acknowledge their existence and try to understand how they occur and what their value might be.

Musical 'flow' arises *when all three levels of the metaphorical process are activated*. Then even experience of music as simple and well-known as 'Strange Countries' can be truly 'moving', 'affecting', 'e-motive'. Whether we want to call this 'aesthetic experience' or 'flow', these peak experiences give music a special place in virtually every culture. Writing of participation in Ghanaian music, Chernoff has little doubt about the fusion of music with the life of feeling.

> In music, the contrasting, tightly organized rhythms are powerful – powerful because there is vitality in rhythmic conflict, powerful precisely because people are affected and moved. As people participate in a musical situation, they mediate the conflict, and their immediate presence gives power a personal form so that they may relate to it. [. . .] In limiting and focusing absolute power to specific forms, they encounter power as a reality which is not overwhelming and devastating but strengthening and upbuilding.
>
> (Chernoff 1979: 169)

Remember Roger Scruton's definition of metaphor, 'bringing dissimilar things together, in creating a relation where previously there was none' (Scruton 1997: 80–3). In Chernoff's account the relationship seems to be between chaotic, arbitrary and pressing feelings and the unifying, consequential and distancing form of music which transcends the immediate.

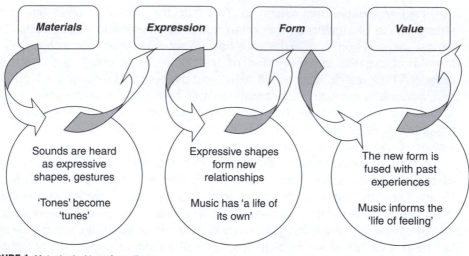

FIGURE 1 Metaphorical transformations.

At this point it may be helpful to consider Figure 1 which is an attempt to summarise in pictorial form the three metaphorical processes implicit in musical experience. The lower level of Figure 1 is of course invisible, unobservable. The psychological processes that constitute metaphorical transformations are hidden from view. But we have evidence of their existence in musical activities and in what people say about music. Out of the hidden processes of metaphor arise four observable layers. These I call *materials, expression, form and value*. I have elsewhere advocated the consideration of the inter-relationship of these four layers as a fertile way of thinking about music and music education (Swanwick 1979; Swanwick 1988; Swanwick 1994). We can now see that they are the manifestations of essential metaphorical processes, giving rise to a strong sense of music's value.

References

Chernoff, J. M. (1979) *African Rhythm and African Sensibility*, Chicago and London: University of Chicago Press.

Csikszentmihalyi, M. and Robinson, R. E. (1990) *The Art of Seeing*, Malibu, California: Getty.

Elliott, D. J. (1995) *Music Matters: A New Philosophy of Music Education*, New York and Oxford: Oxford University Press.

Reimer, B. (1989) *A Philosophy of Music Education* (1989 edn), Englewood Cliffs, N.J.: Prentice Hall.

Scruton, R. (1997) *The Aesthetics of Music*, Oxford: Clarendon Press.

Swanwick, K. (1979) *A Basis for Music Education*, London: Routledge.

Swanwick, K. (1988) *Music, Mind and Education*, London: Routledge.

Swanwick, K. (1994) *Musical Knowledge: Intuition, Analysis and Music Education*, London and New York: Routledge.

Summary

This extract explores the significance of music in the life of young children through the third part of a discussion during which Swanwick analyses what is meant by musical value. Starting with a focus on the materials of music, he argues that musical engagement begins with an understanding of sounds being heard as expressive shapes or gestures; these expressive shapes begin to form new relationships with each other (giving rise to the idea of music having a 'life of its own') and, finally, these new forms are fused with past experiences and ultimately are given value. In this way, music informs the 'life of feeling'.

It is important to recognise that Swanwick presents these three 'stages' as metaphorical shifts that work together to produce a sense of peak experience or aesthetic emotion (what Csikszentmihalyi calls 'flow'). Swanwick is very careful not to present these metaphorical shifts as developmental stages. Rather, he states that 'musical flow varies *when all three levels of the metaphorical process are activated*' (his italics, ibid, p.18). However, in the final paragraph of the extract Swanwick does argue that out of these hidden metaphorical transformations, four observable layers do emerge: materials, expression, form and value.

Questions to consider

1. To what extent can you recognise these metaphorical shifts in your own experience or those of the pupils that you teach?
2. When encountering a new piece or style of music, can you identify any of the psychological processes discussed here as you seek to understand it?

Investigations

Swanwick's notions of musical value and, later on, musical development, have had a big impact on the construction of a particular model of music education within the United Kingdom. In particular, they have impacted significantly on the way that music education is organised around the key processes of engagement, i.e. getting young people engaged as performers, composers, listeners and reviewers. We will be considering these ideas further in following chapters. For now, spend some time looking at the current National Curriculum requirements at Key Stages 1–3. What evidence can you find for some of these ideas in the various statements they contain? If appropriate, read through one example of a Key Stage 4 GCSE examination specification and make a note of any key phrases that resonate with Swanwick's ideas.

Think deeper

Bernard's paper (Bernard 2009) explores these issues of psychological flow within music education in greater detail. Drawing on a framework of ideas from

Maslow's work on transcendence (e.g. Maslow 1971), she also highlights Csikszentmihalyi's work with specific references to music making. In particular, she points to his drawing of:

> connections between the ordering of sounds and the ordering of conscious-ness, and cites historical examples of musicians who achieved flow as performers. Highlighting the powerful role that music plays in all of our lives, and especially in the lives of young people, Csikszentmihalyi laments the fact that music programs are often subject to cuts in educational settings and encourages his readers to get involved in music making (1990, pp. 112–113).
>
> (Bernard 2009, p. 8)

Having explored various narratives of musical transcendence drawn from written responses from her students to three key questions, Bernard's research highlights our responsibility, as music educators, 'to provide opportunities for our students to recall, examine, analyse, and more deeply understand their own transcendent music making experiences as part of their training' (Bernard 2009, p.17). What our students need, she suggests, are 'teachers who can create the conditions that make transcendent experiences possible in their classrooms' (ibid). As we will see, this is a significant challenge.

Think wider

As we discussed above, Swanwick's notions here centre on his play with various metaphors. Quoting Roger Scruton, he suggests that metaphors allow us to 'bring dissimilar things together, in creating a relation where previously there was none' (p. 18). The use of metaphors as tools for teaching and learning have a long history. According to Gorden (1978), one can chart the use of metaphor (and the related concept of analogy which, he suggests, is merely an extended metaphor) back to Greek myths, religious texts and fairy tales which all help readers (or listeners) learn expected conduct. Hoffman (1983) estimated that the average English speaker uses over 3000 metaphors every week as part of their natural language use, and Bowers (Bowers 1993) goes as far as suggesting that all human thinking is metaphorical in some way. It is interesting to reflect for a moment on the number of metaphors that relate to learning itself (e.g. switching on a light bulb, planting a seed, etc.).

As a teaching and learning tool, metaphor can help a teacher relate something unfamiliar to pupils with something familiar. This gets to the Greek root of the word metaphor, *metapherein*, which means to transfer. Metaphors can also be used to specify and constrain our ways of thinking about the original experience. This influences the meaning and importance one can attach to the original experience, the way it fits with other experiences, and the actions that one can take as a result. Pedagogically, this may or may not be problematic. Glynn and Takahashi (1998) warn that metaphors need to be handled carefully within educational situations. Incorrect use of metaphors can lead to greater confusion. Teachers must make sure that the coherence of the metaphor is accurate and clear. There is a responsibility for the teacher, within the classroom setting, of choosing the appropriate metaphor and using it in a way that promotes clear communication.

We will be returning to the whole notion of metaphor in our discussions about curriculum development and how broader approaches to music education can be developed (Chapter 5).

Extract 1.3

Source

Lamont, A. 'Musical identity'. In Macdonald *et al.* (eds) (2002) *Musical Identities*. Oxford, OUP, pp. 41–43.

Introduction

From this milieu of early musical experiences and engagement, musical identities are formed. The following extract written by Alexandra Lamont explores the process by which a child's musical identity develops. As we have already seen, this happens through a process that occurs, simultaneously, internally and externally.

Key words and phrases

identity, self-understanding, self–other understanding, perception, ability, musicality, musical development

Extract

How does a child's identity develop? Two important topics need to be considered when thinking about identity: first, *self understanding*, or how we understand and define ourselves as individuals; and secondly, *self–other understanding*, or how we understand, define and relate to others. Children's development of self understanding and of self–other understanding seems to progress in parallel. For example, at the same point that babies are able to recognize their own reflections in a mirror (about 18 months), they also begin to recognize, and remember, other people in terms of their physical features (Lewis and Brooks-Gunn, 1979).

In early childhood, children's understandings of self and others are characterized by an emphasis on physical, observable features, are inconsistent over time, and are global or generalized. A 4-year-old girl who is good at physical games, for example, is likely to generalize this personal identity to every aspect of her self understanding. She may not have a very accurate understanding of her own abilities, as younger children tend to overestimate what they can do (Harter, 1999). Later in middle childhood, children begin to understand that their identities may be more flexible, yet based on internal and consistent features. The same child at the age of 8 years will appreciate that she may be good at sport but poor at formal academic skills, for example, but that these characteristics remain relatively stable over time (Ruble, 1987). In children's self-descriptions, physical characteristics decline in salience between the ages of 6 and 13 years, whilst social, psychological and activity-related characteristics become more important. Social characteristics in particular dominate at this stage (Damon and Hart, 1988), as children compare their own achievements and attitudes with those of their peers in both self and self–other understanding. Finally, in adolescence, internalized psychological features of self and others achieve a greater prominence (Hart *et al.*, 1993).

We can also separate out the influence of *personal identity*, or our individual and idiosyncratic characteristics, and of *social identity*, which is based on social and particularly group characteristics. Social identity theory explains how interpersonal behaviour (prioritizing individual characteristics, or the personal identity) and intergroup behaviour (prioritizing group membership, or the social identity) are interrelated in self-categorization (Tajfel and Turner, 1979; see also Tarrant *et al.*, Chapter 8). The developmental progression outlined above suggests that personal identity may be more salient in earlier childhood, whilst social identity becomes more influential in the processes of group comparison (Festinger, 1954) that children begin to engage in during middle childhood and particularly in adolescence, in terms of shaping children's understanding of themselves and of others.

The development of identity will thus be crucially shaped by the circumstances that children grow up in (cf. Ellemers *et al.*, 1999). One useful way of understanding these *contextual* influences is Bronfenbrenner's (1979) ecological model (Figure 3.1). The smallest inner circles represent the *microsystems* that children are directly involved in, such as the home or the school. Within each of these microsystems, the individual child is engaged in social processes of negotiation of meaning. The next circle represents the *mesosystems*, which reflect the relationships between microsystems. There may be differences in the processes operating at home and at school, for instance, which will create conflicts in children's lives. The outer levels reflect wider influences on individual children from contexts in which they are not directly involved. The *exosystems* incorporate influences such as government policy and the media. A government policy on working mothers is not something that individual children participate in, but it can have an effect on their upbringing by involving child care from an early age. The *macrosystem* reflects the dominant beliefs of a particular culture, such as the belief in the value of education for all children from a given age, which again influence the course of development.

One change in Western children's lives that may have an important impact on identity occurs around the age of 4 or 5 years, when children begin to come into contact with many more children of the same age at nursery school and

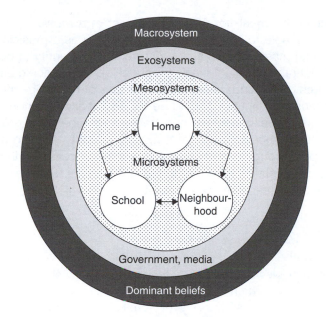

FIGURE 3.1 Bronfenbrenner's ecological model: contexts of development.

school. Before this, children's social identities are shaped largely by their family circumstances. They define themselves in relation to other people within the microsystem of the home, which tends to be a relatively restricted group of parents, siblings, relations and family friends. Perhaps since children are mostly surrounded by people who are more competent than themselves (older siblings and adults), social comparisons are not common in the early years. However, once children have a larger group of peers of similar ages and abilities, social comparisons become more prevalent within the microsystem of the school, having an influence on both self- and self–other understanding (Higgins and Parsons, 1983). Similarly, changes in school systems such as the transition to secondary school are also likely to have similar effects on children's developing identities.

This brief summary of social psychological approaches shows us that identity is based on both personal idiosyncratic features and on social comparative features, and that self and self–other understanding seem to develop in parallel, with some major changes occurring around the age of 7 years (increases in comparative judgements, greater emphasis on social and psychological attributes) and in early adolescence (reduction in activity-related characteristics, increase in psychological comparisons). Personal features dominate younger children's more global identities, whilst social comparisons become more important in older children's more specialized identities, and are particularly influential in adolescence. Context is also an influential factor, and we can conceptualize this at many different levels of influence from the microsystem of the home to the macrosystem of a given society.

What might this mean for the development of a *musical* identity? Children should only be able to develop a specific identity as a musician at the stage when they can master the idea of a differentiated identity (around the age of 7 years). Earlier than this, children's personal identities should be influenced by other features of self understanding which do not relate specifically to music. Children's musical identities should be based initially on external and observable activities and experiences, and being a member of a group involved in music will be an important part of a musical identity. Moving through middle childhood, peer group comparisons will become increasingly important in children's musical identities, whilst attitudes and feelings towards music will come to dominate adolescents' musical identities.

Summary

Lamont highlights a number of binary constructs that affect how a child's understanding of their identity emerges. These begin with a child's focus on physical, observable features which then develop into a broader understanding of their own, or another's, internal features; personal identity and social identity are also highlighted with significant changes in this respect noted around the age of seven. Her conclusions are that a child's identity is based both on personal idiosyncratic features and social comparative features, and that self-understanding and self–other understanding develop in parallel.

In terms of their understanding of a musical identity, Lamont suggests that children should be able to appreciate their own or another child's specific identity at an age when they can master the idea of a 'differentiated' identity – probably around the age of seven. Earlier than this, she suggests, a child's personal identity should be influenced by other non-musical areas of self-understanding; after this, both individual and collaborative musical activities (observable behaviours), peer group comparisons, attitudes and feelings about music will become an important part of a child's developing musical identity.

Questions to consider

1. Lamont is able to identify some specific stages of development in a child's emerging musical identity. How do these stages relate to your own experience or those of your pupils?

2. What consequences can we draw from these observations for the types of music opportunities that we might want to give young children within their music education?

Investigations

Lamont's research described in the rest of her chapter is based on a surprise finding drawn from a survey of 1,800 children aged between five and 16 that explored their cognitive understandings of music (reported in more detail in

Lamont 1998). In responding to factual questions, nearly half the children surveyed described themselves as non-musicians despite regularly participating in class musical activities that included the playing of musical instruments. This issue of how children perceived their role as 'non-musicians', 'playing musicians' or 'trained musicians' varied across the age ranges. In summary, younger children seemed to have a more positive sense of musical identity than those of older children.

As part of a simple investigation, why not ask the pupils you are teaching whether or not they consider themselves musical? How do they describe what a musician is? Which of their friends are musical and why? Like Lamont, you might be surprised by their answers!

Think deeper

The implications of Lamont's ideas about musical identity are important for those of us engaged in the processes of teaching music. We could probably all agree that we would like all children to have a positive sense of their own musical identity. Having a strong musical identity is a cornerstone for one's future musical development as a performer, composer or listener and essential to enjoying music throughout one's life.

However, the social contexts we inhabit in our childhood transmit important messages about the value of music that we cannot ignore as educators: why it is important, who 'owns' it and who it should be for. Thinking deeper about the framework of Lamont's mesosystem, exosystem and macrosystem for music education today, and analysing the impact of each of these on a child's emerging musical identity, is important.

For example, what does it say about the way that society views music education if it is removed from the formal curriculum timetable in a primary school and replaced by an informal set of occasional workshops delivered by visiting staff? Whilst those staff may be highly qualified, will children perceive this in the same way as their 'core' primary school educational experiences? Does it matter if music education is delivered by someone other than their regular class teacher? The psychological dimensions of these changes have been under-researched in recent years.

Think wider

Lucy Green's recent book (Green 2011) takes a broader cultural perspective and includes chapters that focus on these issues drawn from various countries around the world. She emphasises how important it is for music educators to examine, deeply, the broader historical, cultural and societal forces that impinge on the practices of music education. Music education in any country, she argues, is based on an inextricable link between teaching and learning that can be enriched through the facilitation of complementary exchange of ideas between global and more local musical traditions. In her words:

The chapters show how different are the *processes* of musical identity formation, and how varied the *content* of musical identity for individuals and groups in different places; and they illustrate how closely woven musical identity is with music-learning and/or music teaching. They point to a need for music educators and researchers to deepen our understanding of the complexity and multiplicity of the influences on children's, teenagers', adult learners' and our own musical tastes, knowledge, and skills. They suggest that music education can gain in many different ways when it acts in parity and interchangeably with both global and local musical traditions and practices; and that global and local musical traditions and practices can complement and fill many gaps left by more formal approaches to music teaching and learning.

(Green 2011, pp. 17–18, italics in original)

Extract 1.4

Source

MENC 'The value and quality of arts education: a statement of principles'. In Mark, M. (ed.) (2008) *Music Education: Source readings from Ancient Greece to today* (3rd edition). London, Routledge, pp. 344–345.

Introduction

The final extract in this opening chapter comes from the MENC, the national association for music education in the United States of America. It has been chosen deliberately as it focuses on a set of principles for the value and quality of arts education for all children. Adopted and published as an official MENC position statement in January 1999, it was signed by numerous other educational groups across America.

Key words and phrases

policy, principles, values

Extract

We are unanimous in our agreement that all Americans who share our concern about the quality of education in general, and of arts education in particular (dance, visual arts, music, theater), should understand the value of arts education for every child, and we encourage those who will work with us to enhance and support arts education in our nation's schools. To that end, we invite all Americans, both within the professional education community and outside it, to join us in support of the following principles.

First, every student in the nation should have an education in the arts. This means that all PreK-12 students must have a comprehensive, balanced, sequential, in-school program of instruction in the arts, taught by qualified teachers, designed to provide students of all ages with skills and knowledge in the arts in accordance with high national, state, and local standards.

Second, to ensure a basic education in the arts for all students, the arts should be recognized as serious, core academic subjects. The arts should not be treated as extracurricular activities, but as integral core disciplines. In practice, this means that effective arts education requires sequential curricula, regular time-on-task, qualified teachers, and a fair share of educational resources. Similarly, arts instruction should be carried out with the same academic rigor and high expectations as instruction in other core subjects.

Third, as education policy makers make decisions, they should incorporate the multiple lessons of recent research concerning the value and impact of arts education. The arts have a unique ability to communicate the ideas and emotions of the human spirit. Connecting us to our history, our traditions, and our heritage, the arts have a beauty and power unique in our culture. At the same time, a growing body of research indicates that education in the arts provides significant cognitive benefits and bolsters academic achievement, beginning at an early age and continuing through school.

Fourth, qualified arts teachers and sequential curriculum must be recognized as the basis and core for substantive arts education for all students. Teachers who are qualified as arts educators by virtue of academic study and artistic practice provide the very best arts education possible. In-school arts programs are designed to reach and teach all students, not merely the interested, the talented, or those with a particular socioeconomic background. These teachers and curricula should be supported by local school budgets and tax dollars, nurtured by higher education, and derive direct professional development benefits from outstanding teachers and trainers in the organizations we represent. Several national education associations identify the arts as essential learning in which students must demonstrate achievement. (Breaking Ranks, NASSP, 1996, Principal magazine, NAESP, March, 1998.)

Fifth, arts education programs should be grounded in rigorous instruction, provide meaningful assessment of academic progress and performance, and take their place within a structure of direct accountability to school officials, parents, and the community. In-school programs that are fully integrated into state and local curricula afford the best potential for achieving these ends.

Sixth, community resources that provide exposure to the arts, enrichment, and entertainment through the arts all offer valuable support and enhancement to an in-school arts education. As a matter of policy or practice, however, these kinds of activities cannot substitute for a comprehensive, balanced, sequential arts education taught by qualified teachers, as shaped by clear standards and focused by the content of the arts disciplines.

Seventh, and finally, we offer our unified support to those programs, policies, and practitioners that reflect these principles. On behalf of the students we teach, the schools we administer and work in, and the communities we serve, we ask all Americans who care deeply about making the whole spectrum of cultural and cognitive development available to their children to join us in protecting and advancing opportunities for all children to receive an education in the arts.

American Association of School Administrators

With 15,000 members, the American Association of School Administrators, founded in 1865, is a professional organization for superintendents, central office administrators, and other system-wide leaders.

American Federation of Teachers

The American Federation of Teachers, which has more than 2,100 locals nation-wide and a 1998 membership of 980,000, was founded in 1916 to represent the economic, social and professional interests of classroom teachers.

Association for Supervision and Curriculum Development

The Association for Supervision and Curriculum Development is an inter-national, nonprofit, nonpartisan education association committed to the mission of forging covenants in teaching and learning for the success of all learners. ASCD was founded in 1943 and is one of the largest professional education associations in the world, with membership approaching 200,000.

Council for Basic Education

The mission of the Council for Basic Education is to strengthen teaching and learning of the basic subjects—English, history, government, geography, math-ematics, the sciences, foreign languages, and the arts. CBE, with a readership base of 3,000, advocates high academic standards and the promotion of a strong liberal arts education for all children in the nation's elementary and secondary schools.

Council of Chief State School Officers

The Council of Chief State School Officers represents public officials who lead the departments responsible for elementary and secondary education in the states. CCSSO advocates legislative positions of the members and assists state agencies with their leadership capacity.

National Association of Elementary School Principals

Dedicated to educational excellence and high professional standards among K-8 educators, the National Association of Elementary School Principals serves 28,000 elementary and middle school principals in the United States and abroad.

National Association of Secondary School Principals

The National Association of Secondary School Principals is the nation's largest organization of school administrators, representing 43,000 middle, junior, and senior high school principals and assistant principals. NASSP also administers the National Association of Student Activity Advisors, which represents 57,000 members, as well as the 22,000 chapters of the National Honor Society.

National Education Association

The National Education Association is the nation's largest professional employee organization, representing more than 2.4 million elementary and school administrators, retired educators, and students preparing to become teachers.

National Parent Teacher Association

The National PTA, representing 6.5 million members, is the largest volunteer child advocacy organization in the United States. An organization of parents, educators, students, and other citizens active in their schools and communities, the PTA is a leader in reminding our nation of its obligations to children. Membership in the National PTA is open to anyone who is concerned with the health, education, and welfare of children and youth.

National School Board Association

The National School Board Association represents the nation's 95,000 school board members through a federation of state associations and the school boards of the District of Columbia, Guam, Hawaii, and the U.S. Virgin Islands. NSBA's mission is to foster excellence and equity in public education through school board leadership.

There is a demonstrated, direct correlation between improved SAT scores and time spent studying the arts. In 1997, the College Board reported that students with four years of study in the arts outscored students with no arts instruction by a combined total of 101 points on the verbal and mathematics portions of the SAT.

Statistically significant links are now being reported between music instruction and tested intelligence in preschool children. In one widely cited study (Neurological Research, Feb. 1997), after six months, students who had received keyboard instruction performed 34 percent higher on tests measuring temporal-spatial ability than did students without instruction. The findings indicate that music instruction enhances the same higher brain functions required for mathematics, chess, science, and engineering.

As numerous school-based programs have repeatedly reported around the country, study of the arts helps students think and integrate learning across traditional disciplinary lines. In the arts, they learn how to work cooperatively, pose and solve problems, and forge the vital link between individual (or group) effort and quality of result. These skills and attitudes, not incidentally, are vital for success in the 21st century workplace. Sequential arts education also contributes to building technological competencies. It imparts academic discipline and teaches such higher level thinking skills as analyzing, synthesizing, and evaluating both personal experience and objective data. Finally, research findings indicate that arts education enhances students' respect for the cultures, belief systems, and values of their fellow learners.

Summary

This extract about the value and quality of arts education opens with the statement that every child is entitled to an education in the arts. By this, the authors mean a comprehensive, balanced, sequential, in-school programme of instruction taught by qualified teachers and designed to provide all children, whatever their age, with skills and knowledge in the arts.

From this opening statement flow five further assertions:

- The arts should be recognised as serious, core academic subjects;
- They have a unique value that must be recognised by policy makers;
- Qualified teachers and an appropriate curriculum framework are essential to the delivery of a substantive arts education for all;
- Arts education must have elements of rigour, assessment and accountability;
- Although exposure to the arts offer valuable support and enrichment, they are not a substitute for a comprehensive, balanced, sequential arts education taught by qualified teachers.

Questions to consider

1. What would your statement about the value and quality of a music education contain? Are there ideas here that are similar? Would you contest any of the above? Why?

Think deeper

Written in 1999, the extract presents an interesting historical snapshot of the campaign for arts education in the United States of America. More recently, world-wide concerns have been expressed about the value and quality of music education for all our children. For example, the Fellows at the Salzburg Global Seminar 479 on April 5, 2011 wrote:

The future of music education is at risk. Our youth deserves an immediate commitment to music as part of the core education curriculum. We meet at a time when music education, across the world, is under threat. The inspiration and rewards unleashed by music are universal benefits that must be available to all as a human right. All children from the earliest age should have the opportunity to:

- Unlock musical creativity,
- Fulfil musical potential,
- Develop musical expertise,
- Shine for their musical achievements,
- Encounter great music from all cultures, and
- Share their new-found skills of creativity, teamwork, empathy, and discipline.

(Salzburg Global Seminar 2011)

Now, it appears, more than ever, music educators around the globe have to campaign hard for the serious inclusion of music education within every child's educational entitlement. Statements such as those put together by the MENC (Extract 1.4), and those written by the Salzburg Fellows, can be very useful resources for our continued advocacy.

Think wider

The MENC statement makes a significant play on a number of key features for arts education. Not least amongst these are the notions that teachers need to be qualified and that a systematic and sequential curriculum needs to be put in place. Both, the statement asserts, are requirements for the type of arts education it seeks to promote.

This link between the teacher and the curriculum has strong resonances in the educational literature. For Lawrence Stenhouse, there was no curriculum development without teacher development. He was an outspoken critic of what he saw as the de-professionalisation of the teacher through 'objective'-based curriculum models. These, he said, 'rest on an acceptance of the teacher as a kind of intellectually navvy' (Stenhouse 1980, p. 85). An objectives based curriculum, he argued, 'is like a site-plan, simplified so that people know exactly where to dig their trenches without having to know why' (ibid).

For Stenhouse, such curriculum models were a symbol of distrust of the teacher. He worked hard to challenge such approaches. More than that, he developed alternative ideas that reasserted the teacher's role in curriculum planning and development. If, as he wrote, 'it seems odd to minimise the use of the most expensive resource in the school' (Stenhouse 1975, p. 24), it would be better to 'reinvest in the teacher and to construct the curriculum in ways that would enhance teachers' understanding and capability' (Ruddock 1995, p. 5). We will be returning to the ideas of Stenhouse in the following chapters.

Conclusion

This introductory chapter has looked at the power of music. Through the four extracts we have considered what it is to be musical, how our musicality develops in the early part of our lives leading to the formation of our musical identity, and the importance of a sustained and systematic music education for every child. In the following chapter we are going to pick up on one of these themes in more detail, and ask why a music education for every child is so important.

References

Bernard, R. (2009) 'Music Making, Transcendence, Flow, and Music Education'. *International Journal of Education & the Arts*, 10 (14). http://www.ijea.org/v10n14/ [last accessed 5/5/12].

Bowers, C. (1993) *Critical Essays on Education, Modernity, and the Recovery of the Ecological Imperative*. New York, Teachers' College Press.

Csikszentmihalyi, M. (1990) *Flow: The psychology of optimal experience*. New York, Harper & Row.

Gorden, D. (1978) *Therapeutic Metaphors*. Cupertino, CA, Meta.

Glynn, S. and Takahashi, T (1998) 'Learning from Analogy-enhanced Science Texts. *Journal of Research in Science Teaching*, 35, 1129–1149.

Green, L. (ed.) (2011) *Learning, Teaching and Musical Identity: Voices across cultures*. Indiana, Indiana State University.

Hoffman, R. (1983) 'Recent Research on Metaphor'. *Semiotic Inquiry*, 3, 35–62.

Lamont, A. (1998) 'Music, Education and the Development of Pitch Perception: The role of context, age and musical experience'. *Psychology of Music* 26, pp. 7–25.

Lecanuet, J. (1994) 'Prenatal auditory experience'. In Deliège, I. & Sloboda, J. (eds) (1994) *Musical Beginnings: Origins and development of musical competence*. Oxford, Oxford University Press.

Langer, S. (1942) *Philosophy in a New Key*. New York and Cambridge, MA, Mentor Books and Harvard University Press.

Maslow, A. (1971) *The Farther Reaches of Human Nature*. New York, Viking.

Ruddock, J. (1995) (ed.) *An Education that Empowers: A collection of lectures in memory of Lawrence Stenhouse*. Clevedon (Avon), Multilingual Matters.

Salzburg Global Seminar (2011) http://mfym.org.uk/wp-content/ploads/2011/04/Final-Salzburg-Music-Manifesto.pdf [last accessed 05/05/2012]

Stenhouse, L. (1980) 'Product or process? A reply to Brian Crittenden', reprinted in Ruddock, J. and Hopkins, D. (eds) (1985) *Research as a Basis for Teaching*. London, Heinemann Educational.

Stenhouse, L. (1975) *An Introduction to Curriculum Research and Development*. London, Heinemann Educational.

Trainor, L., Celine, M., Gerry, D., Whiskin, E. & Andrea, U. (2012) 'Becoming Musically Enculturated: Effects of music classes for infants on brain and behavior'. *Annals of the New York Academy of Sciences (Issue: The Neurosciences and Music IV: Learning and Memory)* pp. 129–138.

Welch, G. (2005) 'We are Musical'. *International Journal of Music Education* 23:2, 117.

Music Education for All

This chapter explores a number of justifications for music education. As a busy student or teacher, perhaps you have not had the opportunity recently to stop and think why music education is important. Is it important? Is it important for every child? Why? In the previous chapter, we began to consider a range of answers to these questions drawn from various pieces of literature.

In the discussion surrounding the final extract of the previous chapter, the findings of a group of academics who met in Salzburg were discussed. They argued that across the world the threats to a comprehensive and systematic music education for every child as part of their compulsory schooling are becoming increasingly apparent. Writing here in the United Kingdom towards the end of 2012, the National Curriculum is under review and there is a considerable amount of debate amongst the music education community as to whether or not music education will remain a core subject within a new National Curriculum (to be taught in schools from September 2014). Similar debates and discussions are being held in other countries too. The first extract explores these issues within the context of schooling in the United States of America.

Extract 2.1

Source

Goble, S. (2010) *What's So Important About Music Education?* London, Routledge, pp. 7–8.

Introduction

This extract asks a difficult question. Within the United States of America, despite the concerted and well-meaning efforts of music teachers to keep the music education experience they offer to students contemporary and engaging, why are music education classes frequently being cut from the curriculum? The main reason behind these cuts seems to be that the senior managers responsible for the curriculum consider music as not being as important as other subjects within the curriculum. American music educators are having to fight for music's place in the curriculum more vigorously than ever before. But, as our extract explores, therein lies another problem.

Key words and phrases

curriculum, entitlement, justification, principles, advocacy, benefit

Extract

Despite their continuing efforts (such as the Tanglewood Symposium) to keep the subject matter of music education generally relevant to the mainstream concerns of the nation, music classes are periodically and not infrequently cut from the curriculum of the public schools. This often occurs with little advance warning from the school administrators who eliminate them. Music classes are removed from schools usually not for reasons stemming from the cultural and religious differences described earlier, but more typically on the basis that music is not a "sufficiently important" subject (as compared with other subjects) to warrant sustained support.

Music classes are most often eliminated when a school district is suffering financial difficulties or when questions are being raised about a school's effectiveness in teaching the so-called basic subjects (e.g., mathematics and reading). They also may be cut when a school or district undergoes a change in its chief administrators and thus in its guiding educational philosophy. The continuing presence of music education in the schools can be attributed to several factors: to its long, past history of inclusion in the schools, to the positive experiences many parents have had with their children's performance programs and their subsequent enthusiastic lobbying, to the past positive experiences in music education of some school administrators during their own public-school education, and perhaps also to the persistent, publicly visible advocacy of music educators, which stems from their steadfast conviction that the study of music and musical involvement play an important role in the developing lives of young people. The typically strong supporting statements from groups of community members and the often moderate acceptance of many school administrators and government officials even in times of financial crises confirm that some Americans believe music education in the schools to be societally important.

Despite these bases of support, the profession encounters one of its greatest challenges at those times when the role of music in the schools must be explained and its place there justified. When the question is asked, "What place does music have in the education of young people in the United States?", the spectrum of answers given by parents, music teachers, and seasoned scholars in music and education have seemed to many administrators and other listeners to range from such emotion-laden arguments to such disparately biased philosophical positions that they find them difficult to consider seriously. To accomplished amateur or professional musicians, just raising the question of music's importance in education seems odd; the answer seems quite evident to them, though difficult to articulate. Even among the numerous non-musicians who concede the importance of the various arts to society for one reason or another, the role of music in education seems debatable. Some educational writers have pointed out that music is present in nearly all world cultures and that it has been included in the Western educational forum since the time of the ancient Greeks, but arguments that present curricula should necessarily follow practices of the past that have evolved in different social conditions are difficult to accept, though they seem worthy of consideration.

While the importance that citizens of the U.S. ascribe to music education differs widely among individuals and communities, the importance they collectively give to music seems beyond question. It is difficult to find a social situation that does not include "background" music provided by radio or television; food and department stores, restaurants, elevators, offices, and many homes are rarely silent during waking hours. Many citizens participate in musical activities in clubs, theaters, temples, churches, and in their own homes. Sales of musical recordings, while variable over time, are generally very high: In 2008, more than 384.7 million CD album recordings were sold nationally, 568.9 million albums were downloaded, over 1.022 trillion singles were downloaded, and total domestic revenue for the U.S. music industry was over $8.48 billion.[1]

Given the ubiquity of and the widespread interest in music in the U.S., the question inevitably arises as to why music education is not more consistently supported. If one believes that the essential purpose of public education is to help young people learn how to live as successful participants in and contributors to their society, then it must be conceded that most Americans do not now regard musical learning as being as important in the education of their children as study in mathematical, literacy, and vocational-technological areas. While a comparatively small number of children do grow up to pursue music-related occupations, most individuals do not regard musical skill and understanding as being as central to their lives as their skills in these other areas. Still, music's notable presence as a human activity observable in nearly all human societies, its consistent inclusion in Western educational curricula since at least the time of ancient Greece, and the pervasiveness of music listening, record buying, and amateur music making in the lives of U.S. citizens—considered collectively—suggest that music is an important aspect of human life, including the lives of Americans. After so many years of striving to justify and explain the importance of music's inclusion in U.S. schools, the supporters of public-school music education are frustrated with not being able to articulate a single, timeless, unifying theme underlying all of the explanations that would secure a continuing place for it in school curricula.

Notes

1.   2008 Year-End Shipment Statistics on U.S. Recorded Music. Recording Industry Association of America, http://www.riaa.com/keystatistics.php (accessed April 21, 2009).

Summary

Goble's argument is that it is difficult, if not impossible, to provide an adequate summary of the benefits of a music education in a written statement. Therefore, the spectrum of answers that differing groups of people (parents, teachers, students, etc.) produce appear fragmented and disparate. For some, even questioning the importance of a deeply held, life-affirming and integral element of our human nature appears outrageous. This questioning behind the assumptions of the benefits of a music education are, perhaps, even further complicated by the apparent importance attached to music within wider cultural settings. Given, in Goble's terms, the 'ubiquity of and the widespread interest in' music throughout society, it does appear odd that the importance of a music education is not recognised and celebrated more widely. So, given that music is generally felt to be an essential part of human life, why, as a community of educators, do we find it so hard to justify its inclusion within our curriculum frameworks to policy makers?

Questions to consider

1. How does Goble's analysis relate to developments in music education policy in your country? Are there similarities or differences?

2. What common justifications for music education do you hear in your school, university or community? How do these compare to other justifications that you may have read in policy frameworks or other published sources?

Investigations

Look at the work you completed in response to the investigations in the previous chapter. Draw up a new list of the potential benefits of a music education. Categorise these into two main sections: intrinsic benefits (i.e. things that only a music education can provide) and extrinsic benefits (i.e. other 'extra-musical' benefits that a music education can provide). Ask your fellow students, teachers or pupils what benefits they feel a music education can provide and add these to your list.

Think deeper

Intrinsic and extrinsic benefits for a music education are both important. However, there are dangers in creating a divide like this. In particular, the temptation is to appeal to policy makers or curriculum managers through an argument that draws on the extrinsic benefits of music education's wider impact on pupil development rather than on its intrinsic value. However, the other side of that coin is that extrinsic benefits could be more easily dismissed or delivered in other, perhaps cheaper, ways. Getting the balance right in our advocacy is vital.

Think wider

More generally, it is interesting to reflect on the reasons why particular subjects are included within formal curriculum structures. Within the United Kingdom, for example, certain arts subjects such as music and art and design are included; Drama and Dance are not. Tracing back the impact of such decisions on the impact of these subjects in the educational entitlement that pupils might expect to receive is informative.

One of the most recent debates about the exclusion or inclusion of subjects within a specific curriculum framework has centred on the establishment of an English Baccalaureate within Key Stage 4 (pupils aged between 14 and 16) within the United Kingdom. The consequent marginalisation of the arts as schools focused on encouraging pupils (and parents) to choose subjects within the Baccalaureate has led to some call for the arts to be given greater prominence within curricula structures. However, the precise reasons for doing so need to be carefully articulated. Graham Welch provides a good example:

> We need to remember that education in the Arts and Humanities embraces values, tastes, culture, ethics, collaboration, partnerships, aesthetics and self-expression, whilst fostering critical thinking, perceptual and cognitive abilities, creativity and diverse forms of literacy. An 'English Baccalaureate' conceptualization that ignores such curricular qualities flies in the face of history and does our younger generations a disservice. Indeed, an emphasis on STEM [Science, Technology, Engineering and Mathematics] education is unlikely to be the solution to our economic and civic regeneration if this means that the Arts are neglected. As a minimum, we need to insert the Arts into STEM (=STEAM) if we are to ensure that our school curricula are best matched for the realization of the multifaceted potential of all our children and young people.
>
> (Welch 2011, p.249)

Extract 2.2

Source

London DfE (25 November 2011) *Music: Importance Statement*, Music National Curriculum. Available online http://www.education.gov.uk/schools/teaching-andlearning/curriculum/secondary/b00199601/music.

Introduction

Whilst significant changes to the relationships between subjects at Key Stage 4 has been noted due to the imposition of the English Baccalaureate, within the United Kingdom music has enjoyed its place as a statutory subject within the

National Curriculum for the last 20 years. During that time, it has undergone two revisions with the most recent being completed in 2007. The current National Curriculum 'programme of study' for music is prefaced by an Importance Statement. This statement outlines, clearly and succinctly, the key benefits of a music education.

Key words and phrases

curriculum, entitlement, justification, principles, advocacy, benefit

Extract

Music is a unique form of communication that can change the way pupils feel, think and act. Music forms part of an individual's identity and positive interaction with music can develop pupils' competence as learners and increase their self-esteem. Music brings together intellect and feeling and enables personal expression, reflection and emotional development. As an integral part of culture, past and present, music helps pupils understand themselves, relate to others and develop their cultural understanding, forging important links between home, school and the wider world.

Music education encourages active involvement in different forms of music-making, both individual and communal, helping to develop a sense of group identity and togetherness. Music can influence pupils' development in and out of school by fostering personal development and maturity, creating a sense of achievement and self-worth, and increasing pupils' ability to work with others in a group context.

Music learning develops pupils' critical skills: their ability to listen, to appreciate a wide variety of music, and to make judgements about musical quality. It also increases self-discipline, creativity, aesthetic sensitivity and fulfilment.

Summary

The intrinsic and extrinsic benefits of a music education are clearly identifiable in the above paragraphs. The uniqueness of music as a form of communication that can help pupils develop their abilities to feel, think and act are expressed clearly in the first sentence. It is an excellent summary of what music, and a music education, can do for all.

Questions to consider

1. How does the list of intrinsic and extrinsic benefits identified in the Importance Statement compare to your own lists that you made in response to the investigation above? Are there similarities and/or differences?

2. What impact has this Importance Statement had upon the shape and structure of the rest of the English National Curriculum? In particular, how has it helped devise the content of the Key Concepts and Key Processes?

Investigations

Curriculum frameworks like the National Curriculum are fine in theory, but what practical use do they have? Talk to a range of teachers about how they plan for musical learning in their practice. What use, if any, do they make of frameworks like the National Curriculum? What practical benefits does it have for them?

Think deeper

The model of music education that has developed in the United Kingdom owes much to the work of key academics such as Keith Swanwick. Swanwick's notion of 'teaching music musically' (Swanwick 1999) is central to the English National Curriculum. As we will see in Chapter 5, it is something that Ofsted have only just caught up with! It urges us to use what the National Curriculum describes as the Key Concepts and Key Processes of music to inform the very practice of teaching music. In other words, the best way to learn about music is by engaging with music, to 'do' music; for teachers, the best way to teach music is to get your pupils 'doing' music (whether that be performing, composing, listening, improvising or anything else musical).

Think wider

More widely, key definitions of subjects are important in the creation of what might be called a 'subject culture'. It is important to understand the cultural background behind subjects that are taught within our schools. They contain what van Manen called 'ways of being' (van Manen 1977, p. 205) that define our practice as teachers at a fundamental level. For beginning teachers, the opportunity to teach about a particular subject is one of the most important considerations or drivers in their choice to undertake initial teacher education and this continues to affect their ongoing job satisfaction in the early part of their career (Spear, Gould and Lea 2000, p. 52). The generation of appropriate 'subject knowledge' (by which I mean knowledge of a subject but also the knowledge about how to teach it appropriately) is something that all teachers have to undertake throughout their careers. Being unwilling to reflect on and engage with new knowledge and pedagogy about your subject and how it should be taught is very unhealthy for any teacher, however experienced they may be. We will be returning to these thoughts in the following chapter.

Extract 2.3

Source

Hallam, S. (2010) *Music Education in the 21st Century in the United Kingdom.* London, IOE, pp. 2–6.

Introduction

The previous extract focused primarily on the intrinsic benefits of music. It argued that these important benefits shape the structure of music within education and should be reflected on and used to inform ways of teaching about, and learning in, music for all children. The following extract is drawn from the writings of Professor Susan Hallam, a member of the faculty at the Institute of Education at the University of London. In this extract, Hallam explores some of the key benefits of music education for three different and very important wider aspects of a child's development: their language, literacy and numeracy.

Key words and phrases

curriculum, entitlement, justification, principles, advocacy, benefit, language, literacy, numeracy

Extract

Perceptual and Language Skills

Music has long been argued to provide effective experiences for children to develop listening skills. When we listen to music or speech we process an enormous amount of information rapidly. The ease with which we do this depends on our prior musical and linguistic experiences and the culturally determined tonal scheme or language to which we have become accustomed. This knowledge is implicit, learned through exposure to particular environments, and is applied automatically whenever we listen to music or speech. The systems which process speech are shared, in part, with those which process music. Musical experiences which enhance processing can therefore impact on the perception of language. Musical training sharpens the brain's early encoding of sounds (e.g. Patel and Iverson, 2007) impacting on the processing of pitch patterns in language (e.g. Magne *et al.*, 2006). These changes occur relatively quickly. For instance, 4–6 year olds given music training for 25 minutes for seven weeks showed enhanced processing (Flohr *et al.*, 2000), while with just eight weeks of musical training, 8-year-old children showed different patterns of brain activity to the control group (Moreno and Besson, 2006).

Speech makes extensive use of auditory patterns based on timbre (the distinctive character of a musical sound) which enable differentiation between phonemes (the units of sound in a word). Musical training develops skills which enhance perception of these patterns. Learning to play a musical instrument enables children to respond more quickly to the onset of a syllable, and the longer that they have been playing the sharper the responses (Musacchia *et al.*, 2007; Peynircioglu *et al.*, 2002). It also improves the ability to distinguish between rapidly changing sounds (Gaab *et al.*, 2005). This is critical to developing phonological awareness, which in turn contributes to learning to read successfully. A longitudinal study of the effects of music training on brain development and cognition in young children aged 5–7, found that after one year children learning to play an instrument (mainly the piano) had improved auditory discrimination scores compared to controls (Schlaug *et al.*, 2005). Kindergarten children also showed improved phonemic awareness compared with controls after four months of music instruction for 30 minutes a week. This included active music making and movement to emphasise steady beat, rhythm and pitch as well as the association of sounds with symbols (Gromko, 2005). Learning to discriminate differences between tonal and rhythmic patterns and to associate these perceptions with visual symbols transfers to improved phonemic awareness.

Processing of melodic contour, one of the first aspects of music to be discriminated by infants (Trehub *et al.*, 1984), is also important in language (see Patel, 2009). Magne *et al.* (2006) compared 8-year-old children who had musical training with those who did not and found that the musicians performed better on music and language tests. The study showed that pitch processing seemed to take place earlier in music than in language, leading the authors to conclude that there were positive effects of music lessons on linguistic abilities.

Overall, the evidence suggests that engagement with music plays a major role in developing perceptual processing systems which facilitate the encoding and identification of speech sounds and patterns – the earlier the exposure to active music participation and the greater the length of participation, the greater the impact.

Literacy

The role of music in facilitating language skills contributes to the development of reading skills. An early study where music instruction was specifically designed to develop auditory, visual and motor skills in 7–8 year olds over a period of six months, found that the mean reading comprehension scores of the intervention group increased while those of the control group did not (Douglas and Willatts, 1994). Anvari *et al.* (2002), working with 100 pre-schoolers, found that music skills correlated significantly with both phonological awareness and reading development. Moderate relationships have also been found between memory for melody and reading age (Barwick *et al.*, 1989). Butzlaff (2000), in a meta-analysis of 24 studies, found a reliable relationship between musical instruction and standardised measures of reading ability. While, overall, the research showed a positive impact of musical engagement on reading, there were some differences. These may be explained by the kind of musical experiences with which the children were engaged and also their prior musical development. If language skills are well developed already, musical activity may need to focus on reading musical notation for transfer benefits to occur.

Some studies have focused on children who are experiencing difficulties with reading. Nicholson (1972) studied children aged 6–8 categorised as slow learners. Those receiving music instruction had significantly higher reading readiness scores than those who received no music instruction and this advantage was still in evidence a year later. Rhythmic performance seems to be an important factor in reading development. Atterbury (1985) found that children aged 7–9 with reading difficulties were poorer in rhythm performance and tonal memory than normal-achieving readers. Very brief training (10 minutes each week for six weeks) in stamping, clapping and chanting in time to a piece of music while following simple musical notation has been found to have a considerable impact on reading comprehension in children experiencing difficulties (Long, 2007). There are also indications from a range of sources that rhythmic training may help children experiencing dyslexia (Thomson, 1993; Overy, 2003).

Musical instruction can also increase verbal memory, which may support the development of reading skills (Chan *et al.*, 1998). Adult musicians have enlarged left cranial temporal regions of the brain, the area involved in processing heard information, and can typically remember 17 per cent more verbal information than those without musical training. These findings have been supported in a study of boys aged 6–15 (Ho *et al.*, 2003) and appear to be causal – the longer the duration of music training, the better the verbal memory.

Numeracy

It has long been assumed that there is a strong connection between music and mathematics, possibly because musicians are constantly required to adopt quasi-mathematical processes to subdivide beats and turn rhythmic notation into sound. Not all mathematical skills require this type of ability, which may explain why the findings from research exploring the relationship between mathematical skills and music are not always positive. Most research has supported the link between maths and music. For instance, Geoghegan and Mitchelmore (1996) investigating the impact of a music programme on the mathematics achievement of pre-school children found that the children involved in musical activities scored higher on a mathematics achievement test than a control group, although home musical background may have been a confounding factor. Gardiner *et al.* (1996), researching the impact of an arts programme, also found that participating children performed better in mathematics than those who did not, with those participating the longest having the highest scores overall. A study using a national US database also found positive effects for engagement with music. Catterall *et al.* (1999), using the NELS:88 data, compared low socioeconomic-status students who exhibited high mathematical proficiency in the twelfth grade and found that 33 per cent were involved in instrumental music, compared with 15 per cent who were not involved. Focusing on children learning to play an instrument, Haley (2001) found that those who had studied an instrument prior to fourth grade had higher scores in mathematics than those in other groups, although Rafferty (2003) found no effect of the 'Music Spatial-Temporal Maths Program' on the mathematical achievement of second graders.

The contradictory outcomes of the research might be explained by the types of musical activities engaged in and the length of time spent. Cheek and Smith (1999) found that eighth graders who had two or more years of private lessons and those learning keyboard instruments had higher scores than those learning other instruments. Focusing on the length of time engaged with music, Whitehead (2001) found that middle and high school children who were placed in high, moderate and no music instruction groups differed in mathematical gains, with the high-involvement children showing the greatest gains. Overall, the evidence suggests that active engagement with music can improve mathematical performance, but the nature of this relationship, the kinds of musical training needed to realise the effect, and the length of time required are not currently well understood.

Summary

Music has power. New techniques and approaches to educational research are beginning to allow us to understand these more clearly. It impacts on numerous different aspects of our lives. Hallam's chapter explores many of these positive benefits drawn from her consideration of a range of recent research. The strong correlations between music making and language development, literacy and numeracy are clear. As music educators, it is important that we are aware of these findings and use them, constructively, in our discussions with senior managers and policy makers within our educational institutions and more broadly.

Questions to consider

1. What anecdotal evidence can you recall of music's extrinsic benefits in your own life story?
2. Reflect on your teaching experience. What wider benefits have the active engagement in musical activities had on the lives of your pupils or within the context of your school?
3. How can music contribute to the ethos or character of a school?

Investigations

Exploring the links between subjects can be fascinating. As we have seen, each subject has its own particular cultural and contextual background that needs to be respected. But the wider benefits of any particular subject can be felt across many dimensions of a child's life. Spend some time reflecting on these ideas with a colleague who works within a different subject area or has a different subject specialism. What links can be forged between your subjects? In terms of a planning process, what can be done to ensure that a degree of connectedness or collaboration is established to explore these wider, extrinsic subject benefits?

Think deeper

Cross-curricularity in education can take many forms. In its purest form, it is about a way of thinking. Elsewhere (Savage 2011, pp. 8–9), I have described it like this:

> A cross-curricular approach to teaching is characterised by sensitivity towards, and a synthesis of, knowledge, skills and understandings from various subject areas. These inform an enriched pedagogy that promotes an approach to learning which embraces and explores this wider sensitivity through various methods.

This approach to cross-curricularity is not about collaborating with other teachers; neither is it about collapsing subject timetables and exploring a cross-curricular theme for a day. Rather, it is about how an individual teacher thinks about the teaching of their subject and how that thinking informs their pedagogy, i.e. their actions in the classroom. This approach is characterised by respect (being sensitive to the knowledge, skills and understanding of other subject areas); it is about embracing the opportunities afforded by some of the extrinsic benefits that we have explored above, and exploring them in different ways to promote an enriched series of learning opportunities for our pupils. We will consider these ideas further in our chapter on extending and enriching the music curriculum (Chapter 5).

Think wider

Hallam's chapter goes on to consider a range of other extrinsic benefits of a music education. These include positive impacts in the areas of intellectual development, general educational attainment, creativity, physical skills, health, well-being, and social and personal development. The benefits of actively engaging in music making apply equally well to all stages of our lives. As we considered earlier, the paradox is that as music becomes more pervasive in society and our engagement with it becomes more integral to everyday life, the questioning of a need for a formal music education is stronger than ever. Part of your role as a teacher or advocate for music education will be to ensure that its full range of benefits, both intrinsic and extrinsic, are well known and are used to construct high quality educational experiences for all.

Extract 2.4

Source

Mills, J. (2005) *Music in the School*. Oxford, OUP, pp. 3–6.

Introduction

Janet Mill's contribution to music education in the United Kingdom and across the world was invaluable. In this extract, Mills asks a key question: 'why do schools teach music?'. She explores this in two ways. Firstly, schools teach music because they have to. This is not quite as negative as it sounds and Mills addresses this point directly in the opening part of the extract. Towards the end of the extract look out for Mills' explanation of a related but much more powerful question: 'why should music be taught in school?'.

Key words and phrases

curriculum, entitlement, justification, principles, advocacy, benefit

Extract

Once music became compulsory for all students in maintained schools, it could no longer be dismissed as a frippery, a subject only for children thought by someone to be particularly 'musical' (whatever was meant by this!) or something only for children who were not very good at other, seemingly more important, subjects. Until the Education Reform Act of 1988, the only subject that all maintained schools in England and Wales had to teach was religious education. When the Great Education Reform Bill 1987 (known informally as the GERBIL) was published, music made it into the list of ten statutory subjects, albeit at number 10. Music teachers should not have been surprised, as the subject clearly deserves to be in the top ten, if only because of the very high number of schools that were teaching it already. But music teachers have perhaps a tendency to expect to be downtrodden, and some even seem to relish the thought that they belong only somewhere in the twilight corner of school life, and there are many tales of how music made it into the GERBIL, supposedly against the odds. One hears, for example, that a famous musician happened to get into the same lift as a government minister while at Elizabeth House, the building near Waterloo Station that then housed the government Department for Education and Science,[1] so that the minister uttered the word 'music' by association when he went into his meeting on the lofty penthouse floor where many of the decisions that most affected education nationally were then taken. But just who this musician was depends on who is telling the tale, and the musicians who have, at some time or other, got the credit for saving the subject in this way could not all have fitted in the same lift at the same time.

Whatever the reason for music entering the national curriculum, the subject that ministers received was not that which they had expected. Although music's role as an essentially practical subject for all—taught through performing, composing, and listening—had been affirmed for many years through publications such as John Paynter and Peter Aston's *Sound and Silence* (1970), and the government's own *Music from 5 to 16* (DES 1985) and national criteria for their new GCSE[2] music examination (DES and Welsh Office 1985), government ministers and their advisers seemed to expect that the children of the 1990s would be served up the theory of staff notation and 'appreciation' of easy-listening classical works of the ilk of Mozart's *Eine kleine Nachtmusik*, with some dated and occasionally jingoistic songs such as *Hearts of Oak* and *Men of Harlech* thrown in for good measure. In this, they harked back to their worst memories of the personal music education that had left many of them feeling that they were not very good at music, and proposed to recreate this music education anew for another generation. In 1991 the first draft of the new national curriculum for music—itself only a pale copy of the inspirational *Music from 5 to 16* published by the government six years earlier—caused uproar among ministers and their advisers with its seemingly liberal (i.e. musical) approach to music in the curriculum. Expectations of students as musicians diminished further when the National Curriculum Council[3] produced a 'peacemaker' revised version that spoke of offering something not too challenging (or musical) for 'pupils who do not have a practical aptitude for music' (NCC 1992: 16). One wonders who these pupils were, and how they were ever to show the extent of their 'practical aptitude for music', and develop it, if the national curriculum for music did not require them to at least 'have a go'.

The 'non-practical' option within music education did not come to pass. But its residue left a nasty stain on national policy for music education, partly through allowing policy shapers to speak of those who lack 'practical aptitude' without being greeted with the total opprobrium that they deserve. Ironically, the act of bringing music into the national curriculum had diminished notions of what was meant by good practice in music education.

While official expectations of music in schools have mellowed since those dark days, the forces of darkness—or perhaps they are the forces of silence—are still alive. There remain those with purchase on the national curriculum who seem to have had an impoverished personal music education, and to feel that it will do young people good to have a 'backbone-building' similar experience themselves. One sometimes gets the feeling that these people think of education as a matter of survival, rather than as a wonderful opportunity to blossom. Or that they view music as something that they have just found in an old shoebox after many years, or that died out with the Aztecs or the Romans, rather than as a living force that continues to drive and shape people's lives in so many ways, as it has throughout time. One gets the impression from these people that RnB, garage, fusion, Harrison Birtwistle—and even the figures of their youth such as Stephane Grappelli, Ravi Shankar, Stockhausen, Berio, and the Beatles—never existed.

Consequently, despite the fact that schools in many countries teach music partly because they have to, it still makes sense to consider the question 'why is music taught in school' in the second sense of 'why should music be taught in school?'

In 2002 I was asked, among others, by the International Society for Music Education to contribute an answer to this question. This is what I wrote:

Why teach music in school?

There is recorded music almost everywhere in everyday life, but so little music making, and so much misunderstanding of what music is all about. People think that they are 'not musical'. Or that to play an instrument you first have to learn to read music. Or that if they have tried to learn an instrument, but did not make too much progress, this was necessarily their fault. Or that you have to be Mozart to compose. Or that music teachers are only interested in classical music composed by men who are long dead.

Teaching music in school enables us to put all this right before it goes wrong. We build on the natural affinity for and joy in making music—including making up music—that all children bring to their first day at school, and help them on the early stages to achieving their full musical potential. We avoid dogmatic approaches to music teaching that constrain children, but rather guide them as they grow musically, and exceed our very high expectations of them. We make it easy for children to carry on thinking that making music is just as natural as speaking, reading and writing. We show children that there is much more to music than the 'Dance of the Sugar Plum Fairy' or 'Mary Had a Little Lamb'. We engage with the music of children's own culture, and also help them to broaden their musical perspectives. We help the children who become so passionate about music that they want a career in it to achieve their goals. And we also carry on showing all the other children that music can be a major force in their lives, if that is what they want.

We teach music in school primarily because we want children—all children—to grow as musicians. But music, also, improves the mind. While it is hard to catch the results of this in a scientific experiment, or to plan music teaching so that this will necessarily happen, no-one who has had the privilege of observing really good music teaching, and has watched children grow intellectually in front of them, can doubt that this is the case. It may be the raising of children's self-esteem through success in music making that helps them towards achievement more generally. It may be that enjoying music helps children to enjoy school more. It may be that chemical changes induced in the brain by music facilitate learning more generally. Or perhaps the thought experiments that musicians must carry out to improve their performing and composing help children to extend their thinking more generally. I don't much mind what the reason is, but am certain that it happens.

Music making is something that we can draw on to make the bad times in life more bearable. Sometimes this is just in little ways. But I know an elderly man who struggles to make himself understood in words through the fog of Parkinson's disease. The other day, he stood up from the dinner table, moved to the piano, and played the songs of his youth perfectly, and with such communication. I know a much younger man, an outstanding physicist, who has cystic fibrosis. When the frustrations of his life now, and his limited prospects, become too much, he sits down at the piano and improvises for hours and hours . . .

But music is mainly about good times, and making them more frequent and even better. Music is not a gift but a right. (Mills 2002)

Notes

1. In 1987 the Department for Education and Science (DES) was the government department responsible for education in England and Wales. Subsequently the name of the government department responsible for education in England has changed through Department for Education (DfE), and Department for Education and Employment (DfEE) to Department for Education and Skills (DfES). During the same period, education in Wales has increasingly become a responsibility of the Welsh Assembly.

2. The General Certificate of Secondary Education (GCSE) is a national examination taken routinely by students aged 16 in England, Wales, and Northern Ireland, and which relates to individual subjects, e.g. GCSE mathematics, GCSE English, GCSE music.

3. The National Curriculum Council (NCC) was the government agency responsible for defining the curriculum. It was superseded by the Schools Curriculum and Assessment Authority (SCAA), and then the Qualifications and Curriculum Authority (QCA). These latter two agencies also have responsibility for assessment.

Summary

Mills asks two related and interconnected questions in this extract: firstly, 'why do schools teach music?'; secondly, 'why should music be taught in schools?'. She explores various answers to these questions beginning with the mundane and ending with the profound. Mills' final sentence is a call for us to be advocates for music education as an educational right for every child.

Questions to consider

1. If music is not a gift but a right, what are the consequences for the way that music education is organised and delivered within our schools?

2. How would policy makers or senior managers within our schools treat Music if it was either (i) removed from the National Curriculum; or (ii) placed in a second tier or alongside subjects with little or no statutory guidance about what they should include and how they ought to be taught?

Investigations

During this and the opening chapter of the book, we have explored a number of sets of powerful ideas about music and music education. These have culminated in Mills' assertion that access and engagement with music is the right of every child. Drawing on these statements and your own thinking, write your own statement that answers the question that Mills posed in this extract ('why teach music in school?'). As part of the process of writing this statement, why not ask your pupils what their responses would be to this question. What reasons can they give? You might be surprised.

Conclusion

These opening two chapters have explored a range of ideas about music and music education. In particular, they have tried to give a broader overview of some contemporary thinking about the varied and extensive benefits of a music education for every child. In the following chapter we will explore how this can be achieved through the construction of an appropriate musical pedagogy.

References

Savage, J. (2011) *Cross-Curricular Teaching and Learning in the Secondary School*. London, Routledge.

Spear, M., Gould, K. and Lee, B. (2000) 'Who Would be a Teacher? A review of factors motivating and demotivating prospective and practising teachers'. Slough, NFER.

Swanwick, K. (1999) *Teaching Music Musically*. London, Routledge.

van Manen, M. (1977) 'Linking Ways of Knowing with Ways of Being Practical'. *Curriculum Inquiry* 6:3, 205–228.

Welch, G. (2011) 'The Arts and Humanities, Technology and the 'English Baccalaureate': STEAM not STEM'. *Journal of Music, Technology and Education* 4: 2 & 3, 245–250.

3

Your Musical Pedagogy

This sections explores what a musical pedagogy looks like conceptually and practically. Drawing on five extracts, we will consider some of the foundational approaches that you could adopt to construct your own pedagogy for teaching music. Swanwick's maxim of teaching music musically will be central throughout the chapter.

Extract 3.1

Source

Pineau, E. 'Teaching is performance: reconceptualizing a problematic metaphor'. In Alexander, B., Anderson, G. & Gallegos, B. (eds) (2005) *Performance Theories in Education: Power, pedagogy, and the politics of identity*. Mahwah, New Jersey and London, Lawrence Erlbaum Associates, pp. 17–21.

Introduction

How should we describe the act of music teaching? Is it a craft? Is it an art? What metaphors have writers explored for the development of a pedagogy for music teaching? The following extract explores two metaphors that will help introduce us to this chapter focusing on pedagogy: the 'teacher as actor' and the 'teacher as artist'. As with all metaphors, there are elements here that will enhance as well as constrain our thinking.

Key words and phrases

artist, actor, pedagogy, performance, teaching, communication, reflection

Extract

Over the last decade, performance has emerged in educational literature as a metaphor for instructional communication, a method of participatory instruction, and a paradigm for educational experience. Educators have been encouraged to conceive of themselves as 'actors' engaged in instructional dramas (Timpson & Tobin, 1982; Rubin, 1985), as 'artists' operating on intuition and creativity (Dawe, 1984; Hill, 1985; Barrell, 1991), and as 'directors' who orchestrate learning experiences (Park-Fuller, 1991). Theories and methods of kinesthetic learning have been collected in a special issue of *Educational Forum*, and courses that have performance as both the topic and the method of instruction have been published in mainstream education journals (Harrison-Pepper, 1991; Fuoss & Hill, 1992). Reform-minded educators are beginning to use performance to conceptualize educational culture by examining the rules, roles, and rituals that engage its participants (McLaren, 1986, 1988). Despite this burgeoning interest in performance, however, the ways in which educators are playing out the teaching-performance analogy have not recognized the value of performance as a generative metaphor for educational phenomena. To date, most research literature uses performance solely as a method of enhancing instructional communication. These articles, which might be loosely categorized around the 'teacher-as-actor' and 'teacher-as-artist' metaphors, rely on a reductive, actor-centered model that impoverishes both educational and performative experience. In what follows, I sketch in broad strokes some of the characteristics and limitations of these instructional metaphors.

Teacher as Actor

Ironically, many who ground themselves most explicitly in performance terminology are constructing the weakest cases. The teacher-as-actor metaphor is based on an undifferentiated equation of educational and theatrical experiences, and a wholly 'actor-centered' conception of performance phenomena. Performance is reduced to style, and further, to a particular style of enthusiastic theatricality employed to energize one's communicative behaviors. Timpson and Tobin's *Teaching as Performing: A Guide to Energizing Your Public Presentation* is representative of this research. The authors use beginning acting exercises such as physical and vocal warm-ups, emotional recall, and pantomime to enhance paralinguistic and non-verbal communication. In effect, their prescriptive message is that one should strive to 'teach like an actor.' Such studies isolate the performer from the performance context, privilege communicative behaviors over communicative interaction or events, and position students as an amorphous and unreflective body who respond best to accelerated energy—in effect, a 'song and dance.' Not only does this perspective rest on an impoverished sense of performance, it likewise diminishes the complexity of educational interactions. To equate instructional communication with presentational style grossly devalues the intellectual work of teaching and, argues Sprague (1992), is analogous to 'replacing intellectually trained journalists with attractive news readers who project an appealing media image' (p. 8).

This is not to say that performance training is not a valuable method for enhancing classroom communication. As one who has successfully used dramatic techniques to enhance my own and others' expressive repertoire, performance exercises can be an efficient and practical aspect of a comprehensive instructional development program. Nor would I discount the importance of measuring the impact of immediacy behaviors on learning, for it is this body of data that holds us accountable for the idio-syncrasies of our own communicative styles. Studies that highlight a particular performative technique such as storytelling (Cooper, Orban, Henry, & Townsend, 1983), or the impact of humor (Powell & Andresen, 1985), can tell us much about specific communicative strategies. It is to say, however, that an exclusively teacher/ performer-centered model cannot begin to mine the richness of the perfor- mance metaphor, and in fact, can function to close off heuristic interdisciplinary dialogue. It allows critics such as Ralph Smith (1979) to claim that 'if the acting analogy were carried to its logical extreme, a teacher who took it seriously would never have to understand anything' (p. 33). Or to paraphrase a former colleague: 'I used to perform in the classroom, but now I am more concerned with the students' experiences.'

Teacher as Artist

Responding to Dewey's (1927) charge for an aesthetic experience in education that would 'educate the imagination . . . improve sensibilities,' and 'provide peak experiences' for students, many educational theorists play out the metaphor of teacher as artist. These studies advocate the aesthetic sensibility and spontaneous creativity associated with performing artists. The hallmark of artistic teachers, claims Barrie Barrell (1991), is their willingness to 'forego the insistence upon clear-cut behavioral objectives and predictable learning outcomes for the freedom to adjust and to explore new avenues with unpredict- able outcomes' (p. 338). Elliot Eisner (1979), a contemporary forerunner of the teacher-artist movement, emphasizes the human contingencies inherent in learning environments. Artistic teachers cultivate their 'educational imagina- tion'—balancing craft with creativity, systems with spontaneity—to meet the specificity of learners' needs and stimulate their capacity for imaginative conceptualization.

Louis Rubin's *Artistry in Teaching* (1985) attempts to lay theoretical ground for classroom artistry by making a case for education as theater. He draws parallels between theatrical and instructional contexts along the following definitional, structural, and functional lines: (a) Teaching and theater are ephemeral experiences that exist in a 'perpetual present moment'; both are shaped around intellectual ideas illuminated through multiple perspectives, such that aesthetics are used 'to vivify . . . to convince by dramatizing'; (b) education and theater are interactive events that use tension, timing, and counterpoint as organizational principles designed to engage audiences intellectually and emotionally; (c) teachers and actors both function as critical interpreters driven by an 'inner vitality' that stimulates an audience to thought and action (pp. 109–118). Although Rubin's analogy is promising, his experimental study is disappointing. 'Putting content and method temporarily aside,' Rubin led 350 teachers through a series of dramatic workshops and then evaluated their classrooms for evidence of enhanced creativity (p. 103). Not surprisingly, the participating teachers agreed that the workshops had enhanced their communicative style and, therefore, augmented their 'overall technical repertory,' but most concluded that 'artistic teaching requires far more than theatrical devices' (p. 22). Rubin's assumption that theatricality can promote classroom artistry reiterates the reductive component inherent to both the actor and the artist metaphors. Performance functions as a means of enhancing instructional communication, rather than as a generative metaphor for examining educational experience. Ultimately, this offers no genuine challenge to the marginal position of performance in instructional contexts.

Although the teacher-artist conception may be philosophically appealing, it is not methodologically instructive. Indeed, a description of what constitutes artistic pedagogy, or a system for evaluating artistry in the classroom, seems to run counter to the instinctive, nebulous creativity privileged by the model. This theoretical flaw is clearly evident in John Hill's (1985) 'The Teacher as Artist: A Case for Peripheral Supervision.' Hill claims that artistic teachers operate on a level of 'unconscious competence' whereby their interactions with students are guided by instinct, intuition, and innate creativity. Drawing a distinction between artists and craftspeople, Hill claims that 'the teacher-artist is someone so able and so unselfconscious that he or she is unaware ... specific skills are lost between reflective moments' (p. 184). Because artistic teachers instinctively respond 'correctly' to their students, the rationale for their behavior eludes logical reconstruction. In effect, Hill's 'case for peripheral supervision' is based on the assumption that artists are unreflective visionaries who require an external, critical eye to tell them what they are doing and why. In other words, one can be a performing artist, but not a thinking artist, or a theorizing artist. Teacher-performers can engage in creative classroom interactions, but not in scholarly discourse. As one who claims to be both scholar and practitioner of performance, and who struggles diligently to articulate the sources and structures of performative knowledge, I find Hill's profile of artists to be both theoretically untenable and dangerously misconceived. He propounds a view of performative pedagogy that can be too easily and too justifiably dismissed.

Summary

Within the general concept of teaching as a type of performance, Pineau reflects on two metaphors (teachers as actors or artists). Both metaphors have their limitations. However, using these metaphors allows us to consider or refocus on the role of the teacher and their pedagogy. In particular, through her discussion Pineau urges us to ensure that whilst we are engaged in teaching as a type of performance, we also maintain an appropriate degree of reflective and theoretical practice alongside our pedagogy.

Questions to consider

1. What are the strengths and weaknesses of these two metaphors in your opinion?
2. 'I used to perform in the classroom, but now I am more concerned with the students' experiences'. To what extent is this a legitimate concern today?
3. If teaching were to be defined as 'artistry', what specific artistic elements would it contain?

Investigations

Reflect on some of the teachers that have taught you over the years. How would you define their pedagogy? Could any of them be described as actors or artists? Which of them provided the most memorable lessons? Why?

Think back to an engaging performance that you have attended recently. It might be a play, concert, sporting event or something else. What were the features of that performance that made it captivating? Think about the role of the various people within the performance and the context within which it played out. What, if any, implications can be drawn from these reflections to help you imagine what a pedagogy for music education might contain?

Think deeper

As pointed out in the introduction to this extract, metaphors can be simultaneously helpful and problematic. These two metaphors of the teacher as actor and the teacher as artist provide a good illustration of this point. At a practical level, the call to 'teach like an actor' can be highly problematic; yet the performance training associated with being an actor might of considerable valuable to young teachers. Similarly, the aesthetic and creative dimensions of being artists can be seen as both instructive and problematic. The extent to which the artist is cognisant and able to articulate the rationale behind their art is seen as crucial in Pineau's exploration. Critics can too easily dismiss the artist as one who fails to engage deeply enough with the theory behind their practice.

Teachers too, we might reflect, have suffered from these false distinctions that divorce theory from practice in an unhelpful manner. As Pineau says in the closing sentences of the above extract, we need to be both scholars and practitioners to make progress. For our discussion, developing and demonstrating an appropriate pedagogy for music education is important, but being able to analyse and reflect on this too is vital.

Think wider

The literature relating to performance theories for education is fascinating and expanding rapidly. In her chapter, Pineau goes on to explore how educational notions of play can help establish a performance paradigm for teaching.

Many of these thoughts have resonances within the work and practice of music educators. Traditions of music education such as Dalcroze Eurhythmics place the human body at the very centre of musical development and learning. Whilst not every music teacher would necessarily subscribe to a particular approach like this, it is instructive to consider the philosophical and conceptual frameworks that they embrace and how these might help in the development of an individual teacher's pedagogy. We will be examining certain aspects of the Dalcrozian tradition further in Chapter 5.

A key aspect in the development of an individual teacher's pedagogy is their own musical experience, skills and understanding. Given the vast array of music styles and traditions, maintaining a sense of authenticity in relation to your chosen pedagogy is crucial. The importance of authenticity and networking are the two key themes in the following extract.

Extract 3.2

Source

Swanwick, K. (1999) *Teaching Music Musically*. London, Routledge, pp. 99–101.

Introduction

In the above discussion, we considered the application of two metaphors in relation to a teacher's work in the classroom. Performing as a teacher has a metaphorical link to performing as a musician. However, like any metaphor, it can be stretched too far.

One of the key aspects of being a musician that many of us value is authenticity to a particular musical style or tradition. Here, the argument goes, to be an effective music educator it is important to build on one's own musical experience, skills and understanding in an authentic manner. In the following extract, Swanwick explores this concept and extends it through a consideration of how the individual teacher and their work should be located within a musical network.

Key words and phrases

pedagogy, network, authenticity, partnership

Extract

The issue of authenticity

The comment above is indicative of a widespread need. Secondary school music teachers may find themselves uncomfortably veering between their own musical specialism (which may or may not be valued by students) and an insecure 'generalism', for instance, in popular music and what has come to be known as 'world musics'. Although Hargreaves applies a 'specialist-generalist' continuum (Hargreaves 1996) to primary schools, we could equally see this in the secondary school, where music teachers are inevitably specialists in one or two kinds of music but also generalists in the much wider range of music required both by the curriculum and by our culturally diverse society. We might speculate that this lack of musical 'authenticity' accounts in part for the tendency for secondary students to become progressively disenchanted with music in school.

Genuine musical experience has within it something of metaphorical richness. Without this quality of experience music education is impoverished. Indeed, there is a long history of negative attitudes to school music on the part of pupils, especially in secondary schools (Schools Council 1968; Francis 1987; Ross 1995). In a report of a recent study of the arts in five secondary schools, Ross and Kamba assert that for music 'the enjoyment factor remains unchanged and disappointingly low' (Ross and Kamba 1997). We did not find this negative picture among the students in our evaluation of the South Bank Centre programme. Even among those students who were not part of the scheme, attitudes were fairly positive (see Figure 7).

Even so, whether primary, secondary or tertiary, very few schools and colleges can now be musical islands. We might consider how to invest resources differently, for example, involving musicians, individuals and communities as part of a music education network, rather than seeing them as exceptional novelties. Colleges and secondary schools in particular might become facilitating agencies rather than sole 'providers'. Music teaching in inner-city secondary schools is challenging, complex and taxing, whilst there is a richness of resources beyond the school gates if we know how to find and utilise it. The students we studied had access to specialist professional music expertise and to a range of styles which it would not be possible to replicate authentically in every or indeed any school, certainly not on the costly scale of this programme. It so happens that the South Bank Centre programme involved professional musicians. But there are many musicians in communities who could also contribute to the authenticity of music in schools. Most communities have rich seams of music-making ready to be mined. The resources of

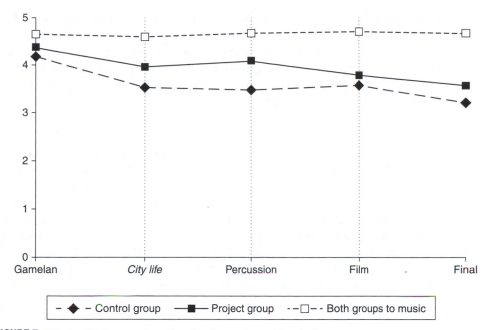

FIGURE 7 Attitudes of both groups to music and each group to music in school.

nearby schools might also be pooled, especially the musical expertise of teachers.

Music is not a single entity easily reduced to work in conventional class-rooms but a multiplicity of activities, each requiring some specialist know-how, varying group size and different levels and types of equipment. How can one teacher and every single school provide access to such musical diversity as, for example, gamelan, steel pans, standard western orchestral instruments in all their variety, a range of choral experience, small groups playing rock and pop and possibly jazz, Indian music and the musics of Africa and the Pacific? Very rarely can students be said to be having a musically authentic experience. No wonder 'school music' appears to many young people as a sub-culture separated from music out there in the world, abstracted by the constraints of classroom and curriculum and subject to very curious arrangements for assessment. We have to do better than this. We should consider involving musicians of various kinds as part of a music education *network,* rather than see them as exotic novelties.

To draw on resources of this kind would require agencies outside of schools to take account of the restrictions of school organisation and to plan carefully and well in advance. It would also be necessary to look critically at the structure and function of schools themselves. If we can achieve this there may be considerable potential for future collaboration between educational and musical agencies. However, the tension between school music and other music is currently amplified structurally within the educational system.

Represented here are two distinct approaches to curriculum innovation which appear to be in tension – the one a nationally engineered, standardised approach to a curriculum devised in non-school settings and imposed with the force of law; the other a locally diverse basket of activities devised in collaborations between professional musicians in school and joined on a voluntaristic basis.

(Kushner 1994: 45)

Saville Kushner sees these collaborative activities as educationally rich, permitting children to engage with music in their own way and at their own speed. There may be little if any curriculum sequencing towards pre-specified learning outcomes. Such projects tend to be broadly process-based rather than geared to narrowly defined and standardised 'products'. Complex music may be 'deconstructed' – for example, involvement over time with an opera production can have different levels of meaning for different individuals. Such musical activities are not only more open-ended but they may also be perceived as 'authentic', involving 'real' instruments, 'real' music, 'real' musicians and 'real' music-making settings, unlike the cumulative and incremental teaching that characterises an institutional curriculum. Although I would link authenticity with the quality of musical experience, there is a sense in which quality depends on a depth of musical understanding which is only likely among insiders to a particular way of 'musicing'.

References

Francis, L. J. (1987) 'The decline in attitudes towards religious education among 8–15 year olds', *Educational Studies* 13, 2.

Hargreaves, D. J. (1996) 'The development of artistic and musical competence', in I. deLiege and J. A. Sloboda (eds), *Musical Beginnings: The Origins and Development of Musical Competence,* Oxford: Oxford University Press.

Kushner, S. (1994) 'Against better judgement: how a centrally prescribed music curriculum works against teacher development', *International Journal of Music Education* 23: 34–45.

Ross, M. (1995) 'What's wrong with school music?', *British Journal of Music Education* 12, 3: 185–201.

Ross, M. and Kamba, M. (1997) *State of the Arts in Five English Secondary Schools,* Exeter: University of Exeter.

Schools Council (1968) *Enquiry One: The Young School-leavers,* London: HMSO.

Summary

Swanwick's argument is developed under the heading of 'authenticity'. All music teachers, he asserts, are uncomfortably positioned between areas of specialism that they have developed (and rightly enjoyed) and an 'insecure generalism' demanded by the contexts within which they teach. His response to this dilemma is to prioritise the adoption of genuine musical experiences within a collaborative or networked approach to music education. The genuine musical experiences that any one music teacher can engage in, Swanwick states, are going to be limited in comparison to the broader range of opportunities that a partnership approach to the provision of music education opportunities could develop. This method would demand a greater degree of collaboration between different agencies, but, he argues, the rewards are considerable.

Questions to consider

1. How can an individual teacher begin the process of creating a network of musical opportunities for their pupils?

2. Swanwick is quick to promote the benefits of such an approach, but are there any drawbacks?

Investigations

Swanwick's call for partnership working was published in 1999. Since then, the creation of musical partnerships between schools and other musical groups in their local communities has moved on quickly. What musical partnerships are you or your school engaged in? How did those partnerships begin? Are they flourishing? How could you develop them further?

Think deeper

The benefits of partnership working are considerable. They have been explored in recent writings by Jayne Price (2012). In particular, she has identified a range of benefits for pupils, teachers, musicians and schools; one of her key notions of success relates to the way in which collaborative projects are integrated within the broader curriculum that the teacher has a responsibility for developing. She writes:

> Impact is enhanced when a project is developed as an integral part of the music curriculum, rather than a 'one-off' event which is intended as a good experience for the students. As part of a unit of work, students get the most benefit from the experience in terms of developing their musical understanding.
>
> (Price 2012, p. 91)

However, despite the enriching aspects of well-integrated musical projects within the curriculum, Price is right to remind us that they are no substitute for the regular, day-to-day opportunities that pupils have to work with an experienced musician – their teacher!

> It is worth remembering that students already work with a musician in the classroom in every music lesson – you! If we model creative processes for the

students and use every opportunity to play or sing for and with them, this will enhance the way they tackle their own projects and develop their musicianship and musical understanding.

(Price 2012, p. 96)

Think wider

There is a tension here. Swanwick is encouraging the adoption of broader collaborative approaches to the provision of musical opportunities in our schools; Price is reminding us, powerfully, that the teacher themselves can be a powerful musical example to their pupils through the adoption of a pedagogy that embodies musical processes in an authentic way.

Within the United Kingdom, a great deal of emphasis has been placed on partnership ways of working. The construction of music education hubs, funded by the Government from September 2012 for three years, is encouraging the integration of music education within schools and a broader range of musical groups – including Local Authority music services, orchestras, bands and others. However, too great an emphasis on partnership can be at the expense of an individual teacher's pedagogy. Suddenly, teachers may begin to think that certain things are not their responsibility, or that they are ill-equipped to provide pupils with a particular set of musical skills or processes. Music teachers need to ensure that their authority, as managers for their pupils' long-term musical learning, is not diminished.

The next extract has been carefully chosen to counteract some of the potential imbalances that an over-zealous approach to partnership working might create.

Extract 3.3

Source

Alexander, R. (2008) *Essays on Pedagogy*. London, Routledge, pp.169–170, 171–172.

Introduction

In the chapter from which this extract is drawn, Robin Alexander introduces us to Douglas Brown, a teacher of English at the Perse School in Cambridge. Alexander was taught by Brown and, in a fascinating account, reflects on what he came to appreciate was the exceptional teaching he received from him.

Key words and phrases

teaching, pedagogy, identity

Extract

One staging post on my own journey, given my struggles against the institutional odds as a would-be musician, was the dialogue (again) between words
and music. Characteristically, Douglas set this up in both familiar and less
obvious ways. So I studied vocal settings, and, naturally, Douglas lent the
necessary recordings and scores so that I could explore what composers did
with words when they turned them into song.

Of these, I particularly recall my first encounter with Britten's stunning
settings of Donne's *Holy Sonnets*, performed by Peter Pears and Britten himself
and culminating in the sustained, defiant, double-forte F sharp of 'Death thou
shalt die'. This contrasted with an account closer to Donne's time, by Purcell's
one-time teacher Pelham Humfrey, of the 'Hymn to God the Father', with its
repeated punning on done/Donne. On Douglas's 78 rpm recording it was
achingly sung by counter-tenor Alfred Deller, and I played it so many times that
I almost wore it out. The less obvious line of enquiry was in the area of musical
and literary form. So, for example, while I was working on T.S. Eliot's *Four
Quartets* Douglas pointed me towards the Bartok string quartets and late
Beethoven and I began, but only began, to tease out the relationship of form,
tension and the crystallisation of feeling.

[The importance of *form* remains a pedagogical as well as a musical, literary
or dramatic preoccupation. It is the act of submitting to but then exploiting and
testing the disciplines and boundaries of form, to and beyond their apparent
limits, which unites some of the greatest composers, writers and painters. So
too with teachers and the elements of pedagogic form: lesson structure, time,
space, organisation, subject-matter, task, activity, interaction, assessment.
Indeed, in making sense of observational, videotape and transcript data from
classrooms in England, France, India, Russia and the United States I have
found the vocabularies of musical composition and performance to be powerfully suggestive of lesson planning which specifies everything in detail to that
which encourages extemporisation on a theme (content) or ground (structure);
teaching in action which ranges from the formally-slavish to the improvisatory;
time conceived as the security of pulse and rhythm combined with the judicious
tempo of cognitive pace rather than the hectic scramble through prescribed
content of what Ofsted and the UK government's national strategies call 'pacy'
teaching; the weaving and recurrence of discernible leitmotifs as a device to
consolidate understanding; the contrast between the rigidity of the three/four
part lesson structure as prescribed by the National Strategies, the formless-
ness of some of the 1970s/1980s teaching to which these prescriptions have
claimed to provide the necessary antidote, and the more episodic formalism of
mainstream European practice, grounded as it is in a pedagogic tradition which
reaches back to Comenius. Comparative analysis of teaching shows that such
applications are far from fanciful – and there are many more – for pedagogy is
an aspect of the wider development of culture and ideas, not separate from
these (Alexander 2001: 306–19).]

But as Douglas surely knew, teaching of that commitment and power leaves its mark and establishes lifelong habits of thought and action, or at least ways of thinking and acting to which one struggles to aspire. His manner of engaging with language and literature, and his close attention to words written and spoken, are with me to this day. His intellect, insight, skill and independence make today's ministerial accolades for politically compliant 'best practice' look utterly tawdry. His moral but never moralistic engagement with literature, music and life render irresponsible as well as contemptible the UK government's injunction to use the dismal pragmatism of 'what works' as the sole touchstone for defining good teaching. His high educational ambitions for his pupils were quite unlike today's teaching 'targets' because we made them our own, gladly, willingly and without the crude panoply of pressures, threats and sanctions upon which the post-1997 target-setting apparatus has depended. In any case, targets may be intended to raise horizons but actually they impose limits and Douglas's aspirations certainly did not. Indeed, they probably far exceeded any targets or attainment levels that might have been thought appropriate to students of the ages he taught – not that we achieved them: aiming high was what mattered. And there's some justice in the fact that after many twists and turns I ended up exploring pedagogy in educational and cultural contexts as far removed from 1950s/1960s Cambridge as it is possible to imagine. For it is that experience that gives me the confidence to assert with more than mere conviction that Douglas Brown was indeed a rare and remarkable teacher.

With Douglas, moreover, there was not one teacher but four: language, literature, music and the man through whom the power of these was unlocked. Not for him the self-important strutting of those teachers whose authority resides in position rather than talent, and whose educational vocabulary neither liberates nor ignites but instead fawns on the clichéd eduspeak of the latest government initiative. He knew, and he wanted us to know, that the words and music mattered much more than he, and in this he displayed the humility of genius and the artistry of teaching at their best.

References

Alexander, R.J. (2001) *Culture and Pedagogy: international comparisons in primary education*, Oxford: Blackwell.

Summary

For Alexander, Douglas Brown was an inspirational and exceptional teacher. But the teaching that he describes throughout the chapter is very different from that which many teachers provide today. For example, earlier in the chapter from which this extract comes Alexander reflects that Brown talked to his classes in a way that today would be considered monological (Alexander 2008, p. 156). In the later part of our extract, Alexander explores Brown's intellectual, moral and pedagogical approaches that resulted, he says, in a display of the 'humility of genius and the artistry of teaching' at their best.

In the first part of the extract, by way of an aside really, Alexander explores the metaphor of musical form as a pedagogical as well as a musical preoccupation. In a fascinating section, he states that the vocabularies of musical composition and performance provide powerful suggestions for the processes of lesson planning. For Alexander, pedagogy (including lesson structure, time, space, organisation, subject matter, task, activity, interaction and assessment) is framed by, and within, the development of culture and ideas, not separate from them.

In the second part of the extract, Alexander presents a wonderful testimony to the work of Douglas Brown, ending with the assertion that he displayed both the humility of genius and the artistry of teaching at their best.

Questions to consider

1. What marks out exceptional teachers today? Are the attributes that Alexander ascribes still relevant and important in teaching today?
2. How do you think that teaching has changed in the context of your lifetime?
3. What other metaphorical insights from the musical practices that Alexander highlights can you draw for the processes of lesson planning?

Investigations

Teaching is an art. In the following extracts we will be exploring this assertion in more detail but, for now, drawing on the account of Douglas Brown and his teaching, we begin to outline the various elements of a pedagogy that can be developed through an application of an artistic metaphor for teaching. What does artistry in teaching look or sound like? How can it be developed? More fundamentally, what type of teacher do you want to be? If you do not want to be an 'artistic' teacher, how would you like to be described?

Think deeper

Words are important in teaching. Alexander reflects on the use of words throughout this chapter. In an obvious sense, as we discussed above, Douglas Brown spoke more than teachers are encouraged to speak today. He would not have found favour with Ofsted. But in deeper ways, and at various points in our extract, Alexander comments that music and language were integrated within Brown's teaching. He explores a specific example in relation to Benjamin Britten's word setting of Donne's *Holy Sonnets*; the broader pedagogical approach he adopted led Alexander to describe him as not one teacher but four (language, literature, music and the man through whom the power of these was unlocked).

It is notable that Alexander chooses to describe him as 'not one teacher but four', rather than 'not one teacher but three'. Brown's sense of personality and identity informed his teaching in powerful ways that recall, for me, Swanwick's notion of authenticity discussed above. The greatest subject that Brown taught was life itself. Douglas Brown did not need to bring a musician into his classroom to bring his teaching of music to light. He did not even need a music lesson as such (in fact, curriculum music at the Perse school in the 1950s left a lot to be desired; according to Alexander it was 'abysmal' (p. 164)). Within his English classes, individual subjects were subsumed through a skilful educational dialogue between teacher and pupil that we would be wise to try and recapture in our schools today. We will be returning to these ideas in Chapter 5.

Think wider

Robin Alexander is one of the world's leading experts on pedagogy. He defines pedagogy as follows:

> Pedagogy is the act of teaching together with its attendant discourse. It is what one needs to know, and the skills one needs to command, in order to make and justify the many different kinds of decisions of which teaching is constituted.

> (Alexander 2004, p. 11)

Within the broader context of partnership working in music education that we considered above, it is essential that music educators rediscover the artistry of teaching through an appropriate musical pedagogy. But like any art, this needs to be studied and practised in order for fluency to develop. If you re-conceptualise pedagogy as a type of performance, as we did in Extract 3.1, and begin to create a rich metaphor for pedagogy of the type exemplified by Swanwick and Alexander, music teaching will be an activity that inspires, equally, your heart and mind throughout your career.

Extract 3.4

Source

Swanwick, K. (1988) *Music, Mind and Education*. London, Routledge, pp. 122–123.

Introduction

In this extract, Swanwick presents two key terms that help us analyse particular pedagogical approaches in more detail. These terms are 'classification' and 'framing'. Classification relates to curriculum knowledge and, in particular, who gets to choose the particular 'knowledge' that is being explored within a teaching episode. Strong classification involves the teacher pre-selecting knowledge; weak classification allows the pupil to choose a particular knowledge area. Framing relates to pedagogy and the degree of control that a teacher may or may not exert over the selection, organisation and pacing of what is to be learnt. Strong framing positions the teacher as the authority on these matters; weaker framing gives control and ownership to the pupils.

Key words and phrases

classification, framing, pedagogy, formal, informal, instruction, encounter

Extract

In order to see classification and framing at work in music education, we could try placing some 'for instances'. For example, running a church choir preparing for a traditional carol service involves strong idiomatic classification—only certain types of music would be acceptable; *and* strong framing—the teacher is likely to function as a 'director of music' rather than a facilitator of individual discovery. We might come to a similar conclusion about a music class lesson in a school, where a teacher has decided to undertake a classroom rehearsal of, say, the chords of the 12-bar blues: once again, strong classification and framing. In both of these settings the teacher exercises considerable power over the idiomatic content—what counts as music—along with control over the pacing and mode of learning. If the work on the 12-bar blues was individualized, with the teacher acting as enabler and adviser rather than instructor, then we might describe this as strongly classified as far as musical idiom is concerned but more weakly framed. This is important: strong or weak classification does not always imply a similar emphasis in framing; there are two concepts here, not one. Any music education event could be placed somewhere within these two dimensions, though in flexible teaching there may be considerable movement between the extremes of weak and strong.

For instance, when someone *asks* how to balance a canoe, or drive a motor car, or finger a guitar, then strong framing may be desirable, necessary and expected. But under these conditions there is an element of 'student' *choice* as to what knowledge is appropriate; he or she has made a decision on classification, what is to be learned, and initiates contractual arrangement with the teacher who will decide on the framing. The problem with formal education in purpose-designed institutions is that this contract may be made indirectly with other agents than the student him-or herself; perhaps with a parent. In our schools, a degree of classification is now enshrined in the laws of the country. Beyond this, the detail of curriculum content and teaching method—what actually takes place is still most frequently left to individual teachers to decide. Even when the learning initiative is handed over to small groups, perhaps engaged in composing, dominant students will tend to influence both classification and framing by the strength of their ideas and force of personality. This is natural and inevitable. As Brian Davies reminds us, the social *is* control.

> One does not choose to live without rules and their consequences, though, at times and in some degree it is possible to choose which rules to live with. To know this is to be freer than not to know it.
>
> (Davies, 1986: 7)

Schools are committed to organize or frame education in some form or other; they are not merely social groups where informal enculturation takes place, but have an ethical and contractual responsibility for the development of *mind*. The obligation to frame knowledge is therefore inescapable, though pupil discovery or encounter might be built into this process. In the previous chapter I emphasized the importance of *choice* whenever music education moves within strongly classified idioms. Here, I want to explore the effect of framing on music teaching, substituting for strong framing the term *instruction* and for weak framing the more affectively charged word, *encounter*.

References

Davies, B. (1986) *Social Control and Education,* London: Methuen.

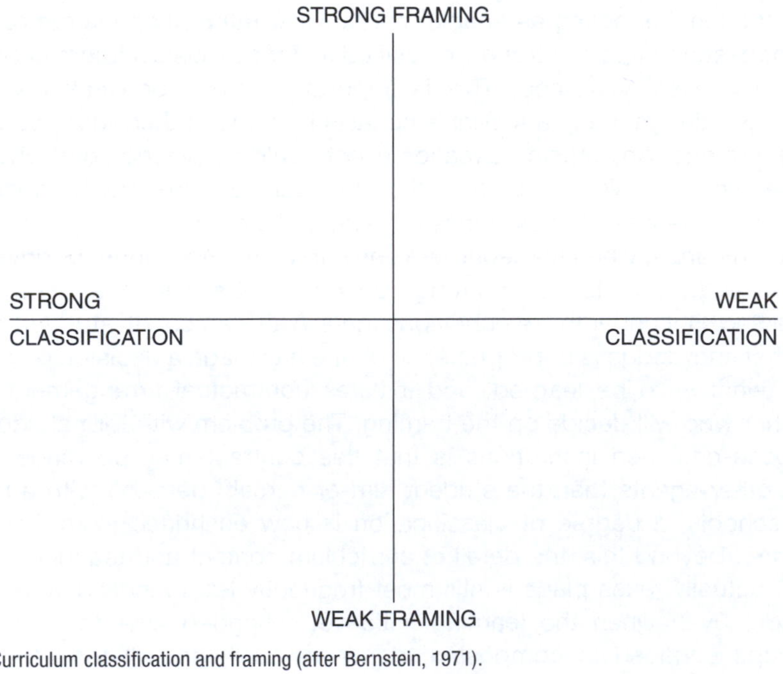

STRONG FRAMING

STRONG   WEAK
CLASSIFICATION   CLASSIFICATION

WEAK FRAMING

FIGURE 3 Curriculum classification and framing (after Bernstein, 1971).

Summary

The extract gives several different examples of classification and framing in various music education contexts. Swanwick highlights that there can be a considerable amount of flexibility in approach, even within one lesson, but ultimately he comments that schools have a responsibility and commitment to organise educational opportunities in a way that develops a pupil's mind. The key question for Swanwick relates to pedagogy: will a stronger or weaker degree of framing result in a greater change for pupils to actually encounter music for themselves, rather than merely be instructed about it?

Questions to consider

1. Reflect back on your own music education for a moment. To what extent was it strongly/weakly classified and strongly/weakly framed? Can you recall any specific moments when there was a significant shift in pedagogy (either classification or framing) and why might this shift have occurred?

Investigations

Swanwick provides a simple x/y graph on which the various combinations of classification or framing within a particular teaching episode can be mapped. At some point soon, either observe some music teaching or, if you have the opportunity, do some yourself and use the graph to chart the perceived degrees of classification and framing throughout the lesson from your own perspective. Try and identify at which points in the lesson the degrees of classification and/or framing change. How would the pupils perceive these matters? Would their graph look the same as yours?

Think deeper

Classification and framing are two specific aspects of pedagogy that help teachers get a handle on choices that they have to make within the classroom. They are dynamic processes that contain various 'mixtures' of both concepts. In their starkest, they are represented by:

- Strong classification and strong framing (top left hand corner of the graph);
- Strong classification and weak framing (bottom left hand corner of the graph);
- Weak classification and weak framing (bottom right hand corner of the graph);
- Weak classification and strong framing (top right hand corner of the graph).

In most lessons it is very unlikely that they would remain unchanged for a long period of time. The key questions relate to when it is appropriate to exert stronger classification and/or framing and when to allow weaker classification and/or framing.

Recent developments in music education, such as Musical Futures, have explored what are commonly known as informal approaches to teaching and learning in music. In Swanwick's terms, these would often exhibit weak classification and weak framing. It is worth remembering Swanwick's wider point that it is the responsibility of educational institutions to frame educational opportunities in meaningful ways. Schools are not, in his phrase, 'merely social groups where informal enculturation takes place' (Swanwick 1988, p. 123). In that sense, even Musical Futures (www.musicalfutures.org), as a form of 'informal' music curriculum, is strongly classified by teacher choice and adoption.

Think wider

The research literature in the field of community music sheds an interesting light on these debates. Jaffurs' research (Jaffurs 2006) starts with the obvious point that formal music learning (which, she suggests, takes place mainly in institutions such as schools) is different from informal music education (which takes place mainly in the home). Understanding the difference is the starting point of a helpful debate about how pedagogical approaches, particularly those within the formal education sector, can develop. However, wholesale adoption is neither possible nor desirable. Her paper ends with a cautionary note:

> As postmodern philosophies come to the forefront of education, universities, schools, community music programs, and all environments that promote the musical development of our children may unite. We have a common goal, the musical development of the whole child, not just when he or she is in the classroom. While it is tempting to suggest that we hop on board the informal approach, we should not ignore formal music education. Yes, there is much to learn from informal music settings, caution should be taken in how we channel and focus our interest.

> (Jaffurs 2006, p.28)

Extract 3.5

Source

Eisner, E. (2002) *The Arts and the Creation of Mind*. New Haven and London, Yale University Press, pp. 48–52.

Introduction

The final extract in this important chapter on pedagogy takes us back to the notion of teaching as artistry and asks an important question: how can artistry in teaching get refined?

Key words and phrases

pedagogy, artistry, reflection, evaluation

Extract

Because the practice of teaching at its best may be conceived of as an art, an art informed but not controlled by the products of social science, we might speculate how artistry in teaching gets refined.[1] One place to begin is to understand how artistry gets refined in the arts. *By artistry I mean a form of practice informed by the imagination that employs technique to select and organize expressive qualities to achieve ends that are aesthetically satisfying.*[2] Artistry—the artistic performance of a practice—is enhanced as artists of that practice learn to see and reflect upon what they have created. This process is enhanced as they receive informed criticism concerning their work from others. The function of such feedback is to enable them to secure a more sensitive and comprehensive grasp on what they have created.

The kind of critical and helpful feedback I am describing is not common fare in most schools. Most teachers face the arduous task of trying to figure out on their own how things went and what might be done better. The task is arduous because the ability to notice what one has done is often impeded by *secondary ignorance*; that is, by not knowing that you don't know. *Primary ignorance*—knowing that you don't know—is far easier to deal with. Secondary ignorance is almost impossible to address. The way to reduce its presence is to organize schools so that they allow colleagues to see and critique each other's teaching, a practice rare but becoming more common in American schools.[3] Good educational criticism illuminates what's happening. In other words, the promotion of artistry in teaching is more likely to be realized not by searching for a formula for effective teaching, but by finding out what one is doing and by imagining how it might be made even better. To indicate that feedback can improve teaching is not to imply that critical feedback must focus on what needs improvement; it can also help teachers recognize what is outstanding in their teaching. It can help them recognize their virtues.

Another important idea about teaching is that its most important effects are located outside the classroom. In most settings students are expected to display what they have learned on tests, in portfolios, and in their commentary about what they have studied. Most of the time these studies are fragmented into disciplinary forms that seldom have much to do with the world outside schools. Yet what we surely want is more than merely knowing whether students can perform well in school. To the extent to which we are interested in their ability to use what they have learned in life outside school—the context that really matters—we must look to their behavior outside school.

We have not yet begun to use such evidence of student learning in American schools, where standardized tests still prevail.[4] And we seem to forget that standardized tests confront students with tasks the likes of which they will seldom encounter outside school. (One of the few other places that require us to take standardized tests of the kind encountered in school is the motor vehicle department, where we apply for a driver's license.) To make matters worse, we take the scores from such tests seriously, as if they were good predictors of what students will do outside school. What such test scores predict best are other test scores. There may be a large difference between what a student can do on a test or in a classroom and what a student will do when he or she has a choice. In education, the really important effects of teaching are located outside the school.

A third idea concerning teaching is related to the previous one, namely, that the effects of teaching may not show up until long after students leave school and in ways the teacher never dreamed of. The way we assess most learning in school is by asking students to perform at a certain time. Yet what students have actually learned may not come to the surface until years after they have finished the course. During the various stages of the life cycle, lessons learned years ago may emerge that one was not aware of learning. Maturity can promote appreciations never before experienced. These appreciations can sometimes be discovered only by looking back. What was learned may be the result of a comment made by a teacher at a particular point in a student's life. It might even be the result of a teacher's or fellow student's half-finished sentence.

When I was in the fourth grade my teacher, Miss Purtle, asked me to have a 'one man' show of my paintings in the classroom. It was an experience that made a difference I will never forget. A nine-year-old having a one-man show of his paintings! What matters is that such occasions, occasions whose importance may be unknown to the teacher, do matter, and may continue to matter long after the child has left the classroom. Although one is not likely to be able to form educational policy on such promissory notes, in our pursuit of evidence of effective teaching we would do well not to forget that our data will always be partial.

In reflecting on the effects of teaching it must be acknowledged, yet again, that students learn both more and less than what we intend to teach. They learn more because of the personal meanings they make of what we have taught. Since meaning is located in the interaction between the student and the rest of the situation, and since each student brings a unique history to that situation, the meanings made by each student will differ from those of others, sometimes in very significant ways. In this sense what students learn exceeds what the teacher intended to teach. But they almost always learn less, as well. Our educational aspirations for students are almost never completely realized. But as Robert Browning said, 'a man's reach should exceed his grasp, or what's a heaven for?'[5]

Notes

1. See Nathaniel Gage, *The Scientific Basis of the Art of Teaching* (New York: Teachers College Press, 1978).
2. Elliot Eisner, "The Art and Craft of Teaching," *Educational Leadership*, 40 (January 1983), 4–13.
3. For a full exposition of how such feedback might be provided, see Elliot Eisner, *The Enlightened Eye: Qualitative Inquiry and the Enhancement of Educational Practice* (New York: Macmillan, 1991).

4. The recognition of the inadequacy of standardized testing procedures for assessing the quality of education is reflected in the term *authentic assessment*. Authentic assessment is by implication a critique of "inauthentic assessment," the kind normally employed in schools.

5. Robert Browning, "Andrea del Sarto (called 'The Faultless Painter')," in *Victorian Prose and Poetry*, ed. Lionel Trilling and Harold Bloom (New York: Oxford University Press, 1973), 543–549.

Summary

Eisner answers this important question by starting with the practices of artists themselves. Artists learn to see and reflect on what they have created. This process of self-reflection is enhanced through the informed criticism of others and helps them secure a more sensitive and comprehensive grasp on what they have created. So it is with teaching. Teachers need to develop an ability to self-reflect on the act of teaching in more sophisticated ways and, at the same time, be open to the informed criticism of other teachers. But, as he goes on to explore throughout the extract, these are by no means easy activities, for pupils learn both more and less than that which teachers intend to teach.

Questions to consider

1. How can I develop my own reflective practice in light of the problems that Eisner touches on in this extract?

2. Uninformed criticism can be harmful, but informed criticism is essential for the artistry in teaching to be refined. How can I nurture a community of teachers around me who can offer me regular, informed criticism of the type needed for my pedagogy to develop? And how can I give this type of informed criticism back to others?

Think deeper and wider

Eisner's work on the generation of reflective and critical approaches for artistry in teaching extend to the ways that we nurture, feedback and assess our pupils' work too. Immediately following this extract, he turns his attention to the forms of intervention that teachers make to help guide their pupils' work in the arts. The 'artistic' approaches to assessment that he outlines here have wonderful resonances for the work of all teachers. Teachers have to choose their words carefully; and not just their words, but also the tone, pace and style of delivery. He writes:

> What a teacher choose to comment upon, and how those comments are made so that they are appropriate for particular students, no theoretical knowledge can prescribe. Knowledge of the situation of which the student is a central part must be considered, and often by the feel of what is likely to

be productive. In the student's response the teacher finds cues – or, better yet, clues – for further comments. The arts have a wonderful open texture that leaves open the entry points for comments.

(Eisner 2002, p. 52)

This is a lovely example of an artistic pedagogy. Within music education we are fortunate to have the opportunity to embrace a 'subjective' approach to assessment, led by our musicality and purpose towards the development of our pupils' emerging musicality and understanding. We will consider these ideas further in Chapter 6.

But as with the other examples we have explored throughout this chapter, this approach does not develop by accident. A powerful, authentic, musical pedagogy is something that every teacher of music should aspire to develop. It is facilitated through an understanding of what an artistic pedagogy entails, is formed through a dedication to exploring what this means in practice, and is honed through careful individual reflections and consideration of the informed criticism of others.

You have already begun this process by getting this far. I would encourage you all to read Eisner's work more widely, starting with this book. There is so much of value here for teachers today.

Conclusion

The development of an authentic, musical pedagogy is central to the process and practice of music education. This chapter has dwelt on this issue at some length and presented a range of ideas and frameworks to help you develop your own pedagogical approach. At whatever stage of your career, and in whatever context you are teaching music, your pedagogy should be your principal concern and focus. As we will see in the following two chapters, a thorough grasp on the pedagogy of music teaching will help pupils develop their musical skills, knowledge and understanding (Chapter 4) and also help you extend and enrich the music curriculum (Chapter 5).

References

Alexander, R. J. (2008) 'Still No Pedagogy? Principle, pragmatism and compliance in primary education'. *Cambridge Journal of Education*, 34:1, 7–34.

Jaffurs, S. (2006) 'The Intersection of Informal and Formal Music Learning Practices'. *International Journal of Community Music*. http://www.intellectbooks.co.uk/Media Manager/Archive/IJCM/Volume%20D/04%20Jaffurs.pdf [last accessed 10/05/12].

Price, J. (2012) 'Working with a Range of Musicians'. In Price, J. & Savage, J. (2012) *Teaching Secondary Music*. London, SAGE, pp. 87–97.

4

Exploring Musical Development

In the previous chapter, we explored five extracts that described, in a general sense, how you might construct an appropriate and authentic musical pedagogy. We explored a number of metaphors for teaching music drawn from key writers, examined a framework for the analysis of pedagogical approaches, read about the work of one exemplary teacher and concluded the chapter with an exploration of the concept of teaching as artistry.

In this chapter, we are going to turn our attention to issues relating to musical development and progression. We might presume that if our pupils are not progressing appropriately, then our teaching is not what it ought to be. But as with any statement of cause and effect, things are seldom that simple.

Extract 4.1

Source

Swanwick, K. (1988) 'Maxims for educators'. *Music, Mind and Education*. London, Routledge, pp. 132–135.

Introduction

In this first extract, Swanwick draws on the work of two music educators from a previous era: Murray Schafer, a Canadian music writer, composer and educationalist; and Mrs Curwen, a Victorian piano teacher. Both, as you will read, had a strong view of what should constitute a musical pedagogy and how their pupils would develop.

Key words and phrases

classification, framing, pedagogy, formal, informal, instruction, encounter, musical development

Extract

Above my desk I have written some maxims for educators, to keep myself in line. They are these:

1. The first practical step in any educational reform is to take it.
2. In education, failures are more important than successes. There is nothing so dismal as a success story.
3. Teach on the verge of peril.
4. There are no more teachers. There is just a community of learners.
5. Do not design a philosophy of education for others. Design one for yourself. A few others may wish to share it with you.
6. For the 5-year-old, art is life and life is art. For the 6-year-old, life is life and art is art. This first school-year is a watershed in the child's history: a trauma.
7. The old approach: Teacher has information; student has empty head. Teacher's objective: to push information into student's empty head. Observations: at outset teacher is a fathead; at conclusion student is a fathead.
8. On the contrary a class should be an hour of a thousand discoveries. For this to happen, the teacher and the student should first discover one another.
9. Why is it that the only people who never matriculate from their own courses are teachers?
10. Always teach provisionally: only God knows for sure.

(Schafer, 1975)

A few educational maxims

Showing the principles on which the method of the *Child Pianist* is founded:

1. Teach the easy before the difficult.
2. Teach the thing before the sign.
3. Teach one fact at a time, and the commonest fact first.
4. Leave out all exceptions and anomalies until the general rule is understood.
5. In training the mind, teach the concrete before the abstract.
6. In developing physical skill, teach the elemental before the compound, and do one thing at a time.
7. Proceed from the known to the related unknown.
8. Let each lesson, as far as possible, rise out of that which goes before, and lead up to that which follows.
9. Call in the understanding to help the skill at every step.
10. Let the first impression be a correct one; leave no room for misunderstanding.
11. Never tell a pupil anything that you can help him to discover for himself.

12. Let the pupil, as soon as possible, derive some pleasure from his knowledge. Interest can only be kept up by a sense of growth in independent power.

(Curwen, 1886)

I notice that Mrs Curwen takes a systematic and sequential approach to what she does, teaching the easy first, the usual before exceptions, proceeding from the known to the unknown. Unlike Murray Schaffer, she has a view as to what is 'correct'. Schafer seems to reject this explicit model of instruction, putting forward a view of music education as encounter. Everything is provisional; there appears to be no continuity; nothing is 'correct'; there is no identifiable subject matter, or even a set of criteria, so far as one can tell. Words like 'failures', 'dismal', 'peril', 'fathead' and 'trauma', reveal his distrust of what I have been calling formal education. We are urged always to teach provisionally since there is no certainty in anything. Against this, Mrs Curwen believes that it is possible to teach *something* and she seems fairly sure as to what this something might be.

Both writers communicate a strong sense of respect for the pupil. Both acknowledge the virtue of 'discovery'. For Mrs Curwen, pupils should never be told anything they can discover for themselves, while for Murray Schafer, a class should be an hour of 'a thousand discoveries'. Both seem to agree that a sense of *encounter* is essential, for that is implicit in the very idea of discovery—propelling ourselves at our own speed towards the, as yet, unknown. The difference lies in the assumptions each of them make about what waits to be discovered. We can be fairly sure that Mrs Curwen knows pretty well what the student will find, whereas Murray Schafer would probably insist that discoveries, by definition cannot be predicted or known in advance by the teacher. Mrs Curwen has enough respect for 'a sense of growth in independent power' to be wary of discovery 'by numbers', and I can imagine her delightedly sharing in the discovery of a chord; or that one of the piano pedals helps to create a kind of musical fog; that a melody still exists even though it be disguised. But she will be predicting the sequence of learning in a firmer way than Murray Schafer; framing knowledge more strongly, leading the student firmly on.

What really marks out the nineteenth-century pianist-teacher from the twentieth-century composer-teacher is her certainty of curriculum *content*, strong classification. Schafer inhabits a world where musical styles and musical language have been overturned, where composers have begun again at the very bottom of the spiral with experimentation at the level of sound quality and sound production. There is no certainty, as he says. Minimalism rules. Consequently, he is neither willing nor able to prescribe the kind of music nor the manner of engagement that might be appropriate for his students. He can only ask questions; encourage experimentation; provoke debate. Inevitable as this appears to him, to Mrs Curwen it would doubtless seem a shocking waste of time.

References

Curwen, A.J. (1886) *The Teacher's Guide to Mrs Curwen's Pianoforte Method*, London: Curwen & Sons.
Schafer, R.M. (1975) *The Rhinoceros in the Classroom*, London: Universal.

Summary

Swanwick presents two contrasting sets of 'maxims for educators'. There are obvious contrasts in cultural and historical setting but, nonetheless, they present an interesting set of ideas that have many resonances with music education today. Schafer's maxims, on a first reading, seem to present a model for music education by encounter; Mrs Curwen's maxims, in contrast, seem more specific, sequential and dictatorial and, Swanwick argues, present the case for music education by instruction.

Questions to consider

1. Which of these individual maxims, if any, characterise your approach to teaching music? Do you know why?
2. What similarities or differences did you notice between the two sets of maxims?

Investigations

Take one of the statements from either set of maxims and reflect on how it could move your own pedagogy in a new direction. If you adopted it and applied it to a forthcoming lesson, what difference would that maxim actually make in practice?

Think deeper

In the paragraphs that follow the presentation of these two sets of maxims, Swanwick argues that there is an interrelationship between their content. Using his framework of musical encounter and musical instruction, he explores some of these links and, later on in the chapter from which this extract comes, states that:

> this tension between instruction and encounter is both inevitable and fertile. These apparent contradictory aspects of human learning are positive and negative poles between which the electricity of educational transactions flow.
>
> (Swanwick 1988, p. 135)

These arguments have significant relevance to music education today. A rigorous musical pedagogy will adopt elements from both sets of maxims – musical instruction and music encounter are both prerequisites for musical learning, development and progression. Approaches to music education that emphasise informality, in terms of their curriculum content or pedagogical style, need to remember that the broader context of musical learning within the school is always determined by the teacher and the ethos of the institution, and that this has a fundamental effect on what occurs within the classroom. Pupils will feel this, and know it, even if their teachers work to mitigate the effect of it. Similarly, those musical styles and traditions that emphasise the role of the teacher as an instructor need to remember that pedagogical approaches that prioritise the acquisition of specific musical skills or knowledge still need to leave room for pupils to engage in meaningful musical encounters. Without this, a musical sterility can develop that leads to disengagement and a lack of musical development.

Think wider

More recently, other researchers have presented similar findings to, and exemplified, Swanwick's classic argument. Sexton's account of the challenges of working with 'informal learning pedagogies' (Sexton 2012) is fascinating. She recounts a journey related to her thinking about the curriculum she was offering to her pupils. This moved, she asserts, from a preoccupation with *what* they were learning (in Swanwick's terms, a concern about the classification of the knowledge contained within the curriculum) to a greater emphasis on *how* they were learning it (Swanwick's notion of framing) (ibid, p. 7). Having worked with a pedagogical approach drawn from the Musical Futures project, her findings are well known:

> Harnessing interest in certain styles and genres and using them in the classroom could potentially have a positive effect on music in schools but it is too narrow minded to think that incorporating current popular music trends into the curriculum is enough to guarantee that pupils will engage with the subject. For the majority of pupils, out of school musical experiences are positive ones as they are not only listening to a different style of music than they are exposed to in school but they are also engaging in more group learning alongside friends and peers with similar interests. To me, it seems critical to acknowledge this way of learning informally and give the pupils opportunities to integrate a variety of musical skills into each task whilst giving them a level of autonomy not normally associated with the formal setting of the music classroom.
>
> (Sexton 2012, p. 10)

Folkestad, in a review of the literature regarding formality and informality in music education, comments that:

> The analysis of the presented research within this area suggests that formal – informal should not be regarded as a dichotomy, but rather as the two poles of a continuum, and that in most learning situations, both these

aspects of learning are in various degrees present and interacting in the learning process. This interaction between formal and informal learning, is quite often described to take place in a 'dialectic' way.

(Folkestad 2006, pp. 143–144)

However, this is never as easy as it sounds because, as he continues to explore, the musical worlds that our pupils inhabit are sharply defined. Using a Hegelian framework, he analyses their musical world within schools (the 'thesis') as opposed to the musical world they inhabit outside (the 'antithesis') before promoting the notion of 'synthesis'. Here, as we considered in our discussion relating to partnership in the previous chapter, teachers need to understand that new ways of musical learning and development occur in both formal and informal settings, while showing a combination of qualities and features of both approaches (ibid, p. 144).

Extract 4.2

Source

Hargreaves, D. 'The social and educational context for musical learning'. In Deliège, I. and Sloboda, J. (eds) (1994) *Musical Beginnings*. Oxford, OUP, pp. 146–150.

Introduction

Starting from Stefani's notion that musical competence can be defined as 'the ability to produce sense through music', the following extract from David Hargreaves' writing provides an alternative set of contextual perspectives through which to consider musical development and the influence of pedagogy.

Key words and phrases

specialist, generalist, pedagogy, musical development

Extract

Stefani (1987, p. 7) has proposed a theory of musical competence that interprets the term as 'the ability to produce sense through music', which is itself defined as 'every social practice or individual experience concerning sounds which we are accustomed to group under this name'. It follows from this that what constitutes music in one society may not necessarily do so in another, and our definition of musical competence correspondingly needs to be able to take into account the cultural, artistic, and educational traditions of particular societies.

Stefani's notion of musical competence derives from semiotic and linguistic theory: 'the ability to produce sense through music' is intended to encompass a variety of approaches within different disciplines. These include what might be called the study of individual musicality, as shown in the predominantly psychological contributions to this volume; of musical techniques, which are possessed and intuitively understood by performers, and which can also be the subject of empirical study; of what might be called musical culture, that is, the historical and stylistic knowledge that is the province of the musicologist; and of social practices, that is, the cultural institutions within which music is performed and heard, and which are the province of the sociologist.

Stefani's theory specifies a series of what he calls *codes*, which are viewed as correlations between the content and expression of particular cultural elements—in other words, as common understandings that relate sound events to cultural experiences that can be connected with them. These range from 'general codes', which represent the basic cultural conventions through which we perceive and interpret sound experiences, through 'social practices', 'musical techniques', and 'styles', through to the most detailed level of 'opuses', that is, single musical works or events. It would not be appropriate here to deal with these codes in any detail, but it is undoubtedly instructive to take the broader social context into account. This is particularly useful here in highlighting differences between commonly used models of music teaching, since these form the immediate context for the development of musical competence in many children.

Stefani also makes the distinction between 'high' and 'popular' competences. The former 'tends to approach music in a way that is specifically and autonomously artistic': it therefore considers the 'opus' level as most pertinent and the 'lower' ones to be less pertinent the lower they are. In contrast, popular competence displays an appropriation of music that is global and heteronomous ('functional'); consequently, it exploits mostly 'general code' and 'social practice levels' (Stefani 1987, p. 17). Some forms of music (for example, opera and 'classical' music) are primarily associated with high competence, some (for example, 'light' or 'popular' music in restaurants or shops) with popular competence, and some fall within a middle ground of common competence.

I have spent some time discussing Stefani's theory because the social dimension that it incorporates provides a useful stimulus for the examination of the prominent pedagogies in music education, and I should like to propose a conceptual model that is based on two dimensions (see Figure 6.1). This formulation draws upon some models proposed by Andrén (1988) and Olsson (1993) that were originally intended as descriptions of the ideological positions of particular educational movements; here they are adapted to a rather more specific description of approaches within music education. The two orthogonal dimensions could be labelled in various possible ways, but I have opted for the terms 'specialist-generalist' and 'control-autonomy'.

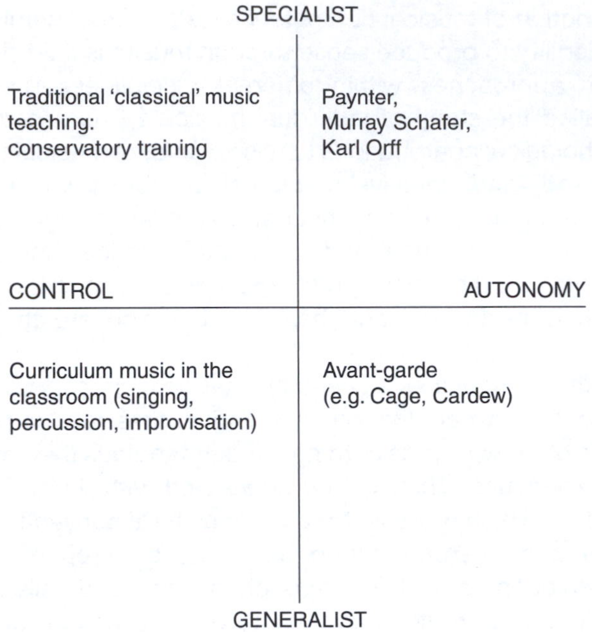

SPECIALIST

Traditional 'classical' music teaching: conservatory training	Paynter, Murray Schafer, Karl Orff

CONTROL ———————————————————— AUTONOMY

Curriculum music in the classroom (singing, percussion, improvisation)	Avant-garde (e.g. Cage, Cardew)

GENERALIST

FIGURE 6.1 A model of teaching methods in music education.

In many cultures there is a long tradition of *specialist* education, within which talented pupils are given tuition, largely on traditional orchestral instruments, and reach high levels of achievement within the 'classical' tradition. This tuition is frequently provided by professional musicians who work with pupils from a relatively wide geographical region, and who deal with only a relatively small proportion of high-ability pupils, many of whom may go on to become professional musicians. This contrasts with what might be called *generalist* music education, which is based on the premise that music can be performed, appreciated, and enjoyed by all pupils at all levels. A high degree of conventional instrumental skill is not seen as a prerequisite for successful participation in music, and its absence does not in any way diminish the seriousness of purpose of the activity.

The specialist-generalist distinction is currently very salient in the UK. Since the introduction of the national curriculum in 1988, it is now statutory for all British children to follow courses in music up to the age of 14, which was not hitherto the case. A new body of teaching provision in 'general class music' or 'curriculum music' has accordingly emerged fairly quickly. Its aims are very different from those of the specialist music teacher, and new staff who are not primarily music specialists are being recruited and trained to teach it. The implications of the specialist-generalist distinction go well beyond the issues of teaching methods, as indicated earlier; they are also linked with questions about the relationship between serious and popular culture and the extent to which these are conveyed by different cultural institutions.

The other distinction, which intersects with this, has been labelled 'control-autonomy'. This refers to the extent to which particular educational practices emphasize creative improvisation on the part of the pupils, perhaps (but not necessarily) with relatively little emphasis on traditional instrumental technique, as compared with the reproduction of music previously conceived, and probably written down, by another composer. This is strongly related to the dimension of 'structuredness' which emerged in some of my own previous research on the dimensions of teachers' views of classroom activities in music (see Hargreaves and Galton 1992). This dimension can be applied to many aspects of class-room music teaching, including the teacher's implicit and explicit structuring of the lesson in terms of day-to-day planning and presentation, the degree to which the content, techniques, and media to be used are specified in advance, and the availability and variety of resources. 'Control-autonomy' can be thought of not only in terms of these aspects of the teacher's work, but also in terms of their corresponding effects on the pupils.

If we now conceive of these two distinctions as orthogonal dimensions, it becomes possible to identify particular pedagogical and/or musical techniques within each of the four quadrants. It is easy to locate traditional conservatory-based training within the 'specialist-control' quadrant since typical 'classical' conservatory training requires a great deal of detailed, high-level study of a relatively circumscribed repertoire of composed music. It is also possible, perhaps slightly more ambiguously, to identify the work of music educators such as John Paynter (for example, Paynter 1992), Murray Schafer (for example, Schafer 1965) and Carl Orff (for example, Orff and Keetman 1958) as representing both 'specialism' and 'autonomy'. These educators are firmly located within 'serious' specialist institutions, but are renowned for their advocacy of an approach that leaves a great deal of creative control in the hands of the pupils, and that therefore goes beyond the standard repertoire.

When we consider the two 'generalist' quadrants, it is easy to identify a good deal of the new material that is being produced in Great Britain to meet the demands of teaching general curriculum music at lower age levels (see, for example, Mills 1993) as being at the 'control' end of this continuum. Although the aim of techniques such as group singing, percussion, and improvisation is to encourage individual expression, it nevertheless takes place within a fairly constrained framework of conventional tonal music. A good deal of pop, folk, and rock music as they are used in the classroom could also be put into this category.

The most difficult quadrant to characterize is that representing 'generalist' music and 'autonomy', perhaps because this is by its very nature the broadest and most open-ended category. The obvious examples that spring to mind are the aleatory techniques of composers such as John Cage, or the 'scratch orchestra' experiments of Cornelius Cardew; these fulfil the description of 'generalist' by virtue of their non-reliance on conventional instrumental techniques. However, neither of these figures is associated with particular pedagogical techniques as such, and both would almost certainly resent being described as 'generalists' if this had any implication of being 'popular' rather than 'serious'. Furthermore, the absence of conventional tonality is by no means a necessary characteristic of music that might be produced by methods within this quadrant so that the categorization is made with a great deal of trepidation. This leads to the more general point that the scheme as a whole is approximate and provisional: it may well be possible to improve upon and refine it.

Summary

Drawing on Stefani's definition of musical competence and through an emphasis on the social contexts within which musical activity occurs, Hargreaves proposes a conceptual model for music education differentiated by two sets of binaries: specialist versus generalist, and; control versus autonomy. Each of the resulting quadrants are briefly considered and examples given of particular approaches within them.

Questions to consider

1. Written in 1994, is this still a helpful framework for the analysis of music education provision? How does it compare to the pedagogical framework from Swanwick's work (classification and framing) presented in the previous chapter?

2. Hargreaves says that the generalist autonomy quadrant is the hardest to characterise. Is this still the case today? How would you characterise this approach from your experiences of teaching music today?

Investigations

Hargreaves writes that his scheme 'as a whole is approximate and provisional'. However we might build on this and make it reflect the current trends in music education today, his key point is that 'the attempt to be more precise about the institutional context within which musical competence is expressed is worthwhile since it has a direct influence on psychological development' (Hargreaves 1994, p. 150). With this point in mind, to what extent do the institutions and wider social contexts that you work within directly affect the types of musical opportunities you present to your pupils? How do they affect your pupils' psychological development within these activities?

Think deeper

Perhaps the greatest exemplification of the 'autonomy' side of Hargreaves' framework in recent years has been the Musical Futures initiative (www. musicalfutures.org), but it is worth considering for a moment whether this falls within his 'specialist autonomy' or 'generalist autonomy' quadrant. What exactly is the role of the teacher when their pupils have significant autonomy over the classification and framing within a lesson?

Winters (2012) provides an interesting reflection on this question.

> As a young learner's tool bag of musical ideas and understanding grows, the role of the teacher becomes that of a guide who allows room for the co-construction of learning to take place, both within the classroom and through acknowledging and valuing the music-making which takes place outside of school through informal learning. In other words the monopoly position of teachers has evolved into one which acknowledges the students' interests and starting places for musical learning. The work of the Musical Futures researchers and practitioners has articulated the role of the teacher within an informal learning model: facilitate, stand back, observe, diagnose, guide, suggest, model, take on students' perspectives, help students achieve the objectives they set for themselves.
>
> (Winters 2012, p. 22)

In other words, even when pupils are experiencing a significant degree of autonomy in terms of classification and framing, there are still skilful decisions and roles being played out by their teachers. Teachers still need to develop a broad, robust and multifaceted pedagogy.

Think wider

The broad early and mid-childhood developmental frameworks that a music education can contribute to have been thoroughly researched and articulated by various writers. Perhaps the best summary of them in recent years has been compiled by Professor Susan Hallam (Hallam 2010). In the previous chapter, we read how a child's musical development can impact their language, literacy and numeracy abilities. Her article goes on to consider the impact on a child's sense of creativity, social and personal development, health and well-being, intellectual ability and general attainment within their broader schooling. She concludes that:

> This overview provides a strong case for the benefits of active engagement with music throughout the lifespan. In early childhood there seem to be benefits for the development of perceptual skills which affect language learning and which subsequently impact on literacy. Opportunities to be able to co-ordinate rhythmically also seem important for the acquisition of literacy skills. Fine motor co-ordination is also improved through learning to play an instrument. Music also seems to improve spatial reasoning, one aspect of general intelligence which is related to some of the skills required in mathematics. While general attainment is clearly affected by literacy and numeracy skills, motivation, which depends on self-esteem, self-efficacy and aspirations, is also important in the amount

of effort given to studying. Engagement with music can enhance self-perceptions, but only if it provides positive learning experiences which are rewarding. This means that overall, the individual needs to experience success. This is not to say that there will never be setbacks but they must be balanced by future aspirations which seem achievable and self-belief in attaining them.

(Hallam 2010, pp. 281–282)

This theme of active, successful engagement will be picked up in our next reading. Within it, we will leave aside our discussion of formality and informality, encounter and instruction, specialist and generalist, control and autonomy, and turn our attention to the general qualities or features that a comprehensive approach to music education might be, and how that can promote a developmental approach to musical learning.

Extract 4.3

Source

Fautley, M. (2010) 'What is developmental learning?'. In *Assessment in Music Education*. Oxford, OUP, pp. 71–73.

Introduction

As a psychological term, 'development' refers to a maturation process during which cognitive and other competencies develop over time. The following extract explores the notion 'developmental learning' within the context of music education.

Key words and phrases

development, psychology, assessment, creativity

Extract

What develops in 'developmental learning'?

In cognitive terms, what is it that develops in 'developmental learning'? From biological and psychological perspectives, we know that as children mature over time changes happen, and we also know that these changes are more likely to occur as phases rather than stages (D. Hargreaves & Zimmerman 1992: 389), the difference being that phases are not hard-edged. Back in 1986 David Hargreaves observed that '. . . music education must have a firm foundation in developmental psychology' (D. Hargreaves 1986: 226). This is still an apposite observation, but the intervening years have not made the task any easier for music teachers! The issue of development raises questions as to what there is that can be developed in terms of musical learning. As in so many areas of music education, development is an issue which is not universally understood. As Pamela Burnard observes, '. . . conceptions of how development proceeds [are] not clear . . .' (Burnard 2006: 359). Building on the work of, amongst others, Hargreaves and Zimmerman (1992), Krumhansl (1990), Davidson and Scripp (1988, 1992), and the innovative Manhattanville Music Curriculum Project of the late 1960s (Thomas 1970), it is possible to propose four main areas for development in music education:

- Generative: original ideas, for example in composing and improvising
- Performance: skills for playing instruments or singing
- Perceptual: listening, appreciating, appraising
- Representational: symbolic representation of music in (e.g.) notation.

These are not discrete areas of potential musical development, but they operate in a complex joined-up fashion. The task for the teacher is to disentangle the various aspects of development that are suggested by each of these, and deal with them accordingly. In this book the first three of the four components of development are given separate chapters, whilst symbolic representation and the role of notation systems is dealt with in a number of places.

It is apparent that there will be some tension between the four proposed areas of musical development, and the knowledge types discussed in previous chapters. There is no obvious mapping between them. To exemplify this, let us consider the role of creativity. Creativity is patently involved in generative processes in music, and also in aspects of performance. Some would argue that listening to music can create new meanings for the listener, thus rendering it a creative act too. The problem with relying on knowledge transmission as a primary function of music education is that creative thinking can be missed, or missed out! Knowledge-based activities, particularly 'knowing about', in music do not always engage the learners personally with the very essence of the subject. 'Since creative thinking by definition goes beyond knowledge, there is explicitly or implicitly assumed to be a tension between knowledge and creativity' (Weisberg 1999: 226). In music education this tension can be readily seen in assessment. Summative assessment of knowledge is much easier to undertake than summative assessment of creative acts. This does not mean that creativity should be excluded because it is harder to assess, but that new ways of thinking need to have new ways of assessing associated with them. In creative music education, tensions between knowledge and creativity are not necessarily apparent, as Weisberg goes on to observe, 'A number of researchers have argued the opposite of the tension view, that is, knowledge is positively related to creativity. Rather than breaking out of the old to produce the new, creative thinking builds on knowledge' (Weisberg 1999: 226). This is clearly the case in the way in which in England the Secondary National Strategy for school improvement in music (DfES 2006b) views development, where skills and knowledge contribute towards musical understanding via the use of generative processes and creativity. In this sense, knowledge is a precursor to creative acts. After all, we would not want to set a class of pupils a creative composing task, and for them to come back with a model of a chair (Fautley & Savage 2007)! This might be a creative response, but it is not domain-specific creativity (Craft 2003; Csikszentmihalyi 1999). Creativity and knowledge acquisition, both participatory and acquisitive, are going to be involved in developmental music education.

Returning to the four areas of development—generative, performance, perceptual, and representational—the role of assessment in developing these needs to be considered. Specifically, how can they develop? There seems to be six main ways in which this can happen:

- Increasing depth
- Increasing breadth
- Enhancing skills (practical and cognitive)
- Allowing for personal engagement
- Formulation and articulation of value judgements
- Developing understandings

Managing all of these at the same time is yet another plate-spinning act for the music teacher to undertake! Realistically, however, development proceeds slowly, and so varying attention between these areas is the most likely way for teachers to deal with this. Indeed, so intertwined are they that atomistic separation sometimes becomes difficult.

Summary

This extract from Fautley's book on musical assessment begins with an assertion that the notion of musical development is a problematic one and not universally understood. From this unpromising start, four main areas for development are identified and described. These areas need untangling for, as Fautley describes, there are areas of tension within and between them. After a brief detour considering the role and impact of creativity within these developmental areas, Fautley asks how each of them can develop in practice. He outlines six main ways in which this can happen before urging his readers not to imply from his argument that these should be separated out for processes of educational assessment.

Questions to consider

1. Do Fautley's four developmental areas represent an adequate summary of the types of activities that you cover within your music teaching? If not, what other main areas would you add to his list?

2. Similarly, do Fautley's six ways through which development can occur provide an adequate framework for the ways in which your pupils can demonstrate their learning in music? If not, what else would you add?

Investigations

Curriculum frameworks for musical learning, such as the National Curriculum and examination specifications, are built upon models of musical development as exemplified by that adopted within the above extract. Spend some time comparing the main developmental areas outlined above with a curriculum framework of your own choice (e.g. the National Curriculum for Music). Before reading on, make a note of the similarities and differences that you observe.

Think deeper

The curriculum frameworks for music education within the United Kingdom have traditionally been built upon a holistic approach to the developmental processes within music education. The current National Curriculum frame-work identifies this holistic integration of practice as the first Key Concept that should be at the forefront of teachers' minds when planning for musical learning in their classrooms. The five Key Processes that the curriculum outlines are:

- performing;
- composing;
- listening;
- reviewing;
- evaluating.

There are obvious similarities here to Fautley's four developmental areas, but the tradition within the National Curriculum has been to assess these processes through one attainment target. In the last two versions of the National Curriculum this target has been split into a number of 'levels of attainment', but teachers have not been required to assess a pupil's ability to perform separately from their ability to compose, or to listen attentively.

The reason for this is that music is perceived, philosophically and conceptually, as being a series of interrelated processes and practices. There are elements of composition in performance; listening permeates everything musicians do; performance abilities require an analytical, evaluative ear. To isolate musical processes would be to diminish them. But, as we will see in Chapter 6, this does cause problems for assessment.

Think wider

There are alternative viewpoints. In a fascinating critique of the National Curriculum as a mechanism for order and control, Kushner (2010) exposes what he sees as some of the falsification behind these kinds of developmental frameworks. At the heart of his criticism is his assertion that the National Curriculum contains an artificiality that prioritises certain forms of logical order over ideas but results, in reality, in inauthenticity. For example:

> The twin pillars of the music national curriculum in England are: (a) the movement from simple to complex; and (b) the iteration of experiences at ever-deepening levels of conceptual challenge – the so-called 'spiral curriculum'. Hence, for example, under (a) pupils learn music by accumulating experience of its building blocks – pitch, rhythm, sequence. This may or may not be appropriate to some pupils and teachers in some situations – but it does not easily admit of alternatives such as moving from the complex to the simple – i.e. taking a holistic piece of knowledge like an opera and seeking its elements. Interestingly, this approach (constructivism through deconstruction) is indeed, typically favoured by musicians who visit schools on outreach projects (Kushner, 1988). Principally, however, this adult preoccupation with building blocks is almost certainly out of kilter with young people who have a less differentiated view of the world, and so imposes an inauthentic rationality on young people's deliberations, co-opts them into a false pattern.
>
> Under condition (b), pupils revisit to those building blocks but in the context of higher conceptual challenges, reinforcing and protecting an inauthentic rationality. Through this means the national curriculum imposes a historical legacy on all pedagogical interactions. The logic of a particular moment in a particular place is denied in favour of the necessity to continue to extend the logic asserted long before in the context of other tasks. Of course, we make choices, we buy into certain curriculum logics which deny us others. This one, in particular – the spiral curriculum— denies us surprise and reduces the independence of the moment. Once again, it foregrounds pattern and is intolerant of unrestrained variation – it is not possible to 'falsify' the logic of the moment without bringing into question the whole structure.
>
> (Kushner 2010, p. 5)

Kushner, in his customary provocative style, explores the consequences for music education in the remainder of this article. It is well worth reading in full and is available freely online.

However, it leaves an obvious question: how should we, as teachers, respond to the legitimate requirement to provide our pupils with an appropriate and developmental set of musical learning experiences? Our final extract provides one interesting answer to this question.

Extract 4.4

Source

Eisner, E. (2005) 'Expressive learning objectives'. In *Reimagining Schools: The selected works of Elliot W. Eisner.* London, Routledge, 34–35.

Introduction

Instructional objectives, or learning objectives, are used by teachers to define, in advance, the learning that pupils will engage in within a particular lesson. Within the following extract, Eisner contrasts this approach with a new one, the use of expressive objectives, which, he argues, should be frequently used within teaching.

Key words and phrases

instruction, encounter, objectives, development

Extract

Instructional objectives are used in a predictive model of curriculum development. A predictive model is one in which objectives are formulated and activities selected which are predicted to be useful in enabling children to attain the specific behaviour embodied in the objective. In this model, evaluation is aimed at determining the extent to which the objective has been achieved. If the objective has not been achieved, various courses of action may follow. The objective may be changed. The instructional method may be altered. The content of the curriculum may be revised.

With an instructional objective the teacher as well as the children (if they are told what the objective is) are likely to focus upon the attainment of a specific array of behaviors. The teacher in the instructional context knows what to look for as an indicator of achievement since the objective unambiguously defines the behavior. Insofar as the children are at similar stages of development and insofar as the curriculum and the instruction are effective, the outcomes of the learning activity will be homogeneous in character. The effective curriculum, when it is aimed at instructional objectives, will develop forms of behavior whose characteristics are known beforehand and, as likely as not, will be common across students – if not at the identical point in time, at some point during the school program.

The use of instructional objectives has a variety of educational ramifications. In preparing reading material in the social studies, for example, study questions at the beginning of a chapter can be used as cues to guide the student's attention to certain concepts or generalizations which the teacher intends to help the student learn. In the development of certain motor skills the teacher may provide examples of such skills and thus show the student what he is supposed to be able to do upon terminating the program. With the use of instructional objectives clarity of terminal behavior is crucial since it serves as a standard against which to appraise the effectiveness of the curriculum. *In an effective curriculum using instructional objectives the terminal behavior of the student and the objectives are isomorphic.*

Expressive objectives differ considerably from instructional objectives. An expressive objective does not specify the behavior the student is to acquire after having engaged in one or more learning activities. An expressive objective describes an educational encounter: it identifies a situation in which children are to work, a problem with which they are to cope, a task in which they are to engage; but it does not specify what from that encounter, situation, problem, or task they are to learn. An expressive objective provides both the teacher and the student with an invitation to explore, defer, or focus on issues that are of peculiar interest or import to the inquirer. An expressive objective is evocative rather than prescriptive.

The expressive objective is intended to serve as a theme around which skills and understandings learned earlier can be brought to bear, but through which those skills and understandings can be expanded, elaborated, and made idiosyncratic. With an expressive objective what is desired is not homogeneity of response among students but diversity. In the expressive context the teacher hopes to provide a situation in which meanings become personalized and in which children produce products, both theoretical and qualitative, that are as diverse as themselves. Consequently the evaluative task in this situation is not one of applying a common standard to the products produced but one of reflecting upon what has been produced in order to reveal its uniqueness and significance. In the expressive context, the product is likely to be as much of a surprise to the maker as it is for the teacher who encounters it. Statements of expressive objectives might read:

1. to interpret the meaning of *Paradise Lost*;
2. to examine and appraise the significance of *The Old Man and the Sea*;
3. to develop a three-dimensional form through the use of wire and wood;
4. to visit the zoo and discuss what was of interest there.

What should be noted about such objectives is that they do not specify what the student is to be able to do after he engages in an educational activity; rather they identify the type of encounter he is to have. From this encounter both teacher and student acquire data useful for evaluation. In this context the mode of evaluation is similar to aesthetic criticism; that is, the critic appraises a product, examines its qualities and import, but does not direct the artist toward the painting of a specific type of picture. The critic's subject-matter is the work done – he does not prescribe a blueprint of its construction.

Now I happen to believe that expressive objectives are the type that teachers most frequently use. Given the range and the diversity of children it is more useful to identify potentially fruitful encounters than to specify instructional objectives. Although I believe that the use of expressive objectives is generally more common than the use of instructional objectives, in certain subject areas curriculum specialists have tended to emphasize one rather than the other. In mathematics, for example, much greater attention historically has been given to the instructional objective than in the visual arts where the dominant emphasis has been on the expressive (Eisner, 1965).

I believe that the most sophisticated modes of intellectual work – those, for example, undertaken in the studio, the research laboratory, and the graduate seminar – most frequently employ expressive rather than instructional objectives. In the doctoral seminar, for example, a theme will be identified around which both teacher and students can interact in an effort to cope more adequately with the problems related to the theme. In such situations educational outcomes are appraised after they emerge; specific learnings are seldom formulated in terms of instructional objectives. The dialogue unfolds and is followed as well as led. In such situations the skills and understandings developed are used as instruments for inquiring more deeply into the significant or puzzling. Occasionally such problems require the invention of new intellectual tools, thus inducing the creative act and the creative contribution. Once devised or fashioned these new tools become candidates for instructional attention.

Since these two types of objectives – instructional and expressive – require different kinds of curriculum activities and evaluation procedures, they each must occupy a distinctive place in curriculum theory and development. Instructional objectives embody the codes and the skills that culture has to provide and which make inquiry possible. Expressive objectives designate those circumstances in which the codes and the skills acquired in instructional contexts can be used and elaborated; through their expansion and reconstruction culture remains vital. Both types of objectives and the learning activities they imply constitute, to modify Whitehead's phrase, "the rhythm of curriculum." That is, instructional objectives emphasize the acquisition of the known; while expressive objectives its elaboration, modification, and, at times, the production of the utterly new.

References

Eisner, E. W. Curriculum ideas in time of crisis. *Art Education*, 1965, 18(7).

Summary

Expressive objectives describe educational encounters. They do not prescribe the behaviour that a student is expected to acquire. They provide the teacher and the pupil with an invitation to explore or focus on issues that are of particular interest at that particular moment. They are evocative statements rather than prescriptive statements. Eisner argues that expressive objectives should feature more in curriculum planning than instructional objectives. This approach characterises the most sophisticated modes of intellectual work and has a proven track record. Ultimately, both instructional objectives and expressive objectives help create a 'rhythm of curriculum', which needs to be created and nurtured through skilful teachers. Both types of objectives are required, but teachers should have the freedom to employ both as and when they see fit.

Questions to consider

1. What examples of instructional objectives or expressive objectives can you find from within your own lesson planning?

2. What is the balance between these two different types of objectives within your teaching? Do you tend to favour one approach over the other?

3. What examples of expressive objectives does Eisner give in this extract? What would a set of expressive objectives look like within a music lesson or unit of work?

Investigations

Although Eisner's identification and formulation of expressive objectives spans across every curriculum subject, there are specific resonances for arts subjects within his writing. At the next available opportunity, why not try and plan a music lesson using two or three expressive objectives rather than instructional objectives. What difference does it make in the process of planning, for the selection of activities within the lesson, or the resources you might choose? Does the lesson itself have a different 'feel'? Do the pupils do anything differently? And how do you assess the learning within the lesson? Can you do this in the same way as you might normally do?

Think deeper

The requirements for teachers to anticipate the learning of their pupils within a particular lesson are strong. It is not uncommon for schools to insist on all pupils being told the learning objectives at the commencement of the lesson, often having to write them down into their exercise books or planners. Such approaches may have developed for legitimate reasons (e.g. it gives the pupils a clear idea of what they are doing in their music lesson today and why), or for other spurious reasons (e.g. to provide an accountability framework for internal or external inspection purposes).

Either way, Eisner's work on expressive objectives provides an alternative approach. The challenge for teachers is to relate the well-known developmental processes in music education (or at least a selection of them) to the construction of appropriately engaging musical activities within which pupils can experience musical success that fuels their intrinsic motivation to carry on getting better. The careful use of expressive opportunities can help frame these opportunities in a way that allows shifts towards more autonomy (in terms of Hargreaves' framework) but with elements of control (the teacher still has an overall responsibility to create an overall sense of direction and assess pupils' development at key stages).

Think wider

Fasting and Helge Sætre (2012) provide a fascinating account of these issues in a case study drawn from their work in Norwegian secondary schools. Their conclusions state that:

> The discussions suggests that both the phenomenon of assessment and the teaching and learning contexts are highly complex, and we argue that empirical, contextual and triangulating research designs are required to account for this complexity. In particular, the relations between teachers' intentions, classroom practice, and pupils' experiences and perceptions are important aspects that must be investigated in order to understand the significance, perils and possibilities of assessment in music.
>
> (Fasting and Helge Sætre 2012)

Note the link between the teachers' intentions, the classroom practice and the pupils' experiences and perceptions. As the last two chapters have demonstrated, our pupils' musical development is inextricably linked to the pedagogies that we choose to adopt and use within our teaching.

Conclusion

This chapter has considered a range of issues associated with musical development. From the outset, it recognised that this is a problematic term with a range of meanings in the research literature. However, music education researchers have explored this in various ways, noting the importance of its social constructs and specific interpretations within different musical processes. One of the key elements of encouraging all pupils to develop their musicality is the adoption and development of a strong, authentic musical pedagogy. As we will see in the following chapter, the key way that the music curriculum can be extended and enriched is as teachers re-conceptualise their own pedagogy as a site for curriculum development.

References

Fasting, R. and Helge Sætre, J. (2012) 'Getting Behind Assessment and Learning in Secondary School Music: A case study approach'. *Bulletin of Empirical Research in Music Education* 3:1. Also available from https://oda.hio.no/jspui/bitstream/10642/1161/1/887949.pdf [last accessed 12/05/12].

Folkestad, G. (2006) 'Formal and Informal Learning Situations or Practices vs Formal and Informal Ways of Learning'. *British Journal of Music Education* 23:2, pp. 135–145.

Hallam, S. (2010) 'The Power of Music: Its impact on the intellectual, social and personal development of children and young people'. *International Journal of Music Education* 28, pp. 269–289.

Kushner, S. (2010) 'Falsifying (Music) Education: Surrealism and Curriculum'. *Critical Education* 1:4, 1–12. Also available from http://ojs.library.ubc.ca/index.php/criticaled/article/view/182240/182307 [last accessed 12/05/12].

Sexton, F. (2012) 'Practitioner Challenges Working with Informal Learning Pedagogies'. *British Journal of Music Education,* 29:1, pp. 7–11.

Winters, M. (2012) 'The Challenges of Teaching Composing'. *British Journal of Music Education* 29:1, pp. 19–24.

5

Extending and Enriching the Music Curriculum

In the previous chapter we explored a number of key curriculum frameworks that have underpinned music curricula, in particular those found within the United Kingdom, in recent years. However, at the time of writing formal curriculum frameworks such as the National Curriculum are under review and it is highly likely that a new, slimmer, National Curriculum will be published around the same time as this book.

In this chapter we will be taking an alternative view of the curriculum. Following the lead of Lawrence Stenhouse and often repeated mantra that there is no curriculum development without teacher development (Stenhouse 1980, p. 85), we will explore how different ways of thinking about the music curriculum can lead to it being extended in various ways. We will do this in two ways. Firstly, we will consider how the 'subject' of Music can link to other subject areas; secondly, we will consider how the role you play as a musician and teacher in the classroom can give pupils a different understanding of what music it is and how it is learnt.

The first extract considers how music, as a subject, might link to other subject areas through the examination of a musical metaphor.

Extract 5.1

Source

Savage, J. (2011) *Cross Curricular Teaching and Learning in the Secondary School: The Arts.* London, Routledge, pp. 165–166.

Introduction

There is a tendency in education today to think of the curriculum in terms of a delivery model. Within this model, teachers are the white-van curriculum delivery service, dropping off pre-ordained packages of curriculum content within a set timetable of deliveries. Thankfully, there are alternative ways of conceptualising what the curriculum is about. Using the metaphor of the 'renaissance curriculum', the following extract explores how subjects might relate to each other in a more holistic way.

Key words and phrases

curriculum development, renaissance, subject cultures, cross-curricular

Extract

Taking a cue from Ross' use of the term 'Baroque' as a metaphor to describe a curriculum which contains 'clearly demarcated subjects, classified by both content knowledge and by the discourse forms appropriate and specific to each discipline' (Ross 2000: 3), a 'Renaissance' metaphor for the curriculum was developed. Renaissance scholars have identified two themes that are pertinent to the possible formation of a 'Renaissance' curriculum model (Cassirer 2000; Kristeller 1990). First, the theme of universal orderliness; second, the theme of universal interdependence. Universal orderliness was premised on the concept that every existing thing in the universe had its place in a divinely planned hierarchical order; universal interdependence held the belief that different segments of this great chain of universal orderliness reflected each other in particular ways in what were known as 'correspondences'. As an example, Renaissance thinkers viewed a human being as being a microcosm of the world as a whole. As the world was comprised for four elements (earth, water, air and fire), therefore the human body was composed of four 'humours' (sanguine, choleric, phlegmatic and melancholy). This had implications for medical science, philosophy and psychology within the period.

The existing curriculum models that permeate schools today could be conceived as presenting an orderly model of subjects, arranged in a hierarchical structure of sorts by perceived academic value (hence we have core or foundation subjects; optional or compulsory subjects at particular ages) akin to Ross' Baroque curriculum model (Ross 2000: 3). For each subject culture within this model, there will be categorisations or levels of knowledge, skills and understanding which are valued, perhaps some more highly than others. As we are only too aware, the arts subjects are often undervalued within schools when placed against other curriculum subjects in this model.

But within the cross-curricular Renaissance curriculum model, the notions of universal interdependence and correspondences become the metaphors for cross-curricularity and a different way of thinking about how subjects relate to each other. They facilitate exchanges or correspondences between subjects that relate to and enforce the natural orderliness found within the particular subject cultures. Whilst there will not be exact parallels (and this is where the metaphor begins to fall down), teachers' sensitivity to working across and between the subjects in this way begins to promote an orderliness in knowledge, thinking and understanding which may help stimulate students' cross-curricular learning and, perhaps, help them situate their learning within ways of thinking that are more closely related to their wider life experiences.

The idea of a 'Renaissance' model of cross-curricular development can be further enhanced when one investigates more closely the nature of the arts in the Renaissance period. For example, the music of the Renaissance period is characterised by polyphony, where composers wrote for many voices as if they were one. They did this by:

- Sharing common melodic materials between the voices.
- Allowing different voices to take the lead at different times.
- Ensuring that the voices were equally important and that one voice did not dominate the music at any given point.
- Handling dissonance (i.e. what could be perceived as 'clashes' in the sound of the music at a particular point) in a specific way, making sure that any of these tensions in the music were both prepared and resolved for the listener.

What would this metaphor of polyphony look like in our Renaissance model for cross-curricular curriculum development? It would allow the individual teacher to take key knowledge, skills and understanding, which are initiated and developed by individual subjects (the voices), and share these in a way that allows them to exist alongside each other with an equal sense of value. Within the context of their own teaching, it would allow a particular subject perspective to take the lead at a particular time, but always within a combined, overall sense of balance, purpose and direction that is in relationship to the whole. Perhaps a specific theme would be highlighted for a certain period and then developed by the various subject perspectives, each one presenting it with its own particular tone or resonance. It could handle potential clashes of knowledge or learning by carefully preparing learners for the potential dissonance, allowing them to enjoy the creative tension that the dissonance allows before resolving it for them in a sensitively managed and appropriate way.

References

Cassirer, E. (2000) *The Individual and the Cosmos in Renaissance Philosophy*, New York: Dover Publications.

Kristeller, P.O. (1990) *Renaissance Thought and the Arts*, Princeton, NJ: Princeton University Press.

Ross, A. (2000) *Curriculum: Construction and Critique*, London: Falmer Press.

Savage, J. (2011) *Cross Curricular Approaches to Teaching and Learning in Secondary Education*, London: Routledge.

Stenhouse, L. (1980) *Curriculum Research and Development in Action*, London: Heinemann Educational.

Summary

As musicians, the musical concepts and style of the Renaissance and Baroque periods of musical history are probably well known. This extract compares and contrasts the two styles, positioning 'subjects' within each style in different ways. In the renaissance curriculum model, knowledge, skills and understanding are characterised in a polyphonic way, with different voices (subjects) taking the lead at particular times; with a sharing of common melodic material (knowledge, skills or understanding) between the voices; ensuring an overall balance within the curriculum and handling dissonances (crises in learning) in a constructive way.

Questions to consider

1. What would a renaissance curriculum model mean in practice? How would it be organised within the school? Could it be practical?
2. Alternatively, what would a renaissance curriculum model mean for my individual subject teaching? Would it be possible to teach in a way that included 'voices' from other subject areas and share their melodic materials authentically? What would the problems in this approach be?

Investigations

Creative and metaphorical thinking of this type are useful ways of exploring new approaches or possibilities for the organisation of teaching and learning within a curriculum. What other metaphors for the organisation of subjects within the curriculum could you adopt towards this end?

Think deeper

There are some writers and thinkers who believe that the concept of individual subjects within a curriculum framework is outdated. Ken Robinson, for example, has stated:

> We need to eliminate the existing hierarchy of subjects. Elevating some disciplines over others only reinforces outmoded assumptions of industrialism and offends the principle of diversity. The arts, sciences, humanities, physical education, languages and maths all have equal and central contributions to make to a student's education. In fact, the entire notion of subjects needs to be questioned. The idea of separate subjects that have nothing in common offends the principle of dynamism. School systems should base their curriculum not on the idea of separate subjects, but on the much more fertile idea of disciplines . . . which makes possible a fluid and dynamic curriculum that is interdisciplinary.
>
> (Robinson 2009)

One example of such an approach is the RSA's Opening Minds project. This claims to promote 'innovative and integrated ways of thinking about education and the curriculum' (RSA 2012). Within this project, teachers design and develop a curriculum for their own schools based round the development of five key competences:

- citizenship;
- learning;
- managing information;
- relating to people;
- managing situations.

The theory goes that a competence-based approach enables students not just to acquire subject knowledge but to understand, use and apply it within the context of their wider learning and life. The RSA also claim that it offers students a more holistic and coherent way of learning which allows them to make connections and apply knowledge across different subject areas.

However, approaches such as those adopted within Opening Minds are rare. The vast majority of schools in the United Kingdom still adopt a subject-orientated approach to their curriculum design. As we will go on to see in the final extract of this chapter, the renaissance curriculum model works best when it is situated and applied to the pedagogy of one teacher.

Think wider

When thinking about extending the curriculum in new ways it is important to address the question of what we think that the purpose of the curriculum is at its most fundamental level. Ross (2000, pp. 81–82) has identified five curriculum types with associated purposes.

1. The *imposed* curriculum is about political power and ideology and is charged with maintaining the status quo;
2. The *social transformative* curriculum is charged with empowering the individual and helping them socially progress through the organisation of learning and knowledge;
3. The *content-driven* curriculum is an academic, subject-based approach that seeks to impose clear boundaries on knowledge and assess it accordingly;
4. The *objectives-driven* curriculum is characterised as utilitarian or vocational (historically it might be for pupils who, for whatever reason, were not deemed fit to work with the *content-driven* curriculum);
5. The *process-driven* is a progressive and developmental curriculum model characterised by an approach that places the pupil at the centre of the curriculum and empowers their choice, giving them the opportunity to discover things for themselves.

In reality, any set of curriculum framework will probably have a mix of one or more of these curriculum types. However, they present a useful set of lenses through which current models of music curricula can be viewed.

Extract 5.2

Source

Eisner, E. (2002) *The Arts and the Creation of Mind*. New Haven and London, Yale University Press, pp. 153–156.

Introduction

Extending the music curriculum by working in partnership with other subjects might be seen as desirable, but it can cause many problems. What is at the root of these problems? In the following extract, one of the leading thinkers in the field of arts education from the United States of America provides an insightful critique of over-zealous, uncritical approaches to positioning subjects together within the curriculum.

Key words and phrases

curriculum development, subject cultures, cross–curricular

Extract

The integration of the arts with other subjects can take more than one form. Perhaps the most common is to bring the arts in touch with the social studies or with history, so that when students are studying, say, the American Civil War or the Jazz Age, they also are being exposed to the painting, sculpture, music, and dance of the period.[1] The point of such contiguity is to provide students with a wider picture than the one they are able to secure through written materials alone. After all, it is extremely difficult to know what the music of a period sounds like without being able to listen to it, or to understand the form painting took during a particular period without being able to see it, or to experience the forms of dance or theater that were created at a particular period without images to consult. The availability of such images can enrich students' experience and their historical understanding.

At times, particularly at the elementary school level, teachers will make it possible for students to produce artwork that emulates the features of the work produced in the culture they are studying. Thus, fish measuring, say, a foot long, are sometimes used in classrooms as 'plates' to be painted with ink so that paper once laid upon them and pressed will yield a fish form, scales and all. Such an activity produces 'Japanese-like' images and is designed to give students the flavor of Japanese culture.

Of course, it is very easy to convert art programs into hand-maidens for learning the social studies or history without providing youngsters with occasions for developing artistic judgment or securing aesthetic forms of experience that mark effective art education. It is possible to dilute art programs and to delude oneself that art is being taught when in fact there is little in the way of artistic activity going on.

To say this is not to suggest that integrated curricula cannot pay attention to both aesthetic and imaginative features and at the same time enrich historical understanding. After all, life is a multimedia event, and the meanings that we secure from life are not simply contained in text; they yield their content through a wide variety of forms. Hence, the utilization of an experientially rich array of resources for understanding some aspect of the human condition is not a bad thing to pay attention to. What must also be paid attention to is the art in the project. Simply exploring materials without encouraging attention to aesthetic matters renders them void of their artistic potential. Such practice results in integration without art.

The practical implications are significant for teachers. They suggest that as much time and attention and effort need to be devoted to enabling students to attend to their work aesthetically as is paid to the social studies or history material they are studying. This means helping students learn to scrutinize their work aesthetically, to make judgments about it, to acquire techniques that will make it more powerful, and to acknowledge achievement by other students in such matters. An integrated curriculum makes more, not fewer, demands upon the teacher.

A second form of integration involves identifying a central, key idea that a variety of fields would examine. Consider the idea 'It is always darkest just before dawn.' Assume that you're a high school art teacher collaborating with teachers of English, history, and one of the sciences. What might be done with a group of high school sophomores or juniors in discussing the meaning of this statement? How might its meaning be expressed in different subject matter forms, and how might these forms of subject matter—English, history, one of the sciences, and the arts—be related to one another to produce a work that utilizes the various fields productively? In other words, how can various fields be instrumental to the illumination of a large idea?[2]

Consider others: 'survival of the fittest,' 'the process of metamorphosis,' 'the constancy of change'—the list could go on and on. Selecting an idea that is open-ended and stimulating to a group of high school students is a basis for thinking about the ways in which various fields address such notions and how those fields might be related to one another to create something that is more powerful than any single field could achieve. What needs to be kept salient in such a conception is the key idea to which works in the various fields serve as instrumentalities.

There has been a longstanding tension in the field of education between the desire to be rigorous in a disciplinary way, that is, to provide programs that initiate the young into the concepts and procedures of the disciplines taught within the school curriculum, and programs that relate field to field and are relevant to the student.[3] Thus, a student studying biology would be expected to understand the basic concepts of biology and the procedures used for biological inquiry. The same aspirations are applied to history or to the processes of writing literature. Students are to understand what needs attention in the construction of narrative and are to have practice in producing it.

Yet even individuals seeking to develop disciplinary rigor acknowledge that most school curricula are highly fragmented, that their parts do not fit well together, that subjects have an independent existence, and that the models that we use to plan programs are designed to produce junior disciplinarians rather than to help students understand the ways in which knowledge is integrated and how it might be used in the practical world that they will occupy. In short, we have broken Humpty Dumpty and cannot put the parts back so that they all fit together as they once did. Integration is, on the one hand, an aspiration and on the other hand a problem when one tries to maintain the 'integrity' of a discipline. How one can achieve both—which, if possible, is desirable—remains to be worked out. The farther students proceed in school, the greater the separation among the various disciplines.

The practical need for time to learn is perhaps made most vivid in the acquisition of skills. It is one thing to survey the pottery of the Han dynasty, and it is quite another to have the time needed to learn how to throw a pot on a wheel. Unless there is sufficient time devoted to learning how to center a ball of clay on a potter's wheel and to pull up a gracefully formed, thin-walled vessel, students are unlikely to reach a threshold that makes it possible for them to understand what throwing a pot entails. In other words, there is an irreconcilable tension between the demands that need to be met in understanding what a discipline requires and, on the other hand, understanding its connection to other disciplines. I have no good resolution to this dilemma.

Notes

1. Marcy Singer, "Sound, Image, and Word in the Curriculum: The Making of Historical Sense" (Ph.D. diss., Stanford University, 1991).
2. See Elliot Eisner, *Cognition and Curriculum Reconsidered* (New York: Teachers College Press, 1994).
3. For a sophistication discussion of curriculum integration and issues related to it see Basil Bernstein, "On the Classification and Framing of Educational Knowledge," in *Knowledge and Control: New Directions for the Sociology of Education*, ed. Michael F. D. Young (London: Collier-Macmillan, 1971), 47–69.

Summary

Eisner outlines two ways in which arts subjects can be integrated with other subjects within the curriculum. The first approach sees the arts in a supportive role alongside another subjects ('handmaidens' in Eisner's terminology); the second approach involves identifying a key idea that a variety of subjects might consider together (with similarities here to, perhaps, the Opening Minds model discussed above). The extract closes with a powerful assertion for the rigour of individual arts subjects. This can be too easily and unhelpfully compromised by approaches that link arts subjects with other subjects. There is, Eisner in closing states, an 'irreconcilable tension between the demands that need to be met in understanding what a discipline requires and, on the other hand, understanding its connection to other disciplines. I have no good resolution to this dilemma' (Eisner 2002, p. 156).

Questions to consider

1. Can you think of any examples of curriculum initiatives that have been implemented in your school that fall into either of the categories that Eisner identifies?

2. More positively, how can you ensure that the integrity of music, as a particular subject, is maintained when it is brought into a relationship with other curriculum subjects?

Investigations

If music was to be taught alongside other subjects in a cross-curricular project, what are the key elements of music education that would need to be preserved or protected? How could you ensure that your pedagogy remains musically authentic within such a collaboration?

Think deeper

Approaches to extending or developing the curriculum in ways that bring subjects alongside other curricula dimensions, as we explored above with the RSA Opening Minds project, are not new. The implementation of the first National Curriculum in 1992 was encompassed by an extensive range of discussion about the inclusion of what were referred to at the time as cross-curricular dimensions, skills and themes.

Eventually, cross-curricular themes such as economic and industrial understanding, health education, environmental education and citizenship were implemented. Writing in 1993, a year after the introduction of the National Curriculum, Pumfrey commented that:

> At present, the National Curriculum is far from fully in place in schools. The way in which various subjects and cross-curricular themes have been introduced into the secondary school syllabus has not been of the highest order. Too little preparation and consultation have led to controversial changes.
>
> (Pumfrey 1993, p. 21)

This sounds quite familiar! Individual teachers struggled to make sense of these monumental changes in curriculum policy and design and had to sideline cross-curricular themes in favour of core subjects. In summary, this tumultuous period demonstrated many things. Firstly, the marriage of subjects and cross-curricular themes within the curriculum is not an easy one. Secondly, the imposition of large changes in curriculum design often means that teachers will focus on what they know, i.e. their subject, and not make the wider links that might have been envisaged by a 'whole curriculum'. Finally, although the benefits of a cross-curricular set of themes and skills were recognised by politicians and educators, the practical implementation of the curriculum itself meant that opportunities were missed and creative links were established between subjects, or between subjects and cross-curricular themes.

Think wider

Perhaps a more constructive way of looking at the issue of how the music curriculum can be extended in meaningful ways is to consider some of the common elements that it shares with other subjects. For example, spoken and written language is a common element in all curriculum subjects. There are a number of key ways in which language mediates teachers' engagement with their own subject. One of these ways is illustrated through the process of planning.

Effective planning is based on the setting of appropriate learning objectives and outcomes, choosing and structuring suitable teaching activities and defining strategies for differentiation and assessment. Within the process of planning, language has a specific part to play at a number of levels:

- At a macro level, as we have discussed already, the division of the curriculum by subject area results in artificial distinctions in language usage, with certain language types or words seen as belonging to a particular subject or discipline;
- Within specific subjects the language patterns and prevailing types of discourse mediate teachers' and pupils' engagement with particular concepts or forms of knowledge;
- At the micro level of the individual classroom, various types of language and talk will exhibit elements of different discourses, including the subject culture and its associated patterns of language use, the formal or informal language types that teachers and pupils adopt, and more besides.

But at each of these levels, language has a provisionality and ambiguity which is at the core of its importance as a tool for thinking and learning:

> The fact that language is not always reliable for causing precise meanings to be generated in someone else's mind is a reflection of its powerful strength as a medium for creating new understanding. It is the inherent ambiguity and adaptability of language as a meaning-making system that makes the relationship between language and thinking so special.
>
> (Mercer 2000, p. 6)

By becoming aware of this inherent ambiguity, teachers can begin to play with language within the planning process in a productive way. This could affect the way they plan their own subject teaching as well as any potential cross-curricular approaches that they are wanting to develop. The richness of language, and the possibilities for multiple meaning making, can be exploited for educational benefits in a range of contexts. Mercer gives us an obvious example from the English curriculum perspective:

> When we are dealing with complex, interesting presentations of ideas, variations in understanding are quite normal and sometimes are even welcomed; how otherwise could there be new interpretations of Shakespeare's plays, and why else are we interested in them? I am sure that my understanding of Pinker's book, despite the clarity of his writing, will not be exactly what he might have intended or expected, and I know that I will not make quite the same interpretation of it as other readers. I expect that many authors are frequently dismayed to discover that readers misunderstand their 'message'; but they should not necessarily take this as failure on their part. The act of reading any text relies on the interpretative efforts of a reader, as well as on the communicative efforts and intentions of the author.
>
> (ibid, p. 5)

The same issues would be true for the majority of subjects. The key point here is to consider how the quite normal and expected variations in thinking that occur when using language as part of planning, or more widely within the classrooms, can be built upon to develop a more extensive music curriculum.

If this is true for the spoken language, how much more so would it be true for the 'language' of musical sound? Not surprisingly, there have been some rich explorations in the extension and development of music curricula that promote a richer engagement with sound than words, spoken or written, can provide. Our next extract will turn our attention to one of these: Dalcroze Eurhythmics.

Extract 5.3

Source

Philpott, C. (2001) 'The body and musical literacy'. In Philpott, P. and Plummeridge, C. (eds) *Issues in Music Teaching*. London, Routledge, pp. 83–86.

Introduction

In the previous extract we explored some of the limitations of certain types of curriculum development that seek to position music alongside other subjects in a detrimental manner. Our chapter on extending and enriching the music curriculum is moving towards a conclusion that positions curriculum development at the heart of teacher development. But in respect of the points that Mercer makes about language, it is important to recognise the uniqueness of music in facilitating communication without the spoken or written word. In the following extract, Philpott explores the connections between the human body and music learning as exemplified in the work of Emile Jaques-Dalcroze. As we will see, these ideas present a very powerful argument for a rethinking of music education and associated curricula.

Key words and phrases

pedagogy, Dalcroze, eurhythmics, dynamic body, curriculum development

Extract

The dynamic body is important to learning and is embodied in music. It should not therefore be surprising that music educators have made explicit links between the body and musical learning. Emile Jaques-Dalcroze felt that the connections between the physical and musical learning are very close, if not synonymous. He became frustrated that his conservatoire students could not play their music fluently, expressively or technically correct to his satisfaction.

> He saw feet tapping, heads nodding, bodies responding to the nuances of the music, following a crescendo, marking an accent. They were allowing the music literally to penetrate them through and through, they were responding to it *in movement*. Here lay the answer! these pupils of his, *they* were the instrument he needed, they *were* the instrument. He realised that to music and rhythm he must add movement, thereby acknowledging the body as man's first instrument of self expression.
>
> (Dutoit, 1971: 9)

For Jaques-Dalcroze all types of rhythmic movement (actual, harmonic, dynamic, tonal, expressive, structural) were the most potent elements in music and the most closely related to life itself. Hence his argument that rhythm is movement, is essentially physical and that musical understanding is the result of a physical experience. Furthermore, every movement involves time and space, and the perfection of physical resources in time and space results in clarity of musical perception.

> Rhythm, like dynamics, depends entirely on movement, and finds its nearest prototype in our muscular system. All the nuances of time – allegro, andante, accelerando, ritenuto – all the nuances of energy – forte, piano, crescendo, diminuendo – can be 'realised' by our bodies, and the acuteness of our musical feeling will depend on the acuteness of our bodily sensations.
>
> (Jaques-Dalcroze, 1921: 60)

It is not possible to do justice to his system of 'eurhythmics' here. In short, he encouraged musical learning through a series of exercises, when moving to music and assuming the expressive quality of the music in actions, e.g. pupils might be asked to take on the shape of the music. While Jaques-Dalcroze felt that rhythmic movement was *the* common and unifying factor in music, i.e. the physical and the cognitive, he also saw music as being capable not only of integrating but ultimately transcending these in a holistic vision of education.

> More than ever [children] should be enlightened as to the relations existing between soul and mind, between the conscious and the subconscious, between imagination and the processes of action. Thoughts should be brought into immediate contact with behaviour – the new education aiming at regulating the interaction between our nervous and our intellectual forces.
>
> (ibid.: x)

Research by Taylor (1989) seems to suggest that moving to music can indeed promote musical learning. She used two groups of children in their early years at secondary school (experiment and control) to listen to a wide variety of short extracts of music, and then asked them to convey 'how the music goes' to a deaf boy or girl. The control group were to jot ideas down while the experimental group were asked to move or use physical gestures to help the deaf child understand the music. The results supported the hypothesis that children using the kinaesthetic strategy would perform better on recognition tests delivered some time later. Taylor's work supplies significant evidence for the important realisation that all understanding is enhanced when the physical and cognitive dimensions are recognised.

The developmental spiral proposed by Swanwick and Tillman (1986) has been heavily influenced by the developmental models of Piaget and Bruner. It is therefore not surprising to find that the first and fundamental 'turn' of *Mastery* is characterised as a phase of development which is dominated by a sensory and manipulative engagement with music. Children are impressed at this level with the physical sensation of sound and with the gross exploration of instruments.

> In the compositions of our very young children. .. we observed a keen interest in very soft and very loud sounds. .. The 'mechanical' impulse can be seen at work when the physical aspects of instruments themselves determine the organisation of the music.
>
> (Swanwick, 1988: 64)

From this early 'bodily' engagement with music children progress to the higher cognitive levels of Expression, Form and Value. However, while this is not the place for a full exposition of the spiral, an important implication of Swanwick

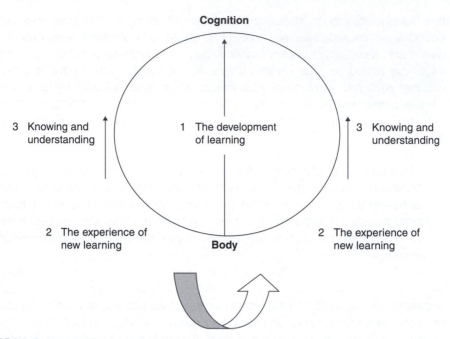

FIGURE 6.1 Body and cognition in musical experience and development.

and Tillman's work is that the sensory aspects of music are never left behind. Thus, the spiral operates in at least three different senses (see Figure 6.1):

1. The musical development of children begins with bodily sense which is then internalised as thought in the higher turns (this is very Piagetian).
2. The spiral is experiential in that it is 'reactivated each time [new] music is encountered' and the 'first and most striking impression of music is always its sensory surface' (Swanwick, 1988: 82).
3. The spiral is also experiential in that the lower turns never leave us in our engagement with music and 'we never lose the need to respond to sound materials, re-entering the spiral repeatedly, no matter what age we happen to be' (ibid.: 67).

While children move on to other cognitive levels, the lowest and most 'physical' turn is always a part of higher understanding. Perhaps this is peculiar to higher levels of musical cognition. Piaget argues that the sensory/active phase is an important stage in development but there is also the suggestion that the phase is then somehow left behind. Once we are able to use abstract conceptual tools, we do not need to engage with the lower levels of development in order to learn. Indeed, the 'body in the mind' at all levels of cognition is often given scant attention, i.e. it has been considered important in early development but is then somehow transcended in higher cognition. However, the notion of the 'body in the mind' can be seen as common to all forms of cognition and this can be explored through the concept of metaphor which is an important vehicle for the transference of bodily understanding into higher cognitive processes.

References

Dutoit, C.-L. (1971) *Music Movement Therapy*, Croydon: Dalcroze Society.

Jaques-Dalcroze, E. (1921, 1965, 1980) *Rhythm, Music and Education*, Croydon: Dalcroze Society.

Swanwick, K. (1988) *Music, Mind and Education*, London: Routledge.

Swanwick, K. and Tillman, J. (1986) 'The sequence of musical development: a study of children's composition', *British Journal of Music Education*, 3, 3, 305–39.

Taylor, D. (1989) 'Physical movement and memory for music', *British Journal of Music Education* 6, 3, 251–60.

Summary

The 'dynamic body' is central to all musical practice. It is also essential within teaching and learning. Herein lies an important link. For Dalcroze, all types of rhythmic movement are at the centre of musical learning. Moving to music is essential to understanding music in a holistic way. The body can understand or feel the music in ways that the mind cannot understand. Philpott gives a short summary of this approach in the extract, before contextualising the work of Dalcroze within the developmental models of music education drawn from the work of Swanwick, Piaget and Bruner. The first stage of 'mastery' is dominated by a sensory and manipulative engagement with sound and this, Philpott argues, is an essential stage for all when encountering new music. More than that, he asserts that this sense of bodily engagement with music never leaves us. We never lose the need to respond to sound in a physical way whatever age we happen to be.

Questions to consider

1. What are the consequences of these ideas for my own teaching of music?
2. In light of Philpott's presentation of the work of Dalcroze, what does it mean to be musically literate?

Think deeper

Drawing on his analysis of Dalcroze's work, Philpott's chapter goes on to consider a range of implications for music education. He suggests that the following themes are important foundations to musical learning and cognition: the dynamic body, sensory-motor experience, the physical, movement, dance, active learning and play (Philpott 2001, p. 87). These themes should be kept in mind as the basics for any process of musical development, for any re-engagement with music at any age and as a constant element of cognition at all levels. In summary, 'the body is always in the mind' (ibid, p. 88).

Ofsted's recent report into music education in the United Kingdom confirms the value of this approach and provides some practical advice (Ofsted 2012). It reinforces one of the key messages of these opening chapters to teach music musically. Ofsted suggest that schools should be encouraged to:

> Promote teachers' use of musical sound as the dominant language of musical teaching and learning by:
>
> ■ Ensuring that lesson planning includes a strong focus on the teacher's musical preparation as well as defining lesson structures and procedures;
>
> ■ Establishing musical sound as the 'target language' of teaching and learning, with talking and writing about music supporting, rather than driving, the development of pupils' musical understanding;
>
> ■ Developing and refining teachers' listening and musical modelling skills, so that they can more accurately interpret and respond to pupils' music-making and show more effectively how to improve the musical quality of their work.
>
> (Ofsted 2012, p. 7)

As with many issues, it is good to see that Ofsted are catching up with key approaches to teaching and learning in music that have been explored throughout the research literature for many years!

Think wider

Paynter's interpretation of these themes focuses on pupils being able to assimilate music through their formal music education. In the following extract, notice how he urges us, like Eisner, to maintain the distinctiveness of music as a subject in its own right, and as a subject of study within formal education, before turning to the key way in which music should be made accessible for all pupils:

> Schools today have to fulfil a variety of needs, social as well as educational, but the core of their responsibility is, as it always has been, the learning that takes place under the guidance of teachers in classrooms. That core is increasingly under pressure, not only from the demands of testing and appraisal but also from expansion (e.g. 'literacy' hours and the reintroduction of 'citizenship' lessons). We ought to be sure that everything we put into the curriculum has educational justification. Time was when we were content to accept music as a relaxation from the rigours of seemingly more demanding

subjects! That was not good enough then, and it won't do now. Neither will it suffice to impose on music a spurious academicism to make it appear rigorous in exactly the same terms as some other curriculum subjects. Apart from anything else, that is unnecessary: music has its own rigour in the demands of sensitivity, imagination, and inventiveness common to all artistic endeavour – qualities which are sorely needed in the modern world. This, I suggest, is what we should expect, first and foremost, from musical education in the classroom – an education accessible to all pupils. The justification for music in these circumstances is not more information to be assimilated but a very important human quality to be exercised and developed: the potential we all have to make art by making up music. There could be no better illustration of the old maxim that 'You cannot teach anyone anything she or he does not already know'. It calls to mind Herbert Read's (1958: 298) often quoted words: 'Appreciation is not acquired by passive contemplation: we only appreciate beauty on the basis of our own creative aspirations.'

(Paynter 2001, pp. 223–224)

Paynter's words are a ringing endorsement for the development of a skilful music pedagogy. This chapter has explored a number of ways in which the music curriculum might be enriched and extended. We started by considering how music might be taught in relationship with other academic subjects. However, this is not without difficulty. Similar problems occur when it is brought alongside other academic themes or dimensions. Philpott's work on Dalcroze represents a much richer alternative. In looking to the core engagement with music that we have all enjoyed as musicians, we can find a richer and more meaningful musical pedagogy that builds on key processes of musical learning that, hopefully, we have experienced ourselves.

Extract 5.4

Source

Savage, J. (2011) *Cross-Curricular Teaching and Learning in the Secondary School.* London, Routledge, pp. 177–179.

Introduction

The final extract of this chapter reasserts the role of the individual music teacher and their pedagogy as the most meaningful way in which the music curriculum can be extended and enriched. Through another metaphor, it encourages you to reconsider your pedagogy and look outwards to new opportunities to connect with music and create an engagement climate of discovery within your classroom.

Key words and phrases

pedagogy, curriculum development, centrifugal teaching, cross–curricular

Extract

Centripetal forces move or direct something towards the centre. In physiology, nerve impulses are sent centripetally to the central nervous system; in botany, the florets nearer the edge of a flower open first and they open centripetally as they move towards the centre. A centripetal approach to life characterises the perspective and attitude of hedgehogs (see Berlin 1953, pp. 1–2) who, despite their many strengths, are unable to see life in any other way apart from through their particular mindset or disposition.

In contrast, centrifugal forces move away from the centre. Centrifugal comes from an amalgamation of two Latin words, *centrum* meaning 'centre', and *fugere* meaning 'to flee'. For Berlin (1953), foxes characterise a centrifugal approach to life. Their thought patterns are, in his words, 'scattered or diffused'. They move on multiple levels, drawing on a vast range of experiences and objects without trying to fit them together within one all-embracing rationale. They are happy to live with the incomplete, the contradictory and, unlike hedge-hogs, thrive on the multiple meanings that life throws at them.

As equally tentatively as I suggested a Renaissance curriculum model, I would like to put forward the concept of centrifugal teaching, which, over the coming years, may provide the best way to develop cross-curricular teaching and learning. What elements define this approach?

Centrifugal teachers are, by instinct, outward looking. They have many interests and they are happy moving between multiple areas of knowledge, pulling together diverse patterns and ideas from different subject areas without worrying too much about a final framework for their co-existence or ultimate meaning. They are willing to pursue metaphors and explore the tensions within them, without closing down patterns of thought too early. For the centrifugal teacher, contradictions between subjects and self-contradictions in their work are creative forces that spur them onwards and outwards to further discoveries. For these teachers, the spiralling, centripetal forces associated with traditional subject cultures and associated pedagogies are an anathema. These suck their creative forces dry and lead them to educational and professional implosions. But centrifugal teachers can often be misunderstood. Their ability to live with uncertainty can be threatening to those who value certainty and see it as a pre-requisite for action. Their pragmatism is seen by some as a lack of ability to establish what is right or wrong within curriculum development; their cautiousness is dismissed as hesitancy, and their self-doubt and provisionality as woolly-headed thinking.

Perhaps you feel that this is a bit strong? Maybe it is. But perhaps there does need to be a significant shift towards a more centrifugal teaching approach if we are to shake the current approaches to curriculum development and pedagogy to their core and develop new curriculum models with cross-curricular pedagogies at their heart. It is easy to meddle around the edges of our subject pedagogies, to do what we have always done and re-package them according to the current educational climate and philosophy.

However, this is not what is required to initiate and sustain a cross-curricular approach to teaching and learning that is sensitive and sympathetic to traditional subject cultures, whilst at the same time enriching, exploring and embracing new pedagogical avenues and directions. As we will consider below, a failure to respond to wider changes in society will result in traditional models of teaching and learning losing currency and value amongst young people.

To return to the metaphors that opened this chapter, teaching seems dominated by hedgehogs. We need more foxes. We need more teachers to think and act centrifugally rather than centripetally. Whilst it is unrealistic and unhelpful to use the term 'educational polymaths', we do need teachers who are able to handle knowledge and understanding from diverse areas with a significant degree of authenticity. Intellectual promiscuity of the type decried by Djerassi (Carr 2009) is not the answer. Nor is intellectual polygamy despite the apparent democratic value it might bestow upon its particular subjects. As we have seen, powerful subject discourses are a real and defining force within our identities and subject cultures, which imbue us with a particular tone or, in Prensky's term, accent which it is impossible to lose (Prensky 2001, pp. 2–3). To return briefly to our discussion of Renaissance polyphonic music, if all the voices in an ensemble sounded the same the result would be bland; a key component of its beauty would be lost. A centrifugal disposition as a teacher will, in part at least, lead to the development of a successful cross-curricular pedagogy. It will also underpin a disposition and ability to collaborate meaningfully with other teachers within a Renaissance curriculum model based on equality of discourse, expression and interaction.

References

Berlin, I. (1953) *The Hedgehog and the Fox: An essay on Tolstoy's view of history*. London, Weidenfeld & Nicolson.

Carr, E. (2009) 'The Last Days of the Polymath'. *Intelligent Life*, Autumn. Available from http://www.moreintelligentlife.com/content/edward-carr/last-days-polymath [last accessed 8 January 2010].

Prensky, M. (2001) 'Digital Natives, Digital Immigrants'. *On the Horizon* 9:5. Lincoln, NCB University Press.

Summary

This extract explores the metaphor of centrifugal forces. Centrifugal forces move away from the centre. A centrifugal teacher is a teacher who looks outwards from their curriculum area and embraces new opportunities for curriculum development and their pedagogy. A centrifugal approach to teaching is a creative approach that can underpin specific approaches to cross-curricularity or other forms of curriculum extension and enrichment.

Questions to consider

1. Metaphorical explorations are fine as far as they go, but what would a centrifugal teacher actually look like in the school where I teach?

2. What aspects of a centrifugal pedagogy could I adopt within my teaching?

Think deeper

This extract makes reference to an interesting classification system explored within an essay by Isaiah Berlin. He classified intellectuals as either hedgehogs or foxes! The hedgehog knows one big thing and tries to explain as much as possible within that conceptual framework. The fox knows lots of small things and is content to improvise explanations on a case-by-case basis.

Are you a hedgehog or a fox? You could work through this short quiz and find out: http://jsavage.org.uk/?p=528. But do not take it too seriously!

Conclusion

Developing the music curriculum, by extension or enrichment, is always linked to the development of a teacher's pedagogy. The curriculum itself as an external framework only has limited impact on pupils' experience in the classroom. Who their teachers are and what they do is much more important. This chapter has charted a process. Starting with how music could be linked to other subjects, it has moved towards the conclusion that you, and your pedagogy, are the key site upon which interesting music education opportunities are constructed.

Do you remember Douglas Brown, who we met in Chapter 3 through our discussion of Robin Alexander's work? He was described as 'not one teacher, but four'. What were the four elements? Language, literature, music and the 'man through whom the power of all these things was unlocked'. Music teachers can too quickly look to others for things that they can actually do themselves. As we will see in Chapter 7, the brokering of effective networks for music education can be very powerful and enriching. But first and foremost, if you are teaching music in a school, day-in day-out, you need to remember that you are the most important musical influence in the lives of the children that you teach. You have great power and responsibility. How you view yourself, how you view music, how you develop, extend and enrich the curriculum you offer, and how you view your role in the classroom (your pedagogy) are all vital considerations. I hope that this survey of the research literature in these areas has given you plenty of ideas for your future development in this crucial area.

References

Mercer, N. (2000) *Words and Minds: How we use language to think together.* London, Routledge.

Ofsted (2012) *Music in Schools: Wider still and wider.* London, OFSTED.

Paynter, J. (2001) 'Music in the School Curriculum: Why bother?' *British Journal of Music Education* 19:3, pp. 215–226.

Pumfrey, P. (1993) 'Cross-curricular Elements and the National Curriculum'. In Verma, G. and Pumfrey, P. (eds) (1993) *Cross Curricular Contexts: Themes and dimensions in secondary schools.* London, The Falmer Press.

Read, H. (1958) *Education Through Art.* London, Faber & Faber.

Robinson, K. (2009) 'Fertile Minds Need Feeding'. *The Guardian* http://www.guardian.co.uk/education/2009/feb/10/teaching-sats [last accessed 12/05/12].

Ross, A. (2000) *Curriculum: Construction and critique.* London, Falmer Press.

RSA (2012) 'What is RSA Opening Minds?' http://www.rsaopeningminds.org.uk/about-rsa-openingminds/ [last accessed 17/5/12].

Stenhouse, L. (1980) 'Product or Process? A reply to Brian Crittenden', reprinted in Ruddock, J. and Hopkins, D. (eds) (1985) *Research as a Basis for Teaching.* London, Heinemann Educational.

6

Musical Approaches to Assessment

Extract 6.1

Source

Eisner, E. (2005) *Reimagining Schools: The selected works of Elliot W. Eisner*. London, Routledge, pp. 210–212.

Introduction

The work of Elliot Eisner has featured throughout this book. He is, in my mind, one of the finest writers and thinkers about arts education of recent years. In this extract from an article written in 2002 (entitled 'What can education learn from the arts about the practice of education?'), Eisner discusses two key elements of 'distinctive forms of thinking' that are rooted in an artistic intelligence. These, he argues, have many resonances for the practice of education and assessment.

Key words and phrases

cognition, knowledge, assessment, context, composition, improvisation

Extract

Not everything knowable can be articulated in propositional form. The limits of our cognition are not defined by the limits of our language. We have a long philosophic tradition in the West that promotes the view that knowing anything requires some formulation of what we know in words; we need to have warrants for our assertions. But is it really the case that what we cannot assert we cannot know? Not according to Michael Polanyi, who speaks of tacit knowledge and says, "We know more than we can tell."[1] And Dewey tells us that while science states meaning, the arts express meaning. Meaning is not limited to what is assertable. Dewey goes on to say that the aesthetic cannot be separated from the intellectual, and for the intellectual to be complete it must bear the stamp of the aesthetic. Having a nose for telling questions and a feel for incisive answers are not empty metaphors.

These ideas not only expand our conception of the ways in which we know; they expand our conception of mind. They point to the cognitive frontiers that our teaching might explore. How can we help students recognize the ways in which we express and recover meaning, not only in the arts but in the sciences as well? How can we introduce them to the art of *doing* science? After all, the practice of any practice, including science, can be an art.

It's clear to virtually everyone that we appeal to expressive form to say what literal language can never say. We build shrines to express our gratitude to the heroes of 9/11 because somehow we find our words inadequate. We appeal to poetry when we bury and when we marry. We situate our most profound religious practices within compositions we have choreographed. What does our need for such practices say to us about the sources of our understanding and what do they mean for how we educate? At a time when we seem to want to package performance into standardized measurable skill sets, questions such as these seem to me to be especially important. The more we feel the pressure to standardize, the more we need to remind ourselves of what we should not try to standardize.

A fifth lesson we can learn from the arts about the practice of education pertains to the relationship between thinking and the material with which we and our students work. In the arts, it is plain that in order for a work to be created, we must think within the constraints and affordances of the medium we elect to use. The flute makes certain qualities possible that the bass fiddle will never produce, and vice versa. Painting with watercolor makes certain visual qualities possible that cannot be created with oil paint. The artist's task is to exploit the possibilities of the medium in order to realize aims he or she values. Each material imposes its own distinctive demands, and to use it well we have to learn to think within it.

Where are the parallels when we teach and when students learn in the social studies, in the sciences, in the language arts? How must language and image be treated to say what we want to say? How must a medium be treated for the medium to mediate? How do we help students get smart with the media they are invited to use, and what are the cognitive demands that different media make upon those who use them? Carving a sculpture out of a piece of wood is clearly a different cognitive task than building a sculpture out of plasticine clay. The former is a subtractive task, the latter an additive one. Getting smart in any domain requires at the very least learning to think within a medium. What are the varieties of media we help children get smart about? What do we neglect?

It seems to me that the computer has a particularly promising role to play in providing students with opportunities to learn how to think in new ways. Assuming the programs can be developed, and it is my impression that many already have been, operations are performable on the computer that cannot be executed through any other medium. New possibilities for matters of representation can stimulate our imaginative capacities and can generate forms of experience that would otherwise not exist. Indeed, the history of art itself is, in large measure, a history studded with the effects of new technologies. This has been at no time more visible than during the twentieth century. Artists have learned to think within materials such as neon tubing and plastic, day-glow color and corfam steel, materials that make forms possible that Leonardo da Vinci himself could not have conceived of. Each new material offers us new affordances and constraints, and in the process develops the ways in which we think. There is a lesson to be learned here for the ways in which we design curricula and the sorts of materials we make it possible for students to work with.

Decisions we make about such matters have a great deal to do with the kinds of minds we develop in school. Minds, unlike brains, are not entirely given at birth; minds are also forms of cultural achievement. The kinds of minds we develop are profoundly influenced by the opportunities to learn that the school provides. And this is the point of my remarks about what education might learn from the arts. The kinds of thinking I have described, and it is only a sample, represent the kind of thinking I believe schools should promote. The promotion of such thinking requires not only a shift in perspective regarding our educational aims; it represents a shift in the kind of tasks we invite students to undertake, the kind of thinking we ask them to do, and the kind of criteria we apply to appraise both their work and ours. Artistry, in other words, can be fostered by how we design the environments we inhabit. The lessons the arts teach are not only for our students; they are for us as well.

Notes

1. Michael Polanyi, *The Tacit Dimension* (London: Routledge and Kegan Paul, 1967).

Summary

Drawing on Polanyi, the first key point that Eisner makes is that we know more than we can tell. The limits of our cognition are not confined nor defined by the limits of our language. In a similar vein, he quotes Dewey's viewpoint that the sciences state meaning but the arts express meaning. What are the consequences of this line of thought for education? Eisner argues that the more we try to standardise learning the more we need to remind ourselves that some things should not be standardised.

The second key area that Eisner explores in the extract is that the resources used in a particular activity constrain and afford certain types of response. The medium within which our pupils are working needs to be carefully chosen and understood by the teacher in order to contextualise the learning that takes place within and through it.

Questions to consider

1. How do Eisner's two points relate to the principles and practices of educational assessment?
2. If pupils really know more than they can tell, what forms of musical expression should teachers help them develop in order for them to find their voice and express it effectively?
3. How can musical processes such as composition or improvisation be taught in such a way as to actively encourage pupils to reflect meaningfully on their experiences?

Investigations

Eisner's second point focuses on the 'medium' that teachers choose. This has some obvious repercussions for the music teacher's choice of units of work and the selection of resources within it. Spend some time reviewing your, or another teacher's, choices in this respect. How do the units of work that pupils are expected to engage with constrain or empower their musical responses? How do the resources that you have chosen to use within the unit affect the ways in which pupils can express their musical voices?

Think deeper

Burnard's response to Polanyi's assertion (Burnard 2000) is to encourage teachers to facilitate authentic forms of music making, e.g. composition and improvisation, whilst giving emphasis to the development of a shared understanding between themselves and their pupils. In her view, musical learning must be experiential and reflection must be integrated within the curriculum. From these general points, Burnard has the following specific advice for the teaching of improvisation and composition that must incorporate:

> examining past and present assumptions about what it is to improvise and compose; (ii) encouraging children to be more reflective by asking children to think about how as well as what they improvise and compose; (iii) ensuring the starting points for improvising and composing are based on children's existing knowledge and experience; (iv) ensuring children have the opportunity to select from a wide range of instruments; (v) sufficient time for children to clarify conceptual modification or changes and to test and extend ideas through their actions and reflections; (vi) a clear distinction between critical appraisal and interpretation of improvised and composed outcomes; and (vii) opportunities for children to confer meaning on the creation of their own music and musical experiences.
>
> (ibid, p. 22)

Similar reflections about the pedagogy of musical performance can be drawn from the work of Bennett Reimer. He argues that musical performance should be considered an integrated part of every pupil's music education for a number of reasons. Musical performance itself can be conceived as an act of intelligence because it is dependent upon, and springs from, the skills of a knowing body, and within musical performance the mind and body are unified. The practice of musical performance is a primary way in which musical problems are dealt with and by which musical thinking takes place. This viewpoint has interesting consequences for the practice of educational assessment. Clearly, what pupils can talk or write about in respect of their musical learning will only be a small fragment of their total understanding. Or, as Reimer puts it:

> Our approach to teaching performance needs to be guided by the fundamental principle that we are developing an inherent human intelligence, in which thinking, feeling and acting are uniquely conjoined in the process of bringing music ideas to sonic fruition.
>
> (Reimer 1994, p. 20)

Think wider

Eisner's first point was that we often know more than we can tell. Leaving aside educational assessment for a moment, this statement has important consequences for the ways in which teachers develop their own skills. As we discussed in Chapter 3, effective teachers need a range of skills including good subject and pedagogical knowledge. But there is an important third area within which all teachers need to develop their competence: the professional characteristics needed to be a good teacher, including social competences and the ability to generate and sustain positive relationships with children. This is often perceived to be the most demanding aspect of a young teacher's work (Johnson and Birkeland 2003).

Here, the concept of 'tacit knowledge', identified by Eisner from Polanyi's work, has some interesting resonances for initial teacher education and continuing professional development. Complex professional knowledge is often tacit and not easily made explicit (e.g. in the formulation of a set of rules for action). One example of such an area might be the strategies needed to promote good behaviour management in the classroom. The work of Elliott *et al.* (2011) has conceptualised tacit knowledge according to three main features:

1. It is acquired without a high degree of direct input from others;
2. It is essentially procedural in nature, concerning itself with how to best undertake certain tasks in specific situations (i.e. it serves to guide action with itself being easily articulated);
3. It is intricately bound up with the individual's own goals and reflects our own circumstances, dispositions and personalities.

(Elliott *et al.* 2011, p. 85).

All of these characteristics of tacit knowledge will become important for the construction of an effective process of musical assessment. Our second extract turns its attention to our chapter's main theme.

Extract 6.2

Source

Fautley, M. (2010) *Assessment in Music Education*. Oxford, OUP, pp. 188–190.

Introduction

The following extract from Professor Martin Fautley's book on musical assessment starts with a reinterpretation of the Polanyi phrase discussed above. Here, 'you know more than you can tell' becomes 'the whole is greater than the sum of its parts'. What are the consequences of this viewpoint for the assessment of a pupil's musical ability or achievement?

Key words and phrases

assessment, formative, summative, composition

Extract

Holistic approaches

The oft-cited idea that 'the whole is greater than the sum of its parts' can be turned on its head in assessment terms. The sum of the parts do not make up the whole, something is missing. This is an important concept when dealing with assessment. The best that can be hoped for is that the wider the range of assessment data that can be accrued, the nearer we will get to understanding the whole, but, and this is crucial, the sum of the assessment-parts will never equal the pupil-whole! What this means for the music teacher is that assessment data should be collected from a range of sources and types, but that this data then needs to be interpreted. Keith Swanwick suggested that the elements of music education can be characterized by the mnemonic C(L)A(S)P: composition literature studies (of and about music), audition (responsive listening), skill acquisition, and performance (Swanwick 1979: 45). In the UK the National Curriculum has codified these into the three areas of performing, listening, and composing. Whatever the local or national context, these elements together will form the basis of a rounded education in music, and so assessment needs to reflect this.

Whilst it is clear that listening will play a central role in music education (Bresler 1995), the development of listening can be undertaken alongside that of performing and composing. Indeed, composing with pupils offers a key methodology for tapping into all aspects of musical learning, and some music teachers are able to construct their entire music curriculum for pupils aged 11–14 years old with a wide range of musical learning stemming from composing-based activities. Doing this is an holistic approach which enables progression in listening and performing to be employed in the service of composing. How this will appear in practice is likely to involve a combination of bottom-up and top-down assessments being employed simultaneously. The three dimensions of assessment which were discussed in Chapter 9 come into play here for bottom-up criteria, and at the same time a top-down overview can be employed for an impression of musicality.

As an instance of how this can work in practice, let us consider an example of summative assessment of a group composing project being undertaken in a Year 7 KS3 music class. The class are composing music in response to a visual stimulus, a picture of a ruined house in a rural setting. The pupils will work in groups composing their piece of music, and will then perform their resultant compositions to the rest of the class. The assessment criteria for this work need to involve a range of competencies and attainments. A short, but not exclusive, list of assessment areas which the teacher and pupils will be concerned with in this composing project are shown in Table 16.1.

There is a distinction to be made here between those aspects of musical attainment which can be summatively assessed during the process of

TABLE 16.1 Assessment areas in composing project.

Composing:	Generation
	Organization
	Revision
	Transformation and development
Performing:	Work-in-progress performances
	Instrumental skills
	Control
	Final performance
Listening:	Reviewing
	Evaluating
	Audiation
Group Work:	Awareness
	Responding
	Ensemble-ness
Musicality:	Expressive-ness (in context)
	Feelingful-ness

composing, i.e. those which appertain to the final product, and those for which a combination of process and product would be the most suitable assessment methodology. At this stage we need to make a clear distinction between formative and summative purposes of assessment. In this example the focus of attention, although focused on summative assessment, also needs to take into account an element of formative assessment, in that the teacher will have been making formative assessments throughout the composing process. These formative judgements are likely to inform some aspects of the final summative assessment decisions. This therefore becomes an assessment which takes into account the *process* of composing, it is not (possibly erroneously) based solely on the final performance of the piece.

Summary

Fautley starts with the assertion that the whole is always greater that the sum of its parts. For processes of assessment, the sum of the assessment parts will never equal the wholeness of what the pupil knows. In other words, the difficulty in identifying or representing tacit knowledge relates directly to the processes of assessment. The assessment data that a teacher collects, however rigorously or carefully, will never tell the whole story.

Fautley explores the consequences of this for music education. Within music education, there is a need to collect a broad range of assessment data from the key processes of performing, composing and listening. He emphasises that this is best done in a holistic way, i.e. a way that integrates these processes together rather than separates them out. He also applies Polanyi's assertion to the thorny issue of whether or not teachers should assess process and/or product. The product of a musical composition, he says, should include a consideration of both the final product itself (a summative judgement) but also a consideration of the process by which it was conceived and put together (a formative judgement).

Questions to consider

1. How can musical assessment be conducted in a holistic way?
2. In terms of the teacher or pupil's focus on their work, what emphasis should be given to product or process?

Investigations

Consider the various assessment processes that you currently use in your teaching. Which ones are summative? Which ones are formative? Are some a mixture of both? Which ones focus on product, and which ones focus on process? Do some focus on both? What would happen if you swapped some of the assessment processes around and used them in a different way? How would that affect how you teach and what your pupils might learn?

Think deeper

Within the United Kingdom, statutory assessment of a pupil's attainment in music occurs using National Curriculum levels, and takes place at the end of the period of study of compulsory music lessons (presently around the age of 14). In common with all subjects within the National Curriculum, there are eight levels, plus one for 'exceptional performance'. The levels holistically delineate the processes of musical learning, including performing, composing and listening. As we have already noted, there are not separate levels for each of these processes; rather, the levels are predicated on the conception music as a holistic practice. The standard expected of all pupils at the end of their compulsory period of study is Level 5, the statement for which reads thus:

> Pupils identify and explore musical devices and how music reflects time, place and culture. They perform significant parts from memory and from notations, with awareness of their own contribution such as leading others, taking a solo part or providing rhythmic support. They improvise melodic and rhythmic material within given structures, use a variety of notations, and compose music for different occasions using appropriate musical devices. They analyse and compare musical features. They evaluate how venue, occasion and purpose affect the way music is created, performed and heard. They refine and improve their work.
>
> (QCA, 2007)

Recent research (Fautley and Savage 2011) has clearly demonstrated that National Curriculum (NC) levels are the principal way that teachers assess their pupils' work at Key Stage 3, with:

> 49% of respondents mentioning them directly. The text from which this analysis is derived reveals that, for some teachers, use of the NC levels was felt to be sufficient in and of itself, with short answers such as these being not atypical: 'Use NC Level descriptors'; 'National Curriculum criteria'; 'KS3 levels'; 'NC orders'. This seems to show that in teacher thinking there exists an unproblematic connection between NC levels and assessment of composing.
>
> (ibid, p.56)

In terms of how often teachers use these levels, the research found that:

> 74% of teachers are employing National Curriculum levels at least once a term. This frequency of utilisation is an issue for music teachers. We then asked whether teachers were assessing frequently because they had to, or because they wanted to. . . . Only about 11% of respondents answered that they assess with this frequency because they wanted to; 36% of respondents were using the NC levels this often because the school required them to.

However, 45% of teachers were using the NC levels as a way of monitoring progress, using them for benchmarking so they could track progress over time.

(ibid, p.57)

Think wider

Teachers' use of a summative assessment tool (the National Curriculum levels) for a formative assessment process is curious. When Fautley and Savage asked why teachers were using the National Curriculum levels in this way, practical issues such as the imposition of demands of senior managers were often cited (see above). But it is important to note that 45 per cent of teachers were still choosing to use this device in a way that it was not intended to be used. Why? Fautley and Savage's view was this:

> Possibly because no other tool exists, they have been subverted for use in ways for which they were never intended. Teachers are trying to assess composing using NC levels, a tool which was never intended for the task. As the folk saying goes, 'when the only tool you have is a hammer, everything looks like a nail'. Music teachers are busy banging at everything with the hammer of NC levels.

> (ibid, p.64)

In other words, the careless imposition of a generic assessment framework has skewed teachers' thinking about other, possibly more musically authentic, assessment methodologies.

However, it is important to emphasise that music teachers are not unusual in this respect! Across our education system, the careless imposition of rigid assessment frameworks and their antithetical effect on the opportunity for pupils to experience authentic educational encounters have been noted by many researchers. Here, for example, is Torrance's view:

> Understanding and addressing key educational issues for the twenty-first century requires much more curriculum flexibility and responsiveness and this requires investment in teacher professional development at local level. Twenty years of increasing central control and regulation have produced a narrow and risk-averse education culture which is the very antithesis of the ostensible purpose of the exercise. Producing higher test scores is not enough, for learners or for governments. The need for better quality educational encounters and better quality information with which to take decisions has never been more acute. We need to stimulate new visions of what might be accomplished by our education system, and new ways to record diverse experiences and outcomes, rather than continuing to insist that all we can achieve is compliance with that which is already known.

> (Torrance 2011, pp. 481–482).

At the time of writing, the National Curriculum framework is under review in the United Kingdom. There are indications that Torrance's call for greater curriculum flexibility and local autonomy may be heeded and the requirement for the 'levelling' of pupil's attainment may be removed. However, will this lead to music teachers being able to re-imagine what musical assessment looks and sounds like in their classrooms. As the following extract explores, even within the music classroom there are intriguing debates about how to apply alternative assessment pedagogies.

Extract 6.3

Source

Green, L. 'Music as a media art: evaluation and assessment in the contemporary classroom'. In Sefton-Green, J. (ed.) (2000) *Evaluating Creativity*. London, Routledge, pp. 101–103.

Introduction

Despite the argument for a holistic model of musical assessment at Key Stage 3 and the various difficulties with misapplication of summative assessment processes for a formative assessment process, as pupils work their way through formal schooling into Key Stage 4 (pupils aged between −14 and 16) the assessment pendulum swings towards the assessment of individual musical processes. Therefore, at Key Stage 4 musical performances are assessed independently from a pupil's composition work; listening skills are assessed through a formal listening examination. The following extract, written by Lucy Green, asks some searching questions about the pedagogy and ideology behind some of the individualised assessment processes.

Key words and phrases

assessment, pedagogy, formative, summative, performance, composition

Extract

The question I want to pose here is: if it is possible to assess the performance of a piece according to criteria which are sensitive to the level of difficulty considered to be involved in the performance, then why not assess the composition of a piece according to the level of difficulty considered to be involved in its composition? This question brings me back again to the three axes around which I've organised this chapter: first, that of whether we focus on 'notes' or 'contexts'; second, whether we develop a range of limited evaluative criteria or one unified set of criteria; and third, whether we attempt to evaluate individual pieces or to evaluate styles.

In attempting to establish a graded system or a difficulty multiplier for composition, one of the most intractable problems for classically educated music teachers, is that traditionally it has seemed as if there is a connection *between* difficulty and 'good' composition. Complexity and intellectual rigour are often valued within the musical canon and seen as justification for quality in and of themselves. This is not the case with performance. As we have seen, in the process of assessment, it is possible for a musician to give a performance capable of being considered 'good' (or even superlative), even if the piece of music being performed is considered very 'easy' (or for that matter, very 'bad'). A graded system or a difficulty multiplier responds at least in part to any unfairness or unreliability in the test, and a performance-candidate will of course always be advised to choose pieces that balance his or her ability with the grade or difficulty multiplier to maximum effect. But the distinction between what is 'good' or 'bad' and what is 'easy' or 'difficult' in composition is more elusive, at least as far as assessment mechanisms are concerned.

Defining 'difficulty' in the assessment of composition cannot just take into account 'technical complexity'. It would be possible for someone to compose a piece that was technically extremely complex, for example highly polyphonic, or totally serialised music, but which from an aesthetic point of view would be deemed lifeless and unattractive. The key issue here is that the kind of difficulty that is pertinent, the difficulty that contributes to musical value in composition, is not technical prowess, but the interaction of technique with those many factors which are impossible to describe accurately in words: factors, depending on the style and era of the music, such as expression in relation to the social and historical origins of the music, originality, or the relationship of the particular piece of music with the general style to which it alludes. Whereas in the assessment of performance, linguistically elusive factors such as 'expressivity' can be separated from the technical difficulty of the piece being performed, in the assessment of composition, they cannot so readily.[1] Here we come again to the conundrum of trying to find a language to describe what is (in music's case as well as other art forms) beyond language.

Another, related problem in the establishment of criteria for assessing composition is that any criteria must be sensitive to what musical possibilities are afforded by the *style* of the piece in question. The piece would then have to be considered in terms of how well or how poorly it represented that style. But so often in the history of music—whether classical, popular, or any other—what has been considered most valuable, is precisely that certain composers do *not* simply represent the style: they go beyond it.

The GCSE exam boards' criteria for the assessment of composition can be difficult to use. This is partly because while the boards mostly allow compositions to be submitted in any style whatsoever, they do not recognise anything akin to a difficulty multiplier with reference to composition, and they do not provide assessment criteria for composition that are tailored to suit particular styles of music.

Instead, they provide that unified set of criteria alluded to in the second of my three axes: universal criteria, which go across styles, and are supposedly pertinent to any style. But what if one style is much more difficult, or requires much more originality, or affords more compositional virtuosity, than another style? I would like to examine this question with reference to four contrasting examples.

Pupil A composes a piece in sonata-form in the style of Mozart; pupil B composes a jazz piece in the style of early Ellington; pupil C composes a rap involving voice, pre-set drum rhythm and a bass line; and pupil D composes a John Cage-style aleatoric piece by throwing dice. All four pieces are to be assessed in terms of a set of unified criteria concerning generalised musical qualities such as balance, form, variety and so on. These criteria give no guidance about differences between musical styles, but in practice, teachers are bound to relate the given 'universal' criteria to the demands of the style of the piece of music in question: see Green (1990). Thus, let us say, all four of these pupils receive a mark of 8 out of 10. But the two pupils who composed the sonata and the jazz pastiche have demonstrated far greater understanding of far more musical *technical* parameters than the ones who composed the rap and the aleatoric piece. Is it valid, then, that they should all end up with equal marks? Clearly not, the reason being that the styles in which they are composing do not allow for equivalent possibilities in terms of technical manipulation. This problem is compounded at school level by the fact that no distinction is made in the National Curriculum or the GCSE syllabus between pastiche and original composition. Whereas the Mozart and Ellington pastiches require a high level of technical proficiency, as pastiche, the exercise does not so much warrant *expressive originality* as faithfulness to a model. By contrast, the rap requires little technical skill, but allows, at least potentially, for a high level of expressivity: it need not be pastiche and could well be original. The aleatoric composition, pastiche again, affords very little of either technical proficiency or expressivity.

The only thing to do then, in the present-day situation where in schools and universities we are often assessing pupils' and students' compositions in a large variety of musical styles, is to establish different criteria for evaluating different styles of music against each other, including a type of 'difficulty multiplier' to distinguish between different styles. Any attempt to do such a thing would be highly contentious and would undoubtedly lead to some heated debate between defenders on one hand, and critics on the other, of the styles involved. But, because educational assessment has to have a degree of not only validity and reliability, but also plain fairness, we *must* surely proceed along lines somewhat akin to awarding different value, in terms of the availability of marks, to different musical styles and compositional exercises.

Notes

1. Green (1997) provides ethnographic evidence to suggest that teachers do in fact devalue pupils' compositions when they consider them to be 'merely' technically

proficient; and that they place most value on those compositions which they deem to be 'imaginative', 'creative', or 'exploratory', even when technical proficiency is considered to be lacking. It will come as no surprise to many people, that in the research, it was overwhelmingly girls who were seen to produce the former type of composition, and boys the latter.

References

Green, L. (1997) *Music, Gender, Education*, Cambridge: Cambridge University Press.

Summary

When assessing a musical performance, it is standard practice to assess the performance against criteria that are sensitive to the level of difficulty considered to be involved in that particular piece. Green asks why similar approaches are not used in the assessment of musical compositions. She explores the notion of 'difficulty' within composition. Difficulty does not equate to 'technical complexity'; but it could relate to many other factors, which, she says, may be difficult to describe accurately in words (notice the link here to Polanyi's tacit knowledge introduced in Eisner's work – Extract 6.1). These unidentifiable features may relate to musical style, historical origins, notions of originality or the sense in which the pupil's composition relates to the general style from which it came.

Against these conceptual difficulties the GCSE examination boards do not do themselves any favours either. In providing a generic or universal set of assessment criteria, together with a difficulty multiplier, Green suggests that problems are compounded rather than resolved. Her answer is to put forward the idea that different criteria need to be established for different styles of music, together with a 'difficulty multiplier' to distinguish between different musical styles.

Questions to consider

1. Green's challenge to the assessment of composition at GCSE level was issued in 2000 and has been largely ignored. Why do you think that is the case?

2. More fundamentally, why do you think musical performance is assessed in a different way to musical composition?

Investigations

In the spirit of a creative investigation, why not try marking several pupils' compositions in the way that Lucy Green imagines in the above extract. Use general assessment criteria of the type found in each GCSE specification, but factor in a 'stylistic difficulty multiplier' of your own design. What, if any, difference does it make to the marks your pupils would be awarded?

Think deeper

Green's article presents an important philosophical and conceptual challenge to the way that the assessment of composition is conducted at Key Stage 4. However, other research has shown that there is little appetite amongst teachers for changes of this type. For example, Savage and Fautley's research (Savage and Fautley 2011) noted that although the assessment of composition preoccupied the vast majority of teachers' time:

> Music teachers are, in general, satisfied with the sorts of assessments which are being done at Key Stage 4. Criteria set by the examination boards for the assessment of composing are universally utilised. There is a feeling that examination board criteria, whilst fit for purpose, do not always reflect the effort that students have put into their work. Some styles which are 'set' by examination boards are seen as being inappropriate for some students to access. Assessment of composing almost invariably entails assessment of the compositional product. There was no wish of teachers to change this. . . . Teachers want to do the best for their students, and they want to know how to improve their learning. There was a general sense of confidence with assessment systems and teachers felt they understood them. There was some concern about using these to show all aspects of a student's learning, but, in general terms, teachers felt here that systems were working to the advantage of their learners.
>
> (ibid, pp. 146–147)

Since the time of Green's writings, there have been little if any changes to the system that she and Savage and Fautley describe. This suggests that, as in Key Stage 3, there is a degree of compliance or complacency being shown by teachers and schools to the assessment frameworks produced by companies that construct GCSE specifications (under the remit of the Department for Education). Sophisticated musicological arguments about the process, as advanced in the extract above, have made little impact on the practice of assessment at this level.

Think wider

Moving beyond the context of music assessment in the United Kingdom, it is useful to review research from elsewhere around the world. One interesting study comes from Finland (Antilla 2010). Here, in a similar observation to those reported in this chapter, he states that:

> Knowledge and skills may be assessed through tests and exams, but the many qualitative dimensions of music studying and learning – such as the love of music, music as a hobby, creativity, metacognitions and other learning skills are much more difficult to identify and investigate. However, all these aspects belong to music teaching and learning and therefore should also be included in the assessment of learning. The quantitative grade (in Finland

from 4 to 10) is arguably a much too one-dimensional means of assessing a pupil's learning. A better means of assessing qualitative learning is the use of process- and self-evaluation.

However, not a single pupil mentioned anything of process- or self-evaluation. They were not in use in Finnish schools, although the core curriculum stipulates their importance in supporting, among other things, the learners' self-knowledge, learning skills and motivation. Self-evaluation is also a good way of supporting pupils' individual musical learning. Each member of the group learns different things in the music lesson. In order to 'catch' the individual characteristics of learning, assessment should be qualitative, taking into consideration various aspects of musical learning.

(ibid, p. 250)

Antilla's observation that a move towards a more qualitative-based approach to assessment provides us with an important link to the final extract of this chapter.

Extract 6.4

Source

Stobart, G. (2008) *Testing Times: The uses and abuses of assessment.* London, Routledge, pp. 145–146.

Introduction

As we have discussed throughout this chapter, pupils know more than they can tell. This includes what they can 'tell' us, as their teachers, and also what they can 'tell' in the context of a formal summative assessment process such as an end of Key Stage assessment of public examination. Therefore, the challenge for music teachers is to find a way of facilitating their pupils' voices so that they can express themselves in different ways. One of the most significant alternative approaches to assessment over the last few years has been described as 'assessment for learning'.

Key words and phrases

assessment, formative

Extract

Overview

Assessment for Learning is best viewed as an approach to classroom assessment, rather than as a tightly formulated theory. In this respect, it is closer to

Learning Styles and Emotional Intelligence than to more fully articulated systems such as Multiple Intelligences. This does not mean there are no theoretical underpinnings; simply that it has not been organised, and may not need to be, into a stand-alone theory. AfL is only one element in a wider system which incorporates curriculum, school culture and ways of teaching. While the terms used are relatively recent ('formative' was coined in 1967 and Assessment for Learning in the mid-1990s), some of the key themes have a far longer pedigree.[1]

What distinguishes Assessment for Learning from the Intelligences and Learning Styles that we looked at in chapters three and four is its emphasis on the *situational* – classroom interaction – rather than on individual learner dispositions. This is a highly significant difference; *it puts the focus on what is being learned and on the quality of classroom interactions and relationships*. In this approach assessment is interpreted broadly, it is about gathering evidence about where learners are, and providing feedback which helps them move on. This evidence can come from observation (puzzled looks, 'penny-dropping' moments) and classroom interactions, as well as from more tangible products. Tests can play a part if the responses are used to identify what has, and has not, been understood, and if this leads to action to improve learning.

One of the central arguments of this book is that assessment shapes how we see ourselves as learners and as people. My championing of Assessment for Learning is based on its emphasis on the learning process, rather than on learners' abilities and dispositions. In Carol Dweck's terms, it takes an *incrementalist* approach to learning which emphasises effort and *improving* competence. This contrasts with an *entity* approach, which attributes learning to ability and is focused on *proving* competence through grades and comparisons.[2] This links to the AfL emphasis on learners becoming self-regulated and autonomous in their learning – a skill which is developed through self-assessment and classroom dialogue.

What is Assessment for Learning?

It is best treated as assessment which is embedded in the learning process.
Five 'deceptively simple' key factors are:

- the active involvement of pupils in their own learning;
- the provision of effective feedback to pupils;
- adjusting teaching to take account of the results of assessment;
- the need for pupils to be able to assess themselves;
- a recognition of the profound influence that assessment has on the motivation and self-esteem of pupils, both of which are crucial influences on learning.

(Assessment Reform Group, 1999, pp. 4–5)

One widely used definition that follows from these is the Assessment Reform Group's:

> The process of seeking and interpreting evidence for use by learners and their teachers, to identify where the learners are in their learning, where they need to go to and how best to get there.
>
> (2002, pp. 2–3)

This approach could be treated simply as good teaching, particularly as the 'evidence' in the definition is construed as a wide range of information, rather than as formal or informal tests. So why this emphasis on assessment? Largely, I think, as a deliberate move by members of the assessment community to reclaim one of the key, and endangered, purposes of assessment. In an era dominated by summative accountability testing, this can be seen as an attempt to rebalance the uses to which assessments are put, by making it *part* of the learning process, rather than standing outside it and checking what has been learned. There is more to assessment than providing a snapshot of what is known at a given moment.

Assessment for Learning is often used interchangeably with *formative assessment*.[3] Assessment for Learning has been introduced as a term partly because of the many misunderstandings that 'formative' generates. One of the most problematic of these is the belief that regular classroom tests, which are used for monitoring progress, are formative. Given their purpose, these are better regarded as mini-summative assessments, as the information gathered is not directly used to modify teaching and learning. The same is true of the marking of classwork, again often described as formative, when in fact its purpose is to provide the evidence for later summative judgements.

Notes

1. This is both in terms of educational theory and the practices found in alternative schooling. These include, from the US, John Dewey's (1938) emphasis on active learning and Ralph Tyler's (1971) emphasis on clear objectives. From Europe, it would include, for example, Montessori's emphasis on learner autonomy and Freinet's on self-assessment.
2. This is Chris Watkins's (2002) useful distinction.
3. I tend to treat AFL as a particular emphasis *within* formative assessment. AfL is primarily concerned with interactive *student* learning, while some approaches to formative assessment focus primarily on *teacher* learning – intended to lead to teaching and curricular changes which improve pupil learning. Paul Black and colleagues make a different distinction. This involves seeing AfL as a *purpose*, while formative assessment is a *function* – 'assessment becomes "formative assessment" when the evidence is actually used to adapt the teaching work to meet learning needs'. (Black *et al.*, 2002, p. i).

References

Assessment Reform Group (1999) *Assessment for Learning: Beyond the Black Box*, University of Cambridge, UK: Assessment Reform Group.

Assessment Reform Group (2002) *Assessment for Learning: 10 Principles*, University of Cambridge, UK: Assessment Reform Group.

Black, P., Harrison, C., Lee, C., Marshall, B. and Wiliam, D. (2002) *Working Inside the Black Box: Assessment for Learning in the Classroom*, London: NFER Nelson.

Dewey, J. (1938) *Experience and Education*, New York and London: Collier-Macmillan.

Dweck, C. S. (2000) *Self-Theories: Their Role in Motivation, Personality and Development*, Philadelphia: Psychology Press.

Watkins, C., Carnell, E., Lodge, C., Wagner, P. and Whalley, C (2002) 'Effective Learning', *NSIN Research Matters*, Institute of Education, London.

Summary

Stobart introduces assessment for learning as an alternative approach to assessment that helpfully relocates 'assessment' as part of a pupil's 'learning process'. As such, it has several identifiable features including the active involvement of pupils in assessing their own learning, the provision of effective feedback and recognition of the profound influence that assessment has on the motivation and self-esteem of pupils. Assessment for learning is not the same as formative assessment although the two terms do have some elements in common.

Questions to consider

1. To what extent do assessment for learning strategies exist within common approaches to the teaching of music already?

2. What other approaches can you imagine for getting pupils more active within an assessment process within the classroom?

Investigations

Assessment for learning is a common strategy in many subjects. Spend some time talking to a colleague who is an effective teacher in a curriculum area outside of your own. How is assessment for learning adopted within their subject teaching? Are there any similarities or differences to how it is applied within music education?

Think deeper

Fautley's book on assessment in music education (Fautley 2010), which was featured in the second extract of this chapter, provides a detailed exploration of assessment for learning in music education. One of the benefits, he posits, is that 'music teachers have long been using it [assessment for learning] as a key element of their work with pupils' (ibid, p. 9). If that is the case, and I think it is, it leads one to wonder why the research presents such a crisis of confidence in the use of such techniques in the work of so many teachers with pupils within two Key Stages (Fautley and Savage 2011; Savage and Fautley 2011).

Looking forward, Fautley's advice for music educators is to privilege assessment for learning techniques at the expense of the summative ones. Whilst no one would advocate non-reporting of pupils' 'progress' through summative devices, as far as possible he urges teachers to emphasise more natural, musical approaches to assessment that are centred on the interactions between teachers and pupils, rather than those being framed by pre-established, decontextualized, criterion-referenced statements.

Assessment has, rightly, always been part our educational system. But, ultimately, the power of assessment rests with teachers and pupils. So 'external data collection, statistical sampling, and pseudo-scientific demonstrations of progression [should not be] allowed to compromise the fundamental relationship between the teacher and the learner' (Fautley 2010, p. 208).

Think wider

Taking a broader historical view, Peter Elbow (Elbow 1983) asks the simple question 'how can we help our students learn more?'. His four-part answer contains much of value for all teachers, regardless of subject:

1. We should see our students as smart and capable. We should assume that they *can* learn what we teach – all of them;
2. We should show students that we are on their side. This means, for example, showing them that the perplexity or ignorance they reveal to us will not be used against them in tests, grading and certifying;
3. Indeed, so far from letting their revelations hurt them in grading, we should be, as it were, lawyers for the defence, explicitly trying to help students do better against the judge and prosecuting attorney when it comes to the 'trial' of testing and grading;
4. We should reveal our own position, particularly our doubts, ambivalences, and biases. We should show that we are still learning, still willing to look at things in new ways, still sometimes uncertain or even stuck, still willing to ask naïve questions, still engaged in the interminable process of working out the relationship between what we teach and the rest of our lives.

(ibid, p. 332).

Conclusion

Starting from the premise that all knowledge is provisional and that it is impossible to 'tell' all that we know, this chapter has explored a range of research within the field of educational assessment. It has identified a number of specific issues within the area of music education and assessment including what has often been reported as the preoccupation of summative assessment processes and techniques that have had a detrimental effect on our understanding of pupils' musical development. Alternative approaches have been explored in the research but, ultimately, the establishment of an open and honest professional relationship between teacher and pupil will be the best platform in helping develop a naturally responsive and regular process of assessment.

References

Antilla, M. (2010) 'Problems with School Music in Finland'. *British Journal of Music Education* 27:3, 241–253.

Burnard, P. (2000) 'How Children Ascribe Meaning to Improvisation and Composition: Rethinking pedagogy in music education'. *Music Education Research* 2:1, 7–23.

Elbow, P. (1983) 'Embracing Contraries in the Teaching Process'. *College English* 45:4, 327–339.

Elliott, J., Stemler, S., Sternberg, R., Grigorenko, E. and Hoffman, N. (2011) 'The Socially Skilled Teacher and the Development of Tacit Knowledge'. *British Educational Research Journal* 37:1, 83–103.

Fautley, M. and Savage, J. (2011) 'Assessment of Composing in the Lower Secondary School in the English National Curriculum'. *British Journal of Music Education* 28:1, 51–67.

Johnson, S. and Birkeland, S. (2003) 'Pursuing a Sense of Success: New teachers explain their career decisions'. *American Educational Research Journal* 40:3, 581–617.

QCA (2007) *Music – Programme of Study: Key Stage 3*. London, QCA (now Department for Education).

Reimer, B. (1994) 'Is Musical Performance Worth Saving?' *Arts Education Policy Review* 95:3, 1–25.

Savage, J. and Fautley, M. (2011) 'The Organisation and Assessment of Composing at Key Stage 4 in English Secondary Schools'. *British Journal of Music Education* 28:2, 135–157.

Torrance, H. (2011) 'Using Assessment to Drive the Reform of Schooling: Time to stop pursuing the chimera?'. *British Journal of Educational Studies* 59:4, 459–485.

7

Music Education Inside and Outside the School

In recent years, a lot of attention has been paid to the musical lives of young people outside formal education. As we have considered in previous chapters, projects such as Musical Futures have encouraged us to plan curriculum opportunities for students from a deeper understanding of the content and approaches to learning contained within a more diverse range of musical styles.

This broadening of awareness has been matched by recent music education policies that have encouraged us to locate and contextualise music within the school as part of a broader network of musical opportunities within our local communities. This raises a number of serious questions for music education. Who should be involved in teaching music? What qualifications, if any, do they need? Do composers, DJs, VJs, world musicians or others have a legitimate role to play within the musical lives of our schools? If so, what is the role of the teacher in working with, or alongside, other professional or community musicians? This chapter explores some of the key questions, starting with the most basic: who should be teaching music in our schools?

Extract 7.1

Source

Mills, J. (2005) *Music in the School*. Oxford, OUP, pp. 27–29.

Introduction

Who should be teaching music in our schools? This is an important question. Do music teachers need a music degree? Do they need to be music specialists? Do they need a postgraduate teaching qualification? In this first extract, Janet Mills discusses these issues as they relate to the teaching of music in primary and secondary schools. She draws on a range of research evidence before coming up with an interesting conclusion.

Key words and phrases

teachers, specialist, generalist, networks, subject knowledge, pedagogical content knowledge

Extract

Music Teachers

> In 1994 there were many primary schools where teachers believed that class music lessons taught by class teachers were necessarily inferior to those taught by music specialists . . . Since 1994 more schools have become aware that good class teaching and poor specialist teaching both exist . . .
>
> (Ofsted 1999: 132)[1]

Who has been doing this 'musical' teaching that I have been describing?

So far in this book, I have avoided referring to any teachers as 'specialists'. I take the view that schools should deploy teachers to teach class music in much the same way as they deploy teachers to teach any other subject. Thus music in secondary schools should normally be taught by music graduates who specialized in music during their teacher training. And the deployment of teachers for music in primary schools should also follow that of other subjects. If a primary school has a culture of 'teacher swops' in later years, so that older students are prepared for secondary school through learning from more than one teacher, and so that teachers can play to their strengths—and there happens to be a teacher who is so good at teaching music that they can do this effectively with a class that they know less well than their own—then it may make sense for music to be included in this arrangement. But if the culture of the school is that class teachers teach everything—a model that reflects and reinforces the ability of all students to do all subjects—then it can damage students' image of themselves as musicians if some special arrangements are made for music.

Categorization of primary teachers as 'specialists' and 'generalists', as in the unfortunately entitled booklet *Using Subject Specialist Teachers to Promote High Standards at Key Stage 2* (Ofsted 1997), frequently carries the implicit assumption that a specialist is necessarily better at teaching than a generalist, and yet it may not be at all clear what the writer means by these terms, and hence what is being compared. For some, a specialist is a teacher who has music qualifications—for example a music degree—that a generalist lacks. For others, specialists are marked out by only teaching music—whether or not they have any qualifications in music. For a few (e.g. MacDonald *et al.* 2002), specialists are thought to plan lessons that are more specialized in some (not always defined) way than those taught by generalists. Whichever way one defines a specialist, it does not follow that their teaching will necessarily be superior to that of other people. Good teaching leads to students learning. That can happen whether or not the teacher has a music degree, and whether or not the teacher also teaches other subjects. When Ofsted compared the quality of music lessons taught in primary schools by children's own class teacher with those taught by someone else (Mills 1994a), they found no difference. A year later, Ofsted observed that:

> many music specialists have not revised the curriculum they offer . . . to reflect [the national curriculum], and overemphasise the use of staff notation, which is not required . . . or singing at the expense of composing and appraising. The highest standards . . . are often found in lessons taught jointly by a music specialist and the class teacher, or when teachers who work for part of their time as music specialists are teaching their own class.
>
> (Ofsted 1995: 18)

More recently, Susan O'Neill and I (2002) investigated the quality of provision in music for 11-year-olds in ten primary schools. We used the term 'quality of provision', like Ofsted, to relate to the quality of teaching (as observed), curricular and extracurricular opportunities, and resources made available to the 11-year-olds. After a consultant had visited the schools to rate their music provision, we divided the schools into three groups accordingly—high, medium, or low—and found at least one teacher deployed as a specialist in each of these groups. So, having a teacher who is deployed as a specialist can be excellent news, but may not be. The school where the provision was best turned out to have a teacher who is a music graduate, and also a well-rounded musician—and who was teaching her own class. So she knew them well, and was confident to work with them in a wide range of musical activities. Clearly, having a teacher who is a music graduate and also your class teacher is an ideal combination that could not possibly be provided for all primary students—unless all primary teachers had to take a degree in music (and mathematics and English and . . .)! But primary students can sometimes be served better by a teacher who knows them well, rather than a teacher who knows music well, but does not know them at all. Even outstanding primary music teachers tend to become a little less effective when they work with a class other than their own.

Some of the finest music teachers that I have observed, particularly, but not only, in primary schools, have no qualifications in music, and teach many subjects—in some cases the whole of the primary curriculum. They may never have learned to play an instrument, and they may not read staff notation well, or at all. What they bring to their music teaching is their ability, typically developed in other subjects, to diagnose where students are, and work out ways of helping them to learn, frequently coupled with a degree of humility about their music skills that leaves them continually questioning how well their students are learning, and whether there are approaches that would enable them to learn more rapidly. They also often bring particular musical skills, interests, and knowledge that are additional to those of the teacher in charge of music at the school, and that enrich the music curriculum of the school. When teachers with little formal training in music teach it, their problem is often confidence, rather than competence (Barrett 1994; Mills 1989). When I work as an inspector in schools, such teachers sometimes try to apologize to me for their teaching before they have even begun, and then the most wonderful lesson unfolds as they focus on the students, closely observe what the students can do and what they cannot do yet, and use a range of skills developed in other subjects to help the students make progress.

Teachers who do not see themselves as musicians often greatly overestimate the range of musical skills—in particular instrumental skills—that music graduates possess. I realized this on my very first day as a teacher, when I got into conversation with a French teacher at my secondary school. He asked me when the school might have an orchestra, and I spoke of starting a violin and viola class when I could get some instruments, and also of enquiring whether the local education authority might be able to send some instrumental teachers to the school to teach other instruments. He was genuinely surprised, as he had assumed that any music graduate would be able to play, and hence teach, every instrument that a student in school might wish to learn.

Jo Glover and Susan Young, when writing of music for children aged 7–11, take a firm line on the need for more than one teacher to be involved in teaching music in any school. They point out that in a single primary school:

> staff musical strengths and interests may include opera, travel, and world musics, guitar playing and folk groups, several orchestral instruments, choral singing, musicals, and dance ranging from tap to Arabic dance and salsa.

They continue:

> Schools are often under-using this kind of whole-staff potential, preferring to rely on the skills of one specialist teacher than draw on those of all staff. Yet however well trained and broad in interests, one teacher presents only one musical personality. Making the most of what each staff member is able to contribute allows for a wider range of working styles in music. It is not acceptable for schools to offer only a single, narrowly defined musical direction for all pupils.
>
> (Glover & Young 1999: 6–7)

This point applies as much in secondary schools as in primary schools. However broad and deep the musical knowledge, skills, and interests of the single music teacher who comprises the music department in many secondary schools, it would be helpful for their students to be able to draw also on the musical enthusiasms of other teachers.

Note

1. The Office for Standards in Education (Ofsted) is a non-ministerial department of the UK government that was established in 1992. It is responsible for the inspection of schools in England, and HM Inspectors of Schools now form part of its staff.

Summary

Mills explores the tension behind the idea of a musically trained specialist teacher being intrinsically better than a non-musically trained generalist teacher. Whilst this has an obvious relevance to primary schools, there are resonances for secondary education too. Mills reviews a range of Ofsted evidence as well as other research and points out that musical skill and expertise exists in a whole range of teachers who may not be identified as a 'specialist'. Her conclusion is that it is not acceptable to offer a single, narrowly defined musical direction for all pupils. An over-reliance on one member of staff for the provision of a musical education entitlement for pupils within a school runs the risk of being mono-dimensional. Schools need to draw on a network of musical expertise.

Questions to consider

1. What are the benefits that having a music specialism bring to the role of being a music teacher?
2. Conversely, what are the benefits that a generalist teacher might bring to the role of music teacher?

Investigations

At the next opportunity, make a list of staff that teach music, in some way, shape or form, within the school where you are working. To what extent are they able to coordinate their work together? Does each member of staff, whether employed by the school or visiting the school, know what the others are up to?

Think deeper

Recent developments in music education across the United Kingdom have emphasised the role of partnership approaches in the delivery of music teaching. The creation of music education hubs in September 2012 which, in the majority of cases are re-configured local authority music services, has emphasised that no one individual teacher can, or should, be expected to deliver the whole of a comprehensive music education entitlement to their pupils on their own.

Whilst this is fine in theory, in practice it has led to a range of questions similar to those included in this chapter's introduction. In particular, the role and purpose of a postgraduate-level, qualified, teacher of music could be seen to be under threat. Indeed, the very location of music education itself could be conceptualised to have shifted as a result of these reforms. Whilst music education hubs are not designed to have replaced the school-based provision provided by a qualified teacher of music, there are numerous examples across the United Kingdom of headteachers reducing their capacity to offer music education through their own staff and formal curriculum organisation, and buying in services from outside providers. Typically, staff working within these music education hubs are qualified to a lower level, often paid less than qualified teachers and do not enjoy the same terms and conditions of employment.

For the music education researcher, these changes in employment, provision and associated pedagogical changes provide an interesting focus. What type of knowledge, pedagogy or experience is required to teach music effectively?

Think wider

Knowledge about a subject is only one of multiple types of knowledge that a teacher requires. For example, Shulman (1994) draws a distinction between 'content knowledge' (e.g. knowledge about music) and 'pedagogical content knowledge'. Pedagogical content knowledge:

> goes beyond knowledge of subject matter per se to the dimension of subject matter knowledge for teaching. I still speak of content knowledge here, but of the particular form of content knowledge that embodies the aspects of content most germane to its teachability. Within the category of pedagogical content knowledge I include, for the most regularly taught topics in one's subject area, the most useful forms of representation of those ideas, the most powerful analogies, illustrations, examples, explanations, and demonstrations in a word, the ways of representing and formulating the subject that make it comprehensible to others. Since there are no single most powerful forms of representation, the teacher must have at hand a veritable armamentarium of alternative forms of representation, some of which derive from research whereas others originate in the wisdom of practice.
>
> (Shulman 1994, p. 11)

Or, in other words, pedagogical content knowledge is the musical knowledge required to teach music in a musical way. It is not good enough for the teacher to know about music or be an expert musician in and of themselves; they have to, in Shulman's argument, have a knowledge of how the subject of music can be taught. This includes several very practical elements including:

> an understanding of what makes the learning of specific topics easy or difficult: the conceptions and preconceptions that students of different ages and backgrounds bring with them to the learning of those most frequently taught topics and lessons. If those preconceptions are misconceptions, which they so often are, teachers need knowledge of the strategies most likely to be fruitful in reorganizing the understanding of learners, because those learners are unlikely to appear before them as blank slates.
>
> (ibid)

Shulman's argument is that teachers need many different types of knowledge in order to teach effectively. To this end, content knowledge and pedagogical content knowledge (together with 'curriculum knowledge' and 'lateral curriculum knowledge') work together to produce a skilful pedagogy in an individual teacher. Simply knowing one's subject is not good enough.

Extract 7.2

Source

Adams, P. 'Resources and activities beyond the school'. In Philpott, P. and Plummeridge, C. (eds) (2001) *Issues in Music Teaching*. London, Routledge, pp. 186–188.

Introduction

The following extract comes from a chapter that explores how the musical life of a school can be enriched by forging relationships with professional and community-based artists, within the school's local area. However, these relationships are not value- or problem-free. In particular, as Adams explores, the skills and experiences of those musicians working within these groups may be called into question.

Key words and phrases

teacher, artist, network, community

Extract

Professional and community based artists are adapting their practice to promote partnership through education programmes. The term Fordism was first used by Antonio Gramsci in 1971 to describe factory production techniques, such as those employed by Henry Ford. What has this to do with organisations such as orchestras and their players? The following informal statement made by a professional orchestral musician during a conversation may give a clue: 'I have sat in this orchestra for twenty years being told what to do and how to do it! I have never improvised or composed or been musically engaged stylistically in other cultural styles and genres outside the orchestral repertoire, until fairly recently.'

In contrast, post-Fordist principles are marked by the development of a qualified and highly skilled labour force used in flexible employment patterns. The words 'highly skilled and flexible' seem here to be the key to surviving change. This may seem a strange and tenuous way in which to view the changing patterns of work for orchestral players, but there are parallels. A number of orchestras are self-managing, having responsibility for marketing and finance, and their players are often involved in projects outside their concert commitments. Contracted work, including first call contracts, are the norm for most orchestral players, many of whom are often not full-time, which means that professional musicians have to explore other avenues in order to earn a living. Orchestras have, through the necessity for survival, adopted a more eclectic style of working. Live concerts on the web are now becoming a real possibility and the word 'flexibility' for some orchestral musicians has become synonymous with 'education work'! The consultation document *Orchestral Education Programmes: Intents and Purposes* highlights changing expectations 'that publicly-funded arts organisations should develop programmes in order to further develop the Arts Council's chartered objectives of developing and improving knowledge and practice in the arts and to increasing the accessibility of the arts to the public' (Lowson, 1999: 1).

Publicly funded arts organisations, including orchestras, have also been expected to incorporate education work into their programmes. It could be strongly argued that the burgeoning of orchestral education programmes has been in response to market forces. In a survey undertaken by the Arts Council of England in 1997, 78 per cent of publicly funded arts organisations were involved in education work, and 68 per cent of whom had a dedicated education officer.

Julia Winterson looks at the aims of the pioneering creative music workshops of the 1970s which involved professional players giving direct support to teachers and enhancing music in the classroom. She perceives the large-scale education projects of the 1990s as 'developing into a full scale industry of their own' and as 'a systematic economic activity' (1996: 61). Such developments, for whatever reasons, have also provided opportunities for a number of musicians to become more involved in, and open to music outside their usual experiences, and to relate directly to schools and the wider community.

Recently published research and consultation reports are examining the interface between the world of the professional and that of the school or community. The Education, Research and Development Initiative (ERDI), supported by the Education and Training Department of the Arts Council in England, was set up in 1995 with a view to exploring ways in which education could be more effectively integrated into and across arts organisations. However, while Education programmes are now reasonably well established, relatively little research has been undertaken into their effectiveness in terms of meeting the needs of the host organisations and their impact on the artistic activity of both clients and providers.

Important and revealing research undertaken by Saville Kushner for the Calouste Gulbenkian Foundation explored the thoughts and responses of children to music, and to professional musicians during a collaborative project undertaken with the City of Birmingham Symphony Orchestra. Kushner believes that important challenges arise out of the differing cultures, traditions and values within orchestral practice, compared to those developed within the school system. He poses the important question, 'How do performing musicians judge the quality of their education work – because here the measure of what is good and worthwhile grows out of different problems and values?' (1991: 14). The reality of school and classroom, where the personal assumptions of adults may be severely challenged and where the culture and values of pupils are vastly different from those of their prospective teachers, presents a range of complex issues. All those who engage with young people need to consider their own teaching agenda alongside the knowledge and interests of their clients. Sue Cottrell's summary of a report and survey commissioned by the London Arts Board in 1994 concludes that 'while musicians do not need formal teaching qualifications to achieve successful outcomes in schools, they do need some teaching skills' (1998: 284). Kushner also suggests that 'artists need to develop educational theories of their arts in schools activities' (1991: 81). The implications are that the professionals organising projects need to develop a careful rationale for partnership which allows all individuals to develop within the context of the wider community of artist, teachers and pupils.

References

Cottrell, S. (1998) 'Partnerships in the classroom', *British Journal of Music Education* 15, 3, 271–85.

Kushner, S. (1991) *The Children's Music Book: Performing Musicians in School*, London: Calouste Gulbenkian Foundation.

Lowson, S. (1999) *Orchestral Education Programmes: Intents and Purposes, Report of the Consultation Process*, London: the Arts Council of England.

Winterson, J. (1996) 'So what's new? A survey of the education policies of orchestras and opera companies', *British Journal of Music Education* 13, 3, 259–70.

Summary

There is a long history of professional and community-based artists working in schools. This extract contains a brief history of some of these developments through the work of the Arts Council England. Towards the end of the extract, Adams cites the work of Kushner and Cottrell, both of whom have examined the interrelationship between teachers and artists and the skills that they bring to particular educational projects. They have also both researched the impact that their work has on the lives of young people. Both researchers conclude that artists need to have a more honed rationale for the educational potential of their subject within such collaborative, educational partnerships.

Questions to consider

1. When working in an educational partnership, what are the specific skills that a teacher and artist bring to the partnership?

2. Do the artists that you have worked with lack that 'pedagogical content knowledge' that Kushner and Cottrell refer to as a weakness? Would you have expected them to have these skills or not?

3. Given that teachers and artists have different skill sets, how can they work together productively? What does effective partnership look and sound like?

Investigations

Talk to a professional or community musician about their work. How do they feel about working in educational settings? How does their view of partnership working differ from yours? Does it?

Think deeper

Richard Hallam, a consultant who has worked for the Department for Education in the United Kingdom on music education policy, has written extensively about these issues (Hallam 2011). The key question for him is how a wide diversity of music experiences can form a coherent music education that enables young people to develop musically and personally. Partnership working, for him (ibid, p. 166), fulfil two key functions: strategic planning and delivery. But effective partnerships need a range of prerequisites in order to function well. These include good leadership, appropriate membership, clear roles and responsibilities and, perhaps most importantly, trust.

Additionally, Hallam makes a crucial, but often forgotten, point about ensuring that partnerships between teachers and artists need to look both upwards and downwards:

> When projects take place in a school or involve young people of school age the importance of decision makers, budget holders and policy makers still applies. The role of senior managers is critical but one that is often overlooked. Young people themselves need to be able to contribute at all stages. Time is an issue. There needs to be sufficient time for planning, ongoing monitoring, evaluation and feedback, so that the value for money and impact of the partnership will not be diminished.
>
> (ibid, p.167).

From my own experiences in this area (Savage and Challis 2002; 2001), I can not overemphasise the importance of getting senior management support for any partnership projects; similarly, getting young people involved in the planning, running and evaluation of the project itself can also be a very rewarding and informative process for all involved.

Think wider

Working from a different artistic background and national context, Hager's article in the *Youth Theatre Journal* (Hager 2010) contains a range of helpful insights for the music education community. Within the United States of America there is a longer tradition of arts residences delivered by professional artists and arts educators within schools. She argues that changing patterns of participation in the arts are transforming the ways that young people gain entry and sustain lifelong learning in the arts and that the maturation of the teaching-artist field is resulting in changes to arts education delivery mechanisms.

All of these factors have implications for arts education training and preparation through higher education and professional development. The questions stated at the beginning of this chapter are highly relevant for music education today. The answers that we give to these questions, and the policies that are developed, will have a powerful effect on the type and quality of music education delivery that our young people receive.

Extract 7.3

Source

Savage, J. (2011) *Cross-Curricular Teaching and Learning in the Secondary School: The Arts*. London, Routledge, pp. 126–127.

Introduction

The previous two extracts have explored partnerships between people. The final extract in this chapter considers a different form of educational partnership, notably the type that can be facilitated through the use of digital technologies. Specifically, cross-curricular ways of working, which include the types of educational collaborations we have been discussing in this chapter so far, can be facilitated through digital technologies. In the following extract, the role of technologies as a formative force within and between subjects is analysed in a pedagogical framework.

Key words and phrases

collaboration, technology, pedagogy, networks

Extract

Developing cross-curricular approaches to the arts through technology is about harnessing the powerful force of new technology within a pedagogy that maintains a firm grip on the broader aesthetic preoccupations of one's particular subject. It is about a balance between remaining true and faithful to the key concepts and process that really underpin one's subject whilst, simultaneously, recognising that subjects themselves are being transformed by new approaches many of which are inspired by the potential of new technologies to blur subject boundaries. Pedagogy has an important part of play in this. Pedagogy is both a 'practice' and a 'process' (Bernstein 1999: 259; Popkewitz 1998: 536) through which certain things can be acquired or through which certain capabilities can be developed. In the accompanying title to this book (Savage 2011), an argument was made that skilful teachers embody a skilful pedagogy. This skilful pedagogy has to be developed at some point. The ideas and practices of developing a pedagogical approach to cross-curricular teaching and learning, inspired by technology within the arts may well, in Bruner's terms, 'compete with, replace, or otherwise modify' your current pedagogical thinking and practice (Bruner 1996: 46).

One of the greatest advocates for pedagogy in recent times has been Professor Robin Alexander, a Fellow of Wolfson College at the University of Cambridge, and Director of the Cambridge Primary Review. His view is that 'it is schooling that has reduced knowledge to 'subjects' and teaching to mere telling' (Alexander 2008: 141). As teachers within creative subjects, it is time for us to rediscover a pedagogy for teaching the arts that transcends subjects and mere telling. Technology can play a role in this. But your involvement as a teacher is crucial. Research done at the University of Bristol pointed to:

> the importance of the teacher and the ways in which technology is incorporated into their pedagogy. This emphasises the importance of the ecological setting of classrooms and how a mixture of teachers' subject and pedagogical understandings act as filters during planning, practice and reflection.
>
> (Sutherland and John 2005: 411)

The role of the teacher was fundamental in incorporating technology within the classroom. One of the key future challenges facing educational communities will be the creation of opportunities for teachers to debate and discuss the educational purposes for, and philosophy underpinning, new technological approaches to teaching and learning. Teachers need to have a meaningful say in this ongoing debate, challenging and critiquing ideas so that the future shape of curriculum initiatives have a greater degree of shared ownership and, it is hoped, a wider impact. Facer calls this a 'curriculum for networked learning' and defines it as '. . . enabling individuals to learn to work effectively within social networks for educational, social and civic purposes and to develop strategies to establish and mobilise social networks for their own purposes' (Facer 2009: 7).

For teachers and learners the degree of personalisation within such a network is significant and should allow for the development of powerful processes for the development of subject knowledge and curriculum development. It will also facilitate the cross-subject exchanges or transactions that we have been discussing above. From the perspective of the learner (and this would include teachers as well as students), such a curriculum might consist of opportunities for:

- Learning and working within meaningful socio-technical networks not wholly within single educational institutions.
- Being assessed in interaction with tools, resources and collaborators.
- Developing capacities to manage information and intellectual property, building reputation and trust, developing experience of working remotely and in mediated environments.
- Creating new, personalised learning networks.
- Reflecting upon how learning is connected with other areas of personal, social, and working lives and manage and negotiate these relationships.
- Exploring the human-machine relationships involved in socio-technical networks.

(Facer 2009: 7)

The days of the individual teacher, teaching their individual subject in their own classroom, with the door closed to the majority of others outside, are clearly numbered. Key technological developments have already facilitated a significant shift in individual subject cultures, curriculum design and delivery. The role of technology within teaching and learning is powerful. Allying technology to the promotion of a cross-curricular approach to teaching and learning makes sense in many ways, not least in the educational benefits that it brings to students and teachers and the way that it reflects the wider use of technology outside the world of education. Networking and collaborative approaches are a key way forward.

References

Alexander, R. J. (2008) *Essays on Pedagogy*, London: Routledge.

Bernstein, B. (1999) Official knowledge and pedagogic identities, in F. Christie (ed.) *Pedagogy and the Shaping of Consciousness*, London: Cassell.

Bruner, J. (1996) *The Culture of Education*, Cambridge, MA: Harvard University Press.

Facer, K. (2009) *Educational, Social and Technological Futures: A report from the Beyond Current Horizons Programme*, London: DCSF and Futurelab.

Popkewitz, T. (1998) *Struggling for the Soul: The Politics of Schooling and the Construction of the Teacher*, New York: Teachers' College Press.

Savage, J. (2011) *Cross Curricular Approaches to Teaching and Learning in Secondary Education*, London: Routledge.

Sutherland, R. and John, P. (2005) Affordance, opportunity and the pedagogical implications of ICT, Educational Review, 57(4): 405–13.

Summary

Using any piece of technology in an educational context requires a certain amount of balancing. There are trade–offs between the subject itself, the technology being used, and the teacher's pedagogy that need to be analysed and understood. This extract reinforces the role of the teacher as the mediator for technological applications and usages within the classroom. Even within

networks facilitated by digital network technologies, the personalised pedagogical approaches that teachers adopt have a formative power in creating
opportunities for learning and a facilitative role in ensuring that pupils, and
others, can work effectively. The extract closes with an assertion that the days of
individual teachers working in their individual classrooms are well and truly
numbered. Networking and collaborative approaches to teaching and learning
will only become more predominant in the future.

Questions to consider

1. To what extent have I exploited the potential of digital networked technologies in my own teaching?
2. What have been the advantages or disadvantages of these tools in my own
   or others' teaching?

Investigations

What are the social networks that underpin current practices in music education? How can these be usefully extended to assist the development of subject
knowledge and to help processes of curriculum development?

Think deeper

Leong (2011) makes a passionate case for a different form of music education
suitable for the interconnected digital age within which we live. Specifically, he
argues that:

> Music education should re-position itself tuning into the emerging trends
> and developments. As more emphasis is given to creativity and the arts, music
> education practices need to devote more attention to developing learners'
> digital literacies, analytical and critical thinking, and the other twenty-first-
> century skills with reference to the realities of the cultural and creative
> industries. Curriculum priorities should focus on nurturing the creative,
> reflective and intuitive abilities of learners, utilizing web-based and game-
> based pedagogies, developing communities of learners as well as teaching
> them how to make use of the vast information and knowledge bases that are
> available and growing exponentially. Technology-enabled learning should
> go beyond accessing rich online resources and providing a publishing and
> distribution environment to value deep and collaborative learning as well as
> knowledge building. Learners should be helped to cultivate a keener cultural
> sensitivity and appreciation that would enable them to draw on diverse
> cultural ideas during the processes of creation and innovation. Indeed, music
> education should extend its localized horizons to make stronger links with
> the global knowledge economy in the digital and conceptual age.
>
> (ibid, p. 240)

Clearly, this is a potential vision for every music educator. It is not solely about the use of music technologies for a particular purpose. In this sense, Leong argues that it is not about the technology at all:

> The learning of music technology should go beyond the 'core' study areas – such as sound and its properties, basic audio processing, introduction to MIDI, digital audio basics, basic recording techniques and introduction to music sequencing – to explore ways of applying these skills and knowledge in empowering artistic expressions, and strategies that locate music effectively as an essential, integral and vibrant aspect of human lives and civilization.

> (ibid, p.241)

Instead, it is about harnessing the power of digital networked technologies to help make, create and connect together in new ways. This focus on nurturing creativity is something that the work of our final writer within this chapter has also been concerned with.

Think wider

Gauntlett (2011) takes a historical perspective on creativity and argues that it has always been about connecting people. Whilst he recognises that many writers and thinkers have located creativity within the context of the individual human mind and its capacity to think and develop new thoughts (e.g. with Csikszentmihalyi's work as we described earlier), his broader analysis of what creativity is ties up with the concept of making. Early in his book he argues that creative people engage in making, but that this making is in fact part of the same process of connecting with others. How? He summarises it in three ways:

- Making is connecting because you have to connect things together (materials, ideas or both) to make something new;
- Making is connecting because acts of creativity usually involve, at some point, a social dimension and connect us with other people;
- And making is connecting because through making things and sharing them in the world, we increase our engagement and communication with our social and physical environments.

> (ibid, p. 2)

Gauntlett's focus on the process of creativity, expressed through making with its integral element of connecting, leads him to a very different definition for creativity. He focuses, perhaps unsurprisingly, on the everyday process of creativity that combines making and connecting in an integral manner. But he also focuses on the feelings that arise when one is involved in a creative process:

Everyday creativity refers to a process which brings together at least one active human mind, and the material or digital world, in the activity of making something. The activity has not been done in this way by this person (or these people) before. The process may arouse various emotions, such as excitement and frustration, but most especially a feeling of joy. When witnessing and appreciating the output, people may sense the presence of the maker, and recognise those feelings.

(ibid, p. 76)

In a very obvious and simple sense, teachers are engaged in making things. Following Gauntlett's thesis, if we are involved in making things then we are involved in connecting with things too. Gauntlett applies his theory to education specifically, and says:

This [an anticipated] future education system recognises the characteristics of powerful learners: they are curious about the world, and wish to understand the how and why of things; they have courage, which means they are willing to take risks, and to try things out to see what happens; and they recognise that mistakes are not shameful disasters but are just events that can be learned from. They like to explore, investigate, and experiment. Tinkering with things is a way of learning. They have imagination, which is grounded by reason, thoughtfulness, and the ability to plan. They have the virtue of sociability, which means they know how to make use of the potent social space of learning. Finally, they are reflective, and are aware of their own strengths and weaknesses in the learning process.

(ibid, p.239)

Gauntlett is a little less clear about the ways in which this transformation will be made possible. In terms of the role of the teacher in all this, he says that pupils will be 'inspired by their teachers, who are no longer just the holders of the "answer book" but are visibly also learning new knowledge and skills in their own lives' (ibid, p. 237).

Conclusion

This chapter has explored some key questions about who should be involved in the teaching of music. The importance of content (subject) knowledge, pedagogical content knowledge and pedagogical knowledge itself have been highlighted. Working with other professional or community artists can have many benefits, but these collaborative partnerships do not succeed by accident. Everyone involved needs to understand the key features of successful partnership working and the range of thinking, skills and abilities that different individuals bring with them to such projects. Similarly, technology is not a neutral force, but digital networked technologies have much to offer the aspiring music educator.

They help us, and our pupils, make, share and connect in new ways and help facilitate a new way of working – for teachers and pupils.

References

Gauntlett, D. (2011) *Making is Connecting: The social meaning of creativity, from DIY and knitting to YouTube and Web 2.0*. Cambridge, Polity Press.

Hager, L. (2010) 'Youth Arts Residencies: Implications for policy and education'. *Youth Theatre Journal* 24, 111–124.

Hallam, R. (2011) 'Effective Partnership Working in Music Education: Principles and practice'. *International Journal of Music Education* 29:2, 155–171.

Leong, S. (2011) 'Navigating the Emerging Futures in Music Education'. *Journal of Music, Technology and Education* 4:2 and 3, 233–243.

Savage, J. and Challis, M. (2002) 'A Digital Arts Curriculum? Practical ways forward'. *Music Education Research* 4:1, 7–24.

Savage, J. and Challis, M. (2001) 'Dunwich Revisited: Collaborative composition and performance with new technologies'. *British Journal of Music Education* 18:2, 139–149.

Shulman, L (1994) 'Those Who Understand: Knowledge growth in teaching'. In Moon, B, and Shelton Mayes, A. (eds) *Teaching and Learning in the Secondary School*. London, Routledge.

Technology and Music Education

This chapter explores the use of technology within music education. The following four extracts have each been chosen because they illustrate concepts that relate to the key practice of using technology within the processes of teaching and learning in music. They are not about the nitty-gritty of what to do with a particular piece of technology nor how to use it within your teaching, but rather address the bigger themes that writers and researchers have explored that should impact on your future work in this area.

Extract 8.1

Source

Somekh, B. (2007) *Pedagogy and Learning with ICT.* London, Routledge, pp. 40–42.

Introduction

Nothing that schools do takes place in a vacuum. This is especially true when we consider something that is as prevalent in our lives as technology. Yet within music education it is curious how often we seem to forget that young people's musical lives – as performers, composers and listeners – outside the school are often initiated and sustained through their engagement with a range of techno-logical devices, including hardware and software. For this reason, our first extract is drawn from the work of Professor Bridget Somekh, one of the leading educational researchers in the field over the last 25 years. In this extract, Somekh explores some of the differences between learning in the home and learning in the school.

Key words and phrases

technology, formal, informal, home

Extract

A key difference between using ICT at home and at school is between informal and formal learning, hence we should not be surprised to find a replication of Lave's (1996) finding that learning in informal settings is ubiquitous and continuous whereas 'it often seems nearly impossible to learn in settings dedicated to education' (ibid., p. 9). What is at stake then becomes the nature and quality of the learning in informal settings. In the various research studies, ICT is observed entering homes and becoming embedded in family life, at first with some uncertainty about its purposes. Downes (2002), reporting on a study carried out with 500 children in Australia between 1995 and 1998, said that they thought of the computer as either a toy or a 'playable tool' – saying things like, 'I played typing stories' and 'I played the encyclopaedia'. From their descriptions it was clear that they used the computer for 'exploratory learning and "learning by doing", demonstrating the co-agency of the relationship between computer and child' (ibid., pp. 30–1). Similarly, in the ImpaCT2 evaluation we found that students habitually referred to their computer use at home as 'playing games' and reserved the word 'learning' only for activities that they engaged in at school: when they were asked to list their ICT activities at home it was clear that 'games' was a generic term used for a wide range of activities and categorised in this way because the computer was perceived as a site for leisure and autonomy. Facer *et al.* (2003), reporting on research between 1998 and 2000, describe how adults construct the family computer variably through discourses of entertainment, education and work, which parallel the fluidity of their constructions of childhood. Facer *et al.* provide photographs showing the various locations in which computers are positioned in the homes they visited, suggesting that 'ownership' varies: sometimes the computer is perceived as a shared resource for all the family and sometimes as more personally owned by a child, a sibling or a parent. They suggest that key features of ICT, such as the volume and speed of information and varied forms of interactivity, create a 'life on the screen' which is 'powerfully engaging' but that these features are not apparent from young people's accounts of using ICT at school. The problem they suggest is that 'at present, in school, computers are seen primarily as a *resource* for learning rather than a *context* for learning' (ibid., p. 232). At school, computer use is planned to support more rapid and more effective acquisition of a prescribed curriculum, whereas it is clear from the way that it is used at home that the computer's appeal to young people is that it accords them the same status as adults and gives them access to choices. The Internet allows them to take control, provides direct links with popular culture through accessing music and images, and keeps them in contact with their friends through messaging services and chat rooms. Since Downes (op. cit.) and Facer *et al.* (op. cit.) completed their studies most young people in England have acquired MP3 players and mobile phones and are able to access the Internet away from home. The technologies are merging: phones are turning into digital cameras and becoming Internet-enabled, MP3 players are extending to store and play back video films as well as music.

This mismatch between ICT use at home and at school is a cause for concern, mainly because it indicates the extent of the lost potential for ICT to transform schooling. A closer examination also reveals that there are aspects of ICT use that home does not provide, and moreover that ICT use at home is strongly differentiated between homes, not so much through what is traditionally called 'the digital divide' (access or non-access to a computer and the Internet) as through the family's cultural ambience or 'habitus' (Bourdieu 1977, pp. 183–5). Angus *et al.* (2004) describe the wide variation in computer and Internet use by four families, three of which were recipients of a special offer that aimed to 'make technology affordable for all Australians' and one which had already had a home computer and Internet access for some time. Differences in the patterns of family life and inequalities of aspirations quickly led to different patterns of computer use, with the least-advantaged family making much less use of the educational advantages offered by the Internet. This was compounded by a lack of empathy among teachers for the children from the most disadvantaged home, manifested for example in their failure to recognise and value the ICT skills of the family's teenage boy. The mother in this family used ICT to enhance her social life through participation in chat rooms, but this did not add to the family's cultural capital in any way. In another of our own studies (Lewin *et al.* 2003) we found, similarly, that the real digital divide was not between those with and without access to ICT at home, but related to the purposes for which home computers were used: only the students from advantaged homes used ICT for school-related work, either of their own volition or because their parents suggested it. Had teachers requested that ICT should be used for homework many others would have had the facilities to do so, but teachers operated a *de facto* policy of not setting ICT-related activities for homework for reasons of equity. This differential between kinds of use, rather than merely access to, ICT has been called by Natriello (2001) the 'second digital divide'.

The implications of all this research are clear: schools need to find ways of using ICT that give young people the transformed learning opportunities that some are already experiencing with ICT at home. This would involve giving students more time for extended engagement with ICT and encouraging them to use it to extend their creativity and productivity and take greater responsibility for their learning. At present the support for ICT use in the home is very unequal. There are also areas of ICT use, such as work with spreadsheets and calculations, that are virtually absent from patterns of ICT use even in homes with high cultural capital (Facer *et al.* 2003, pp. 235–6). It is clear from these research studies that there is a vital role for schools to play in helping children to acquire new digital literacies: skills in searching for, and selecting, websites, identifying their provenance, discriminating between their qualities and using them appropriately to produce new knowledge representations. November (2001) urges the importance of teaching essential digital literacies without which students using the Internet are open to misinformation and deception. Kerawalla and Crook (2002) in a study which shows strongly differentiated patterns of ICT use in homes and a prevalence for games playing, even in homes where parents have purchased the computer and software with specific educational purposes, recommend that schools should 'respect and locate within the classroom children's spontaneous achievements on home computers' and incorporate ICT more prominently into the school–family dialogue'.

References

Angus, L., Snyder, I. and Sutherland-Smith, W. (2004) 'ICT and educational (dis)advantage: families, computers and contemporary social and educational inequalities', *British Journal of Sociology of Education*, 25(1): 3–18.

Bourdieu, P. (1977) *Outline of a Theory of Practice*. Cambridge and New York: Cambridge University Press.

Downes, T. (2002) 'Blending play, practice and performance: chidren's use of the computer at home', *Journal of Educational Enquiry*, 3(2): 21–34.

Facer, K., Furlong, J., Furlong, R. and Sutherland, R. (2003) *ScreenPlay: Children and Computing in the Home*. London and New York: RoutledgeFalmer.

Kerawalla, L. and Crook, C. (2002) 'Children's computer use at home and at school: context and continuity', *British Educational Research Journal*, 28(6): 751–71.

Lave, J. (1996) 'The practice of learning', in S. Chaiklin and J. Lave (eds) *Understanding Practice: Perspectives on Activity and Context*. Cambridge, New York and Melbourne: Cambridge University Press.

Lewin, C., Mavers, D. and Somekh, B. (2003) 'Broadening access to the curriculum through using technology to link home and school: a critical analysis of reforms intended to improve students' educational attainment', *The Curriculum Journal*, 14(1): 23–53.

Natriello, G. (2001) 'Bridging the second digital divide: what can sociologists of education contribute?' *Sociology of Education*, 74(July): 260–5.

November, A. (2001) *Empowering Students with Technology*. Glenview, IL: Skylight Professional Development. See also www.anovember.com/alan.html (accessed 16/10/06).

Summary

This extract explores differences in the use of technology between the home and school environments. It argues that the difference between informal learning (within the home) and formal learning (within the school) is only part of the problem. Whilst there can be an obvious digital divide between those that do and those that do not have access to technology, Somekh cites research indicating that the uses to which technology is put within the home can be equally as divisive as whether or not a child has access to technology at all. Her finding is that there needs to be a greater degree of school–family dialogue about the uses of technology and a greater degree of understanding about the skills of digital literacy that young people need to acquire.

Questions to consider

1.   How does the general discussion about technology and its use in the home and the school relate to your work as a music teacher? What, if any, uses are

pupils making of technology for musical activities in the home and how will these impact on their work with you in the classroom?

2. Somekh lists a range of digital literacy skills towards the end of the extract. Are any of these particularly suited for, or applicable to, a music education? What other digital or technological skills would you want pupils to acquire throughout their music education?

Investigations

Draw up a list of some of the potential applications of technology that you make in your own musical practice (as a musician and teacher). How many of these can be done within the school context? How many can be done within the home context? To what extent are these uses dependent on particular pieces of technology? Can you imagine ways that they could be 'translated' from one context into the other, perhaps given the use of alternative or similar technologies?

Think deeper

Notions of informal or formal learning are problematic. They create an un-necessary binary division that can cause more problems than they solve. Somekh equates informal learning with the home, and formal learning with the school. However, others present alternative ways of thinking about this. After all, there is no golden rule that says all learning in the school needs to be formal, or vice versa! Many pieces of research that have considered future uses of technology seem to have found that the physical location of learning (whether you are in the home or the school) is, perhaps, less important than how you are connected.

The Beyond Current Horizons project (http://www.beyondcurrenthorizons. org.uk/) hypothesised a range of scenarios for learning with technology. Many of these emphasise how learners will create connections in terms of their location, their actions and their autonomy (i.e. to what extent they conceptualise themselves as an individual or part of a learning community). So, Facer (2009, p. 7) talks about a new curriculum that gives pupils an opportunity to:

■ Learn and work within meaningful socio-technical networks but not wholly within single educational institutions;

■ Develop experiences of working remotely and in mediated environments;

■ Create new learning networks;

■ Reflect upon how learning is connected with other areas of personal, social and working lives and manage and negotiate these relationships;

■ Explore the human–machine relationships involved in socio-technical networks.

Think wider

Somekh's work draws on an earlier piece of research conducted by Facer and others in 2003. This research drew on data generated through observations of children using technology in the home environment between 1998 and 2000. But the observations drawn from this research are still relevant today. In particular, Somekh picks up on one observation that is very applicable to our contemporary use of technology. Computers, she says, can be seen 'as a resource for learning rather than a context for learning' (Somekh 2007, p. 40).

What are the implications of this statement for music education? Technology, generally, could be conceptualised as a 'resource for musical learning' rather than a 'context for music learning'. In the first phrase, technology is external to the process, it is something that facilitates or encourages musical learning; in the second, it is integral to the process and provides a venue or location for a young person's emerging musicality to develop. Which is preferable? Are both necessary?

To unpick these questions we need to get a clearer idea about what particular musical skills or attributes technology can help facilitate. Towards this end, our next extract paints a provocative picture of what being a 'digital musician' might mean.

Extract 8.2

Source

Hugill, A. (2008) *The Digital Musician*. London, Routledge, pp. 2–5.

Introduction

In this extract, Hugill outlines the attributes of what he calls the 'digital musicians'. These, he suggests, are a discrete class of musician who exhibit certain characteristics that make them stand out from other musicians who may make occasional use of technologies within their musical activities. As the extract unfolds, keep track of the various 'types' of musician that Hugill discusses and, towards the end of the extract, note the specific characteristics of a 'digital musician' that he presents.

Key words and phrases

digital, technology, musicianship, performer, composer, identity

Extract

There are, of course, many different musical traditions and many different ways of classifying musicians according to their background. Some classifications are made by musicians themselves, others are made by writers, critics or academics. No single way is really satisfactory, because music tends to seep through its own porous boundaries. It is highly likely that a musician will show characteristics of more than one type.

Many musicians who knowingly work within highly established traditions, such as 'classical' music and certain forms of 'folk' music, take *pitch* as a starting point for their musical training. These musicians generally play an acoustic instrument as their main practice, and they travel a prescribed career path that involves the gradual evolution of technique and musicianship. The criteria for recognizing virtuosity are clearly established, and there is broad agreement among listeners about the level that an individual musician has attained.

Indian *raga*, Javanese *gamelan*, Chinese folk music, Western classical music and some forms of jazz, are all examples of such established traditions. What these systems have in common is an established set of skills and a standard practice. The relationship with pitch is a constant, whether it is the microtonal *sruti* of the *raga*, the harmonious relationship between the instruments of the gamelan orchestra, the modal inflections of Chinese folk music or the twelve notes to an octave of Western music. The first piano lesson generally begins with the note 'middle C', just above the keyhole in the piano frame, the middle of the keyboard. From this fundamental understanding, a pianist's training can begin. The student follows a path prescribed by experts, usually supervised by a teacher who gives 'one-to-one' guidance through the various levels of technical mastery to the full realization of musical potential. So 'technique' is acquired.

Another type of musician may begin with *rhythm*, or at least *beat*. This includes rock and most forms of popular music. Musicians working within this tradition tend to show a relative lack of interest in pitch when compared to the first type, although of course they do not ignore it completely. Bands without some sort of percussion section are rare, and, when they do appear, the instruments often emphasize rhythmic content in order to compensate. There is also general agreement about what constitutes a good musician in this field. The path to success is just as difficult as that for other musicians and is also mapped out by convention and experts.

As you look around the world today, it is clear that this kind of musician is the most prevalent. On the island of Zanzibar, most musicians are drawn to rap, rather than the traditional *Taarab*; in Bali, the young people perform punk rock in shopping malls, in preference to gamelan under pagodas; in Iran, the underground-rave and heavy-metal scenes flourish in spite of attempts by the regime to limit expression to traditional Iranian forms such as the *Radif*. But in many of these cases, the musicians are concerned to introduce traditional instruments and sounds into the more Western forms. Globalization is complex, and there is more going on here than just a Westernization of world culture. A musical commitment to traditional music does not necessarily prevent an involvement in bands, or vice versa. Recent musical history is peppered with examples of 'classically trained' popular musicians or popular musicians who have found a voice in classical forms. Jazz seems to sit somewhere between the two. These categories are not rigid.

A third tradition starts from *timbre*. This type of musician is harder to pin down, for the simple reason that many timbre-focused artists do not consider themselves to be musicians at all, or do not use the word 'music' to describe what they produce. Into this category can be placed the majority of those working in electronic and electro-acoustic[1] music, but also sonic art, sound-art, sound design and various forms of radiophonic[2] and speech-based work. By dealing with *sounds* rather than *notes*, these musicians have changed the nature of music itself, raising questions about what is 'musical'. The conventions of music seem inadequate to describe their activities. These musicians may even begin to challenge music's very existence, since so much of their prime material is *audio* and lacks the expressive intention and cultural baggage of 'music'.

This third type of 'musician' generates and manipulates sound using electronic means. For the majority of the relatively short history of this kind of music, they have done so using non-digital technologies. The fixed elements of the music – the microphone and the loudspeaker – remain (and presumably always will remain) *analogue*, that is to say, transducers that convert sound waves into an electrical signal (in the case of the microphone) or an electrical signal into sound waves (in the case of loudspeakers). The arrival of digital technologies has effected a rapid change in, and expansion of, the techniques available to this musician.

It might be assumed that these 'technological' musicians most naturally fit into the class of 'digital musicians', but in fact this is not necessarily the case. All types of musicians have always worked with technology, and all musical instruments are an example of technological innovation and development. Even the human voice may be thought of as a technology by the singer. For each of the three types of musician described above, a new situation exists, because so many people are now faced with digital technology at some stage in their working lives. The challenge is how, and to what extent, to engage with these technologies.

'Digital musicians' are, therefore, not defined by their use of technology alone. A classical pianist giving a recital on a digital piano is not really a digital musician, nor is a composer using a notation software package to write a string quartet. These are musicians using digital tools to facilitate an outcome that is not conceived in digital terms. However, if that pianist or composer were to become intrigued by some possibility made available by the technology they are using, so much so that it starts to change the way they think about what they are doing, at that point they might start to move towards becoming a digital musician.

The phrase 'digital musician' itself is only descriptive. It is the intention of this book to address a new class of musicians, but not necessarily to rename them. 'Computer musician', 'sound artist', 'sonic artist', 'sound designer', or even just a qualified 'musician' are among the possible names for people from this group. A digital musician is one who has embraced the possibilities opened up by new technologies, in particular the potential of the computer for exploring, organizing and processing sound, and the development of numerous other digital tools and devices which enable musical invention and discovery. This is a starting point for creativity of a kind that differs from previously established musical practice in certain respects, and requires a different attitude of mind. These musicians will be concerned not only with *how* to do what they do, or *what* to do, but also with *why* to make music. A digital musician, therefore, has a certain curiosity, a questioning and critical engagement that goes with the territory.

Although the digital musician could not have existed without the new technologies, that does not mean that he or she uses them exclusively. A digital musician might play an acoustic instrument, or use a non-digital electronic device, as part of their activities. In fact, this will almost certainly happen and be advantageous when it does. The difference is that those technologies will be used in conjunction with or *informed by* the digital. This 'informing' is a consequence of the changes in the state of the mind of the musician outlined above.

So what specifically distinguishes 'digital musicians' from other musicians? What skills do they possess? To be a digital musician requires:

- *aural awareness* (an ability to hear and listen both widely and accurately, linked to an understanding of how sound behaves in space and time)
- *cultural knowledge* (an understanding of one's place within a local and global culture coupled with an ability to make critical judgements and a knowledge of recent cultural developments)
- *musical abilities* (the ability to make music in various ways – performance, improvisation, composition, etc. – using the new technologies)
- *technical skills* (skill in recording, producing, processing, manipulating and disseminating music and sound using digital technologies).

These are not absolute categories: 'aural awareness' may be considered 'musical', acquiring 'cultural knowledge' will require some 'technical skills' and so on. Their interdependency is crucial, and the digital musician will not neglect any one of them. In all respects, the digital musician will be distinguished by *creativity*.

This creativity seems closest to sculpture, as the musician finds and shapes, manipulates and processes, sonic materials. To borrow the title of a book by the great Russian filmmaker, Andrei Tarkovsky, it might be called *sculpting in time*. Tarkovsky himself remarked about music: 'I feel that the sounds of this world are so beautiful in themselves that if only we could learn to listen to them properly, cinema would have no need of music at all.' The creative process perhaps also resembles alchemy: combining and recombining sounds, transforming them all the while, seeking the right mixture, the ideal combination.

These are musicians in a digital world and a digital culture in which sound has joined image and text as information or data, capable of endless mutation and transformation. They are musicians brought together by shared interests in a particular musical idea or form, often regardless of national boundaries or cultural heritage. The main medium is digital technology: the personal computer in all its many manifestations, from the desktop machine to the mobile phone; the network, from local area networks to the Internet; virtual worlds and artificial intelligence; multimedia and new media; software instruments and modified hardware.

Today's digital sound recording and its associated distribution and dissemination media has made all sorts of music readily available. This is far more than just a curious by-product of the development of digital media. It has fundamentally changed the cultural landscape. It affects all types of musician, but the digital musician will be the first to take this for granted, the first for whom the digital world is as 'given' as the physical world around them. For the digital musician, it is not just the technologies that are defining, it is the way they are used.

The world the digital musicians inhabit is both a perpetual horizon and a labyrinth of connections or links to the next meaningful encounter. The great challenge is to have *integrity*, to know who they are, where they are, what they are. They are on a journey without a clear destination. Perhaps they will come to a stop one day, but probably not today. The next encounter looks too intriguing, too exciting, to stop now, to stop here. Driven on by a relentless curiosity, the snail trail of their progress maps their identity as they accumulate ideas, information, stimulations and music. They move perpetually from the known to the unknown. This is what digital musicians are.

Notes

1. The word 'electro-acoustic' comes from engineering, where it is defined as 'an adjective describing any process involving the transfer of a signal from acoustic to electrical form, or vice versa'. B. Truax (ed.) *Handbook for Acoustic Ecology*, 1999. Online. Available HTTP: http://www.sfu. ca/sonicstudio/handbook/Electro-Acoustic.html(accessed 7 October 2011).
2. 'Radiophonic' refers to the experimental use of sound in radio.

Summary

Hugill begins by making the obvious point that throughout history, musicians have always defined themselves according to their particular backgrounds or traditions. Broad characteristics of musicians who are primarily concerned with pitch, rhythm or timbre are outlined. Many musicians make use of technology at some point but these are not, according to Hugill, digital musicians. Rather, digital musicians are those who embrace the opportunities presented by new technologies to engage in musical invention and discovery of a type unlike any previously established musical practices.

Questions to consider

1. To what extent are the categories of musicians that Hugill presents helpful? Which category best describes you and your abilities in music?

2. Are the attributes of the digital musician any different to those of a non-digital musician?

Investigations

As a teacher, you will have a range of existing musical skills. Whatever particular 'category' you placed yourself in response to the question above, how can you broaden your approach through the constructive use of digital technologies? In particular, how can you begin the process of exploring how digital technologies develop, extend and transform more traditional musical activities and, as such, become the context within which musical learning is embedded? This is very different from an approach that uses digital technologies to reinforce (and resource) a traditional model of music education delivery.

Whilst both digital and non-digital approaches to music education have many strengths (and both will be appropriate at particular moments), these technologies offer you an opportunity to work with pupils and conceptually relocate music education in a new place (outside the home and the school and beyond those traditional stereotypes).

Think deeper

Hugill's notion of a digital musician is a helpful set of ideas and principles which, in practice, it would be difficult to apply in any meaningful way. In this language, digital musicians exhibit a range of attributes, notably a creative and entrepreneurial sense of enquiry, that drive them forwards from one encounter to another. Their relentless curiosity is insatiable and they constantly move forward from the known to the unknown. To be honest, I think this describes every serious musician I know, whether they are a performer, composer or improviser; classical, popular, jazz or world musicians all have these attributes in their musical identity.

However, whilst it is easy to pick holes in such a schemata, there is much of value here too. As we have already discussed, the opportunities afforded by technology do present a cogent and powerful set of opportunities that should move us away from considering them as a 'resource for learning' and see them as a 'context for learning'. To this end, Hugill's aspirations for the digital musician help us gain an insight into the specific, facilitative dimensions of digital technologies and how they impact on musical practices. This is valuable work.

Think wider

Specifically, towards the end of this extract Hugill highlights the interdisciplinary nature of the digital musician. He uses a number of metaphors to explore this, notably the work of the alchemist and sculptor. The working practices of the digital musician are by nature interdisciplinary, because digital materials, whether sound, text, image or video, share at their root the same digital 'stuff' that allows them to be treated through similar processes.

These reflections have interesting correspondences to our work as music educators. Digital technologies do allow us to approach the activity of music education in a new way; they open new doors and create new spaces within which we, and our pupils, can work. The interdisciplinary potential of these technologies should be acknowledged and built upon. However, it is important not to overstate the uniqueness of digital technologies alongside traditional approaches. As Théberge wrote:

> Although there are certainly fundamental differences between electronic or digital technologies and acoustic instruments, such differences do not inevitably separate them from the broader continuum of musical expression; only the crudest technological determinism could support the argument that musicians approach these new technologies without bringing with them at least some of their own accumulated sensibilities with regard to their music making.
>
> (Théberge 1997, p. 159)

Extract 8.3

Source

Sefton-Green, J. (1999) *Young People, Creativity and New Technologies*. London, Routledge, pp. 146–148.

Introduction

This extract picks up on the notion of the 'digital' in a different way. It relates it to the concept of the 'digital arts' and explores some of the tensions that occurred when the notion of the 'digital arts' as a subject area collided with the reworking of the National Curriculum in England in the final years of the twentieth century. It presents an interesting case study of the way in which a new 'subject' tried to position itself within a traditional framework of ideas.

Key words and phrases

digital, technology, arts, curriculum, curriculum development

Extract

The British educational system has always had a rather schizophrenic approach towards the traditional and the modern and there are many instances where contemporary needs and ambitions are in conflict with conventional values and practices (see Education Group 1991). From this point of view digital arts becomes yet another 'subject' caught up in this debate. On the one hand, politicians and educationalists extol the values of digital technology and advocate the use of computers within the curriculum; on the other, there is a belief that the school system should provide a solid foundation of basic skills and that these are best prepared through tried and tested methods. Equally, whilst cultural and curriculum modernisers embrace the spirit of the digital age, so the traditionalists advocate old-fashioned humanist values and a belief in the civilising function of high culture. These contradictions will take time to resolve. Whilst we live in a country that is still trying to figure out how best to use calculators in mathematics, it may be at best naïve to imagine that digital arts will play a central part in the curriculum.

However, the enthusiasm and excitement generated by digital arts projects is evident from all the accounts collected here and given that these tensions are not going to be 'solved' one way or the other, it is important that these case studies can stand as evidence for the value of this work. Only by making the argument that this kind of work offers a unique educational experience can we hope to influence the educational agenda. Yet, at times, these projects can appear complicated and time-consuming. Indeed, one slightly negative conclusion, to be drawn from all work, is just how much effort by staff and resources must have gone into these projects. This is not to say they weren't worthwhile—again, all the chapters bear evidence of the value of the students' experience—but that they are the product of individual vision and commitment. The fact that so many of these projects were supported by additional financial resources is also pertinent. On the one hand, these examples strongly imply that you need a very high level of input to achieve results; but on the other it may be reasonable to imagine that as more and more teachers do become familiar with the technology and interested in the field, so it will become that much easier to develop projects of this nature. Ultimately, as I suggested in the last chapter, the problem of resources will not stand in the way of developing digital arts in the curriculum—there is a host of pressures that is encouraging their growth— but it will hinder their development *equally* across all sections of the educational system.

Finally, I want to suggest here that there is much to indicate that multimedia is well on the way to becoming a new cross-curricular subject; and that this development should be treated with caution as well as optimism. I am referring to the fact that multimedia projects are often devised as a way of delivering ICT and that they are often valued for the ways they enable general educational activities to occur. Many of the case studies here identify a number of these: working in groups; the value of pre-production planning; the fact that students who are traditionally excluded from our education system can participate; the high premium placed on discussion, decision-making and negotiation; the fact that other core skills (for example, numeracy, design work, keyboards) are used in the production; and finally the fact that the product can be displayed and used by a peer audience. This is very reminiscent of how drama in education was developed in the 1970s as a tool for learning, almost as a multipurpose medium, for working in any subject. So, it is suggested, multimedia can act as a similar servant to the curriculum, in that it offers a means to explore other subjects in an imaginative and motivating fashion.

On the one hand, multimedia thus feeds into a shared notion of a 'creativity curriculum', that is, those general arts activities which develop not only a range of transferable skills but develop children as individuals. Like drama, multimedia teaches a host of salient modern competencies, which are both specifically vocational (in that young people are likely to work with some kind of digital technology in the future) and pre-vocational (in that they embody a way of working which will be of general use). Equally, multimedia offers an inventive and innovative way into traditional subject knowledge.

References

Education Group 11 (Department of Cultural Studies, University of Birmingham) (1991) *Education Limited: Schooling, Training and the New Right in England since 1979* London: Unwin Hyman.

Summary

Technology and location have been prominent themes within this chapter. This extract reflects on a number of innovative digital arts projects (recounted earlier in Sefton-Green's book) and draws some concluding thoughts together for future practice. Given that it was written around 15 years ago, it provides an interesting historical perspective on certain issues. Firstly, Sefton-Green highlights the schizophrenic approach to technological innovation that is inherent within our educational system. This causes all sorts of problems: Should we be teaching the subject not the technology? Should uses of technology (e.g. calculators) supplant the requirement of more traditional methodology (e.g. mental maths)? Worryingly, none of these issues seem to have been resolved in recent years.

But more fundamentally, the extract tells the story of a new, young subject (digital arts) that is trying to get a foothold locating itself in the mainstream educational context. There is a tension inherent within the discussion between the 'digital arts' (which, as Sefton-Green argues is unlikely to take hold in any meaningful way within a National Curriculum that is dominated by traditional subjects) and the skills of using multimedia technologies (which, he argues, could become akin to a cross-curricular subject area). At the time, 'multimedia' offered much to those concerned with creativity within the curriculum – a specific set of vocational-type skills and an inventive, innovative way to reconsider traditional subject knowledge.

Questions to consider

1. What can this historical snapshot tell us about the current situation facing music educators as they seek to implement new uses of technology within their teaching?

2. What is the appropriate 'location' for the use of digital technologies within music education? Should they be located within 'music' as a curriculum subject, or somewhere else?

Think deeper

This extract contains some important lessons for us relating to the location of knowledge, skills and understanding. Firstly, there is a danger of creating a new subject (e.g. the digital arts) and trying to get it embraced within a traditional curriculum structure. Secondly, there is a problem with trying to create a subset of cross-curricular 'skills' (e.g. multimedia) and trying to get them embedded across other subjects. Thirdly, there is an issue with re-conceptualising key pieces of multimedia learning as 'salient modern competencies' that would have wider vocational relevance in young people lives. All of these have largely failed (there is not a subject called 'digital arts' within the English National Curriculum; 'multimedia' as a term was dated and has no cross-curricular standing today and many commentators are dismissive of the academic/vocational divide in terms of knowledge types).

So, what is the alternative? The more considered approach is to start with you, the teacher. Stenhouse's phrase that we considered in Chapters 3 and 5 comes to mind: 'there is no curriculum development without teacher development' (Stenhouse 1975, p. 142). For Stenhouse and for many of us who have followed in his wake, the only meaningful and lasting curriculum development takes place when teachers are able to rediscover their professionalism and exert it through curriculum planning and development. Many contemporary curriculum frameworks not only tell teachers what to teach, but also how to teach it. This has led to a culture of shallow thinking about curriculum development.

As we considered throughout Chapter 5, developing appropriate curriculum opportunities for the use of digital technologies in the music curriculum must, if it is to have any lasting impact and value, start with you and your work as a musician and teacher. You have to spend the time with the technology; develop the 'accumulated sensibilities' with it that Théberge writes of; consider the broader musicological and cultural impacts it might have and how it links to other traditional forms of musical practice; and skilfully produce a curriculum framework that locates the new knowledge, skills and understanding that digital technologies facilitate in an appropriate place that your pupils can access easily.

Think wider

More widely, it is worth reflecting on the current state of affairs in respect of our examination system. The stark divisions that have opened up in recent years between the study of music and music technology for pupils at Key Stage 4 and above can only be harmful to the future of a coherent provision of music education. Simultaneously, the division raises artificial barriers between forms of musical expression whilst creating groups of those who feel they can and those who feel they cannot use digital technology appropriately. It is worth pausing and asking the question why no other curriculum subject has followed down the road to a similar division?

Extract 8.4

Source

Armstrong, V. (2011) *Technology and the Gendering of Music Education*. Aldershot, Ashgate, pp. 132–135.

Introduction

One of the more unfortunate consequences of the division between 'music' and 'music technology' in our education system has been what Armstrong has called the 'gendering of music education'. Her recent book provides a fascinating account of technology in contemporary music education and the gendered processes and practices that surround its use. This extract comes towards the end of the book where Armstrong discusses certain elements surrounding the classroom practice of teachers she observed.

Key words and phrases

technology, identity, gender, digital

Extract

The problems of single-sex classes

My findings suggest that the ways girls approach learning about technology is slightly different from the approach taken by boys, and often reflects their out-of-school digital activities and interests. In line with other research, girls in my study said that they would appreciate more structured help and training with new music software but I have some reservations about advocating that this take place in single-sex settings as some researchers have advocated (Colley et al., 1997). As Culley (1988) has noted, in taking such an approach, there may be a tendency to 'ghettoize' girls-only sessions, particularly when taught by staff not perceived as particularly technologically proficient, and this clearly has serious implications for classroom practice. While Culley acknowledged that girls may be less inclined to use computer rooms where boys dominate (and this was certainly the case at Crossways Independent and New Tech Comprehensive), girls-only schemes may serve to further diminish girls' access because the 'open' sessions continue to be dominated by boys. I am concerned that, by providing separate sessions for girls, there is a serious risk of producing a subordinate female subculture in which 'female technology' might be unfairly compared to 'male technology'. This concern is reinforced by the observation I made that a significant number of the girls within my study stated that they had not been given the same training in certain types of software as the boys in their class, resulting in fewer girls expressing the confidence or having sufficient knowledge to use the more complex and highly valued sequencing packages in their work. My findings suggest that the meanings around music software are also highly gendered, therefore certain types of software may be more compatible with and reflect gendered assumptions about the user. The more complicated the software the more likely it was to be associated with a male expert user in contrast to simpler notational software which boys (and some girls) were less likely to associate with 'real' music technology. Boys in my study are expected to be secure in their identity as computer users, which in part is associated with the ability to use more complex music software and its association with masculine characteristics of skill and expertise. Therefore it was a worrying observation that boys were often the recipients of more 'complex' technological information whereby teachers tended to introduce boys to advanced sequencing software on an 'ad hoc' informal basis. There were certainly boys within my study who were not proficient technology users but they were less likely or less willing to express any sense of 'lack'. Therefore, by offering more structured approaches to learning about music software so that extra support can be provided to both male and female pupils, all pupils will have access to the same degree of technological information that may help to reduce this inequality of access to different types of music software. In addition, it may also lead teachers to re-examine their perceptions about 'male expertise' that presupposes that all boys are more interested and capable users of technology, and to provide girls with the same opportunities to demonstrate expertise on more sophisticated software.

Greater awareness about how male and female teachers and pupils are differently positioned in the technologized classroom

Throughout this study, I have emphasized the central role played by the teacher in constructing gendered technological discourses. I have argued that men's symbolic association with technology is an important aspect in constructions of masculinity, and my study demonstrates that male teachers and pupils positively align themselves with all things technological. This affords them greater control to name what counts and who counts in technological spaces, and who can be constructed as the technological expert. Game and Pringle (1984) state that men have more power to say what they will and will not do, and consequently have a greater influence over the cultural and material practices within the workplace. Men's experiences feed into pre-existing masculine cultures from which women are already excluded. In addition to these formal male networks are those informal networks around which 'masculine' cultures develop. Few women either wish to or are able to participate in them and are thereby left out of an important part of the loop. As Lamb (1993: 175) observes, 'it becomes apparent that men, as a class, define the structures of power and maintain the relations of ruling within music and music education'. This in turn impacts negatively on pupils' perceptions of female teachers. Female teachers are considered less interested and less able to engage with music composition technologies. Where they do so, their engagement is perceived as requiring very little skill or technical expertise, such as printing off parts for rehearsals. This contributes to the ways in which male teachers and male pupils work together to produced gendered discourses to which female teachers and female pupils find themselves unable to contribute. Pupils' perceptions will be significantly influenced by the gender of the teacher to act as a role-model (Green, 1997). It is therefore important for teachers to begin to develop self-awareness as to how their social interactions around technology are perceived. As I demonstrated in my discussion of the construction of the pupil expert, female teachers can often undermine not only their own authority and identity but also that of their female pupils when they insist on privileging boys' technical knowledge over that of girls. Male teachers should attempt to encourage girls to participate in technological discussions that are more often than not monopolized by boys. This would send out a clear message that girls' knowledge is equally valued, and their technological interactions will be more overtly recognized.

Using older girls to mentor younger girls and boys may also reduce the masculine connotations of computers and music software. If girls are seen to talk about and use technology knowledgeably and confidently, the symbolic associations of technology with masculinity could perhaps be minimized. Female role models are important to other women, as the following comment by a female audio production postgraduate student illustrates:

> The few female teachers that I have encountered during my four years in music/technology education have been tremendous role models for me. I don't think they were trying to be role models. It is often enough that they are there.
>
> (Whistlecroft, 2000: 5)

By encouraging more confident technological girls to work with less confident girls during composition lessons, their knowledge, and indeed their very presence in the music technology suite, may serve to alter negative perceptions about girls' technological competence.

Providing greater flexibility in the compositional process

Throughout the book I have attempted to show why it is important that pupils have some level of control over their digital and non-digital interactions in their compositional processes. It is vital that teachers, wherever possible, do not equate 'composition' with 'music technology suite'. It has been highlighted that such a strongly circumscribed approach to the use of technology poses particular challenges for girls but it is certainly not unproblematic for some boys too although, as my findings suggest, they appear to have access to a wider range of acceptable forms of masculinity (such as the 'rock' musician) that were not available to the girls. If other modes of composition are available, students should be offered the opportunity to use these rather than compel all students to compose in the same way.

While Haraway's cyborg as a concept for feminist analysis continues to stimulate our imaginations, I have suggested that as a political image it has been less successful. As Squires notes, persuasive rhetoric alone will not be sufficient to alter the distribution of power. Like many feminists, she does not deny the usefulness of the cyborg image but feels that it has been 'submerged beneath a sea of technophoric cyberdrool' (2000: 360). She rightly asserts that the image of the cyborg can only be salvaged if it is seen 'as a metaphor for addressing the interrelation between technology and the body, not as a means of using the former to transcend the latter' (2000: 360). This observation highlights the tensions between cyberfeminists who have seized on the cyborg as the ontological future and those feminists, and here I include myself, who wish to see the body included in discussions about technology. Without this sense of the corporeal, we are in danger of losing the political plot. Whatever the acts of 'cyborgian' engagement envisioned by Haraway, these are all initiated from the corporeal, and it is this that grounds us in real, lived, social relations. The idea that the materiality of our existence could or should be extinguished seems to be a frantic attempt to align us with technology, as if our 'cyborgian' selves were entirely transcendent of material concerns. Rather worryingly, it further suggests that the corporeal (and here I am referring to both men's and women's bodies) can be re-drawn *at will* via a new technological embodiment which transcends (or ignores) cultural markers or by attempting to obliterate the body completely. Neither of these formulations appears satisfactory because notions of identity become completely divorced from our real, lived, social relations. I therefore maintain that we must focus on the *materiality* of human–machine amalgams and focus on the degree of choice and level of agency afforded to these young composers in my study.

Summary

The extract starts with a discussion about separation. Is it appropriate for teachers to adopt single-sex classes when introducing a piece of new music software? Armstrong repudiates this approach which can clearly, in her view, do more harm than good. Her discussion moves on to consider the role of the teacher. Whether male or female, the teacher has a key role to play in constructing a gendered technological discourse. Teachers need to understand what this is and seek to mediate the effect of it appropriately.

Questions to consider

1. To what extent are the examples that Armstrong cites in her writing true of your own experiences of music education, either as a pupil or a teacher?
2. What links does Armstrong make to broader societal or cultural issues in her analysis of how technology has gendered the use of music technology in the classroom?

Investigations

At the next opportunity that you have, spend some time observing young people at work with technology in a classroom environment. How does the teacher organise the pieces of technology (where are they located, how are they presented to the pupils and are there support materials available?) and how has the teacher organised the pupils (are they working individually, in same-sex pairs or groups?)? Secondly, what role does the teacher's pedagogy and identity in the classroom play in encouraging all pupils to access the pieces of technology? In Armstrong's words, what does a 'gendered technological discourse' look like in practice?

Think deeper

Armstrong illustrates very clearly how the work that we do as teachers within the classroom is tied to the perceptions, practices and discourses that we inhabit outside the classroom. Our chapter opened with the notions of formal (the classroom) versus informal (the home). These artificial distinctions allow us too easily to excuse the more complex (and interesting) continuum that exists between our lives as teachers and pupils within and outside the school. The genderisation of technology is a broader societal and cultural issue, yet its resonance and influence are clearly observable in our work as teachers and in the lives of our pupils. We need to respond in a positive manner as teachers and Armstrong's work provides some useful starting points in this respect.

In a similar way, our discussion about the categorisation of differing types of musician in Hugill's work also has resonances here. Armstrong's use of the cyborg metaphor is built upon an understanding of the human–machine interface as part of an intimate, synchronous and symbiotic relationship. The two cannot be separated. For me, there is a clear analogy here to the work of the performing musician. In the act of musical performance, the instrument and performer become one. It is impossible to imagine one before or above the other. They are both indispensable. The very things that we value about an expert musical performer are intrinsic to the relationship that has been established between them and their instrument over many years of practice, rehearsal and performance.

Think wider

Finally, the distinctions of 'digital' or 'non-digital' technologies fade into insignificance when compared with the broader musical, cultural and societal discourses that we have discussed in this chapter. It seems to me to be a nonsense that certain types of technology (e.g. digital tools) are examined in one place (a 'music technology' examination) while those of another type (e.g. a clarinet) are examined elsewhere. This causes more problems than it solves. As a subject culture, music has many strengths. It is a broad church with many different voices and points of view within it. Why has it marginalised one and not the others? The sooner we can work towards and establish an integrated approach to music within our classrooms and examination specifications the better – with or without digital technologies.

Conclusion

In Chapter 1 we explored the viewpoint that every child has the right to a music education. I would also argue that every child has the right to a music education that incorporates the use of digital technologies in a pedagogical, helpful way. It is too often the case in our educational systems that those who can, do, and those who can not, use music technology. This is wrong on so many levels and the educational research in this area has highlighted these problems. It is up to us as teachers to show a different way.

References

Facer, K. (2009) 'Educational, Social and Technological Futures: A report from the Beyond Current Horizons Programme'. London, DCSF & Futurelab.

Stenhouse, L. (1975) *An Introduction to Curriculum Research and Development*. London, Heinemann Educational.

Théberge, P. (1997) *Any Sound You Can Imagine: Making music/consuming technology*. London, Wesleyan University Press.

Researching Music Education

The next two chapters present some ideas about how to conduct research into the processes of music education. Whether you are going to carry out some research with a capital 'R', perhaps as part of a higher degree, or with a lower-case 'r', perhaps as part of a process of curriculum development, the following extracts will provide some basic ideas to help frame your work.

Extract 9.1

Source

Campbell, M. *et al.* (2010) *Constructing a Personal Orientation to Music Teaching.* London, Routledge, pp. 133–135

Introduction

For most readers of this book, your research will co-exist alongside your role as a music teacher. For this reason, the first extract starts with how research can be framed within the context of curriculum development.

Key words and phrases

research, curriculum development

Extract

On an ongoing basis, music teachers design educational experiences for students through lessons and rehearsal plans, but they also serve as the architects of entire music programs. Like an architect, the teacher strives to build a strong foundation of knowledge. Like an architect, the teacher begins with a general plan in mind and oversees the construction of such a plan, sometimes making modifications along the way. Of course, the actual nature of this work varies depending upon the setting, and may involve a team instead of one person, relying on close collaboration with other music teachers or a music supervisor within a school district. In the beginning stages of a career, music teachers strive to gain confidence and comfort with daily and weekly planning. With experience, perspectives broaden (to return to the architectural metaphor, you see not just the features of a particular room but the shape of the entire building). Teachers develop and refine their expectations for the overall coherence and impact of the musical offerings supported by the school. When this important shift occurs, teachers often examine their music programs to evaluate whether the curriculum is **comprehensive, balanced, sequential,** and **relevant**. The first three of these adjectives have been cited most frequently and historically within the profession (Barrett, 2009; Mark and Gary, 2007); the concern for relevance reflects more recent dialogue (Kratus, 2007; Williams, 2007).

A **comprehensive** music curriculum is broad enough in scope to provide students with an equally broad range of ways to encounter and experience music. Through the curriculum, many types of *musical engagements* are made possible, including:

- Performing music through singing and playing instruments, as well as various settings for performance, including solo, small ensembles and chamber groups, and large ensembles we commonly know as bands, choirs, and orchestras;
- Listening to the music performed by others, including the development of skills and sensibilities to perceive musical qualities, think in sound, analyze music, and describe it with acuity and sophistication;
- Creating music through various forms of improvisation (from free improvisation to more structured or genre specific improvisation), arranging, composition;
- Representing music through the use of symbol systems (standard musical notation; graphic scores) or digital means;
- Studying the historical and cultural roots of music, the contributions of composers and cultures, the paths of influence and interrelatedness of musical ideas, forms, practices, and styles;
- Relating music to other forms of human expression and achievement, noting its commonalities with subjects 'outside' of music as well as its distinctive qualities; and;
- Deepening our capacity to respond to music's expressive forms and feelings, and enhancing the meanings we derive from musical experience.[1]

A comprehensive music curriculum also reflects a teacher's (or overall music program's) wise sampling of musics to study that are drawn from the panoramic range of *musical styles, practices, and works* accessible to students. There are worlds of musics to explore, particularly when you start with a music teacher's personal and professional experience with music and expand that to embrace the realms of musical interests and experience that students bring with them to the music classroom. More than ever, due to the proliferation of musical ideas made accessible through live performance and mediated outlets, teachers can select increasingly diverse repertoires of works to perform and study. Imagine how these repertoires are expanded by the works that students create and choose themselves. Reimer's criteria of craftsmanship, sensitivity, imagination, and authenticity might be useful to guide this selection of music for classroom exploration.

A comprehensive music curriculum also addresses the **elements and forms of music.** Traditionally, these elements have included melody, rhythm, harmony, timbre, articulation, dynamics, texture and the ways that these elements are combined through varying musical forms and structures. Sound is the definitive core of the music curriculum, distinguishing music education from the rest of school subjects. Learning how properties of musical sound shape the patterns and complexities of music is integral to curricular work. Student understanding depends on how music moves and works.

If a comprehensive curriculum embraces a wide variety of musical engagements; musical styles, practices, and works; and musical elements and forms; then *balance* in the curriculum is a matter of emphasis. Balance is achieved when teachers align their curricular goals with the resources, opportunities, and constraints that influence curricular decisions, and make informed decisions about what to include and what to exclude. A balanced curriculum also involves weighing curricular decisions in light of the overarching philosophy of the school and community, teacher expertise, student interests, and practical considerations of space, funding, instructional time, and scheduling. No single school program can encompass the ever-expanding array of musical possibilities. A balanced program requires wisdom and care. A mixed sampler of offerings that is too eclectic can result in a music curriculum that merely introduces students to musical ideas through fleeting and superficial exposure. A program that is too narrowly focused at the other end can result in a restricted menu of opportunity and understanding. Questions related to balance focus on the proportion of elective and required courses, the range of opportunities offered, and the degree to which they are available for students at various levels of experience and interest.

A *sequential* music curriculum attends to the development of key understandings, skills, and habits in a systematic fashion to support students' musical development. The path for encountering musical ideas, from simple to complex, is chosen based on teachers' deliberations concerning:

- Students' development, and knowledge about their capabilities from early childhood through adolescence;
- Musical considerations, as teachers make decisions based on the challenges and sophistication of the music to be studied;
- Sensitivity to determine *when* learners best encounter certain musical ideas; and

■ Personal knowledge, experience, and preferences of teachers, who organize the content in ways that make sense.

A classic notion of curricular ordering has been that of the spiral curriculum, in which students form increasingly differentiated and sophisticated understandings of music by encountering key ideas repeatedly but at more challenging levels (See Thomas, 1971).

Finally, *relevance* is a relatively new adjective to be cited in speaking about the music curriculum. The inclusion of relevance reflects the profession's desire to bridge the gap between the musics students encounter in school with the musics they encounter outside of school. Such efforts seek to incorporate popular, or vernacular, musics in the curriculum, as well as a range of cultural traditions and musical practices that have not traditionally been included in school music programs. Another aspect of relevance has to do with the role of music in the lives of individuals. Children's early years are infused with musical experiences, even before they enter formal schooling. The influences of the home, extended family, community, media, and societal milieu constitute a platform of understanding; the young child builds on this platform when making sense of a music class.

Relevance also speaks to the way that music programs prepare students to continue their musical involvements once they are no longer enrolled in school music programs. To account for relevance, teachers must keep in mind the lasting impression of making and studying music, and how the student moves toward an independent and fulfilling musical life beyond the boundaries of the program itself. Relevance is a key principle in the contemporary movement within the profession to foster lifelong learning, community music, and adult engagement in music. The school curriculum can be the foundation for this long and satisfying presence of music in our lives.

Notes

1. You may want to compare this list with the National Standards in Music Education.

References

Barrett, J. R. (Ed.). (2009). *Music education at a crossroads: Realizing the goal of music for all*. Lanham, MD: Rowman & Littlefield Education.

Kratus, J. (2007). Music education at the tipping point. *Music Educators Journal, 94*(2), 42–48.

Mark, M. L., & Gary, C. L. (2007). *A history of American music education* (3rd ed.). Lanham, MD: Rowman & Littlefield Education.

Reimer, B. (1991). Criteria for quality in music. In R. A. Smith & A. Simpson (Eds.), *Aesthetics and arts education* (pp. 330–338). Urbana, IL: University of Illinois Press.

Thomas, R. B. (1971). *MMCP synthesis: One of the major products of the Manhattanville Music Curriculum Program*. Elnora, NY: Media.

Williams, D. A. (2007). What are music educators doing and how well are we doing it? *Music Educators Journal, 94*(1), 18–23.

Summary

Starting with an application of a metaphor (the teacher as architect), this extract considers four aspects of the curriculum that music teachers will need to consider as they evaluate the impact of their work:

1. The 'comprehensiveness' of the curriculum will raise questions as to whether the educational opportunities are broad enough to provide all students with an equal range of ways to encounter music;

2. The 'balance' of the curriculum relates to the alignment of particular curricula goals with the resources, opportunities and constraints that a specific context for teaching and learning affords;

3. The 'sequential' nature of the curriculum is about the systematic development of pupils' musical skills, knowledge and understanding; and

4. The notion of 'relevance' considers the joined-up approach to music education within the school to that of pupils' musical experiences outside the school.

Questions to consider

1. To what extent do these four terms encompass the particular issues of curriculum development that you consider in your work? Are there any others that you would want to add to the list?

2. What key questions can you draw from this extract about your own work in designing and delivering a music education curriculum? What personal challenges can you identify?

Investigations

This extract provides an alternative way of thinking about the curriculum. Whether your music education is written down in units of work and lesson plans, or solely exists in your own head and is delivered informally on a pupil-by-pupil basis, the key adjectives identified in the extract should help you rethink your approach in a constructive way.

Identifying a focus area for research, and then formulating a clear research question, is one of the most important skills a researcher needs. Review your responses to the above questions. If pushed into a corner, what is the single most important challenge to your own work that the extract revealed in your mind? Try and turn this into a simple question that you can reflect on further. That's the start of a research process linked to curriculum development.

Think deeper

It is not enough that teachers' work should be studied; they need to study it themselves.

(Stenhouse 1975, p. 143)

Enquiry counts as research to the extent that it is systematic, but even more to the extent that it can claim to be conscientiously self-critical.

(Stenhouse 1985, p. 15)

Education is a complex activity. It involves many different elements, including people, tools and ideas. Watching education in action within a classroom or other learning environment is fascinating. As teachers, I think we often take this for granted. Stenhouse emphasises the requirement that teachers' work is worthy of study. But not only that, it is worthy of study by teachers themselves! To this end, Stenhouse equates systematic enquiry to a form of educational research, particularly when it involves teachers being self-critical of their practice.

To this end, research can be an integral part of teaching. It can be a tool that teachers can use to investigate their own practice in a systematic and self-critical way. It can also be a tool that teams of educators employ to investigate specific pieces of curriculum development. It is important to remember that research is a skilful activity that can be done poorly and done well. The degree of self-criticality that one is able to engender may be a criteria of the success of the piece of research. But there will be many other criteria that you will need to consider as well. Towards this end, it is worth reflecting a while longer on what research is actually about.

Think wider

Like education, research involves many processes. It includes looking at things, asking questions, listening to others, describing events and making interpretations. It is definitely a skilful activity. Some writers relate it to an art form. As an activity, it has many benefits when taken into an educational setting, but there are some important things to consider before doing so.

Firstly, research is about making public things that are often private. This can be uncomfortable and challenging. When thinking about starting a piece of research, it is vital to consider the conditions under which it is carried out and to ensure that it maintains respect for people and their privacy.

Secondly, research is not solely about educational programmes, initiatives or curriculum development. Although it is often used in this way to justify new ventures, it is important to reflect on the roles that people play. In research, people are central. In an educational setting, this would include teachers, pupils and other adults working within the school setting. When done well, research can capture the life experiences of those within an educational project.

Thirdly, whilst research may start with a particular question or issue that you have identified and perhaps shared with others, it is important to recognise that it extends from this into all kinds of other contexts. Research projects, big or small, contain complicated sets of aspirations, values and experiences within which individual's biographies, political values, contextual influences and much more beside, conflict. This can cause difficulties for people on occasion.

Finally, and perhaps most importantly, no piece of research will find out the truth. Although the notion of truth is attractive, a more pragmatic approach to educational research acknowledges that 'truth' is always difficult to establish in a complex set of circumstances like those found in a classroom. This is not to say that research should not be truthful in its application. In fact, having an ethical approach to the collection of research data and the processes by which judgements are made about that data is essential. But in terms of outcomes, there is unlikely to be one 'truth' that the research will uncover.

Extract 9.2

Source

Phelps, R. *et al.* (2005) *A Guide to Research in Music Education*. Oxford, Scarecrow Press, pp. 3–6.

Introduction

If the above has whetted your appetite for researching something within your own teaching practice, the next step might be to read in more detail what the actual research process might contain. As you do so, one thing will quickly become apparent. Educational research is full of jargon! The following extract provides an introduction to two pairs of terms that you are likely to encounter early on.

Key words and phrases

research, methodology, methods

Extract

The researcher in the arts and music can anticipate encountering certain terms and/or concepts relating to procedures of research. Those that refer only to specific types of research will be discussed in appropriate chapters in this book. Others, which are common to all types of research, follow. An understanding of these terms is important to the logical organization of a research study.

When matriculated, especially at the doctoral level, students are required to make a distinction in their program of studies between an emphasis that will enable them to pursue a project with a *pure* research emphasis and one that may be labeled *applied*, usually referred to as *action* research. Action research can be used at all levels of instruction in order to improve performance, state Gall, Gall, and Borg.[1] Pure, sometimes known as 'basic' or 'fundamental' research, is based on the accurate reporting of results, usually with little or no attempt to incorporate practical applications of the findings of the research. Those who read the reports are expected to make whatever use or application of the data that seems appropriate to their own situation. *Pure* research, often concerned with the development of a theory or model based on previous models, is desirable in almost all fields of endeavor, but frequently is not the type to produce answers to questions facing arts educators in the classroom. A history of eighteenth-century English secular choral music most likely would be classified as pure research, provided the study was conducted according to the tenets of 'basic' research. Applied, frequently labeled 'action' research, is conducted in such a way that the investigator includes practical suggestions for applying the results of the study to a teaching situation. An anthology of eighteenth-century English secular choral music would be classified as applied research because an anthology, by implication, may consist of compositions that have been collected and edited for a specific group, with rehearsal suggestions also incorporated in the study. The anthology quite properly could contain a history section, but this factor alone is not significant enough to change the character of the research, since the focus of a study of this type is to present practical suggestions for utilizing the results.

Clarke composed choral settings to selected psalms based on Jamaican folk melodies, rhythms, and harmonies for an action research project. He reviewed three centuries of Jamaican history and culture to determine the influence of African and European immigration to that Caribbean island. Nine psalm settings were arranged for three voice parts with piano, guitar, and percussion accompaniment. The settings, explains Clarke, are appropriate for Jamaican students in secondary schools, churches, or music festivals.[2]

Of the research methods discussed in this book, experimental/quasi-experimental, quantitative, and descriptive studies would usually be classified as applied research and historical, philosophical-aesthetic would fall under the pure research rubric. Beware, because it is dangerous to assign any one of these methods to either pure or applied research. How the research is conducted and the results obtained should determine which category the studies fall under. The purpose and the data collected ought to indicate how the research is classified. Pigeonholing can be frustrating, but researchers who, during the process of planning, consider their research with either a pure or applied emphasis will find it much easier to organize and develop.

'Qualitative' and 'quantitative' are terms frequently referred to in research jargon and may have different meanings. As used in this book, they refer to procedures for looking at information. In the former, research results are largely subjective, that is, not easily translated into scores, whereas in the latter, objective data based on the scores of some type of measurement are given. If one were to count the number of bassoon players in all the public schools of a given state, qualitative data could be obtained. In other words, 'kinds of information' rather than their evaluation. The mere counting of bassoonists would not indicate how proficient these bassoonists were. Some type of objective evaluation of the proficiency of these bassoonists would be necessary—this would result in quantitative data, a most desirable practice when it is possible to do so. Leedy ascribes qualitative research to inductive analysis and deductive analysis studies to those that are quantitative.[3]

While it is possible for a research project to be so organized that it would contain only qualitative data, it would be virtually impossible for a study to contain quantitative but little or no qualitative data because even in research where data obtained are the result of some type of measurement, narrative is necessary to explain the theoretical rationale for the research, and a rationale is a type of research.

In reviewing research in music education, sometimes one can find studies that contain qualitative data only, with quantitative data omitted, when there is every indication that both types should have been included. Such research is weak usually because the investigator has not proceeded thoroughly and carefully to the next significant step of quantifying information. For instance, a qualitative study might be undertaken to learn which school systems in a given state have instrumental music programs. These data, readily available by questionnaire (written or online), could be useful to school administrators who do not have an instrumental music program. They could then report to their boards of education that such a program is needed if students in the community are to receive the same cultural experiences that youngsters in neighboring school systems have. To music teachers, by contrast, these data might be relatively useless because they give little or no indication of the actual content of the instrumental music programs surveyed. They merely indicate the presence or absence of instrumental music in the school systems reviewed. Music directors more likely would be interested in determining how the curricular offerings in their schools compare with those of other schools.

Since music is largely concerned with the development of skills, the question of competence in performance often arises. This problem is largely quantitative, and answers would depend on using a specialized instrument of measurement in conjunction with a questionnaire. Such an investigation would be proper under certain conditions. The investigator would need to establish criteria for comparison in order to ascertain how well the groups performed. Researchers who organize their projects to obtain quantitative data are in a much better position to produce a significant piece of research when qualitative data also are obtained. It should be clear by now, that both qualitative and quantitative research may produce valid results, although different techniques are used for each.

Notes

1. Joyce P. Gall, M. D. Gall, and Walter R. Borg, *Applying Educational Research: A Practical Guide*, 4th ed. (New York: Longman, 1999), 469.
2. Arthur E. Clarke, "Jamaican Folk Psalms: Choral Settings of Selected Psalms Based on Jamaican Folk Melodies, Rhythms, and Harmonies, Suitable for Jamaican Students in Secondary Schools, Churches, and Musical Festivals" (Ed.D. diss., New York University, 1988), UMI 8812527.
3. Paul D. Leedy, *Practical Research: Planning and Design*, 6th ed. (Upper Saddle River, N.J.: Prentice Hall, 1997), 107.

Summary

In the sentence immediately before this extract, the authors define research as

> A carefully organised procedure that can result in the discovery of new knowledge, the substantiation of previously held concepts, the rejection of false tenets, and the formal presentation of data collected.
>
> (Phelps et al. 2005, p. 3).

Moving from that basis, two key terminological binaries are explored throughout the extract: pure/applied, and quantitative/qualitative. As the authors state at various points throughout, categorisations of the type represented by these terms can be dangerous. However, in a general sense, it is important to get an understanding for the range of research methodologies (the broad 'stances' for research) as well as the particular research methods (the actual research 'tools' that you might use within a particular project).

Given that the majority of readers of this book will be teaching music in some capacity and thinking about doing a piece of research structured within their teaching, it is highly likely that most will do a piece of 'applied' research, using a mixture of quantitative and qualitative methods.

Questions to consider

1. Following my response to the investigation above, which particular research methods would be most appropriate to help collect the data needed to provide an answer to your research question? Would these methods be quantitative or qualitative, or a mixture of both? *Note: methods could include observation, interview, focus groups, sampling, questionnaires, etc.*

Investigations

Having considered some of the writings of Burnard, Oldfather and West, and others, what changes would you make to your initial selection of a research methodology and associated methods in the question detailed above?

Think deeper

One of the exciting elements of doing a piece of educational research is that there are so many potential choices in terms of a methodology and methods. Burnard's introductory article to a special edition of the journal *Music Education Research*, which focused on exploring research methodologies and methods in music education, examines this broad range of choices in some detail (Burnard 2006). Drawing on Bassey (1992), she categorised each of the journal's articles as illustrating one of three broad types of research:

1. Reflective research, in which the findings of empirical research become the starting point for review and argument about a specific educational issue;

2. Empirical research, where the collection of data is paramount and the drawing of conclusions from an analysis of this data is of central importance;

3. Creative research, in which new systems are devised, novel solutions are sought and the formulation of new ideas are achieved through systematic and critical enquiry.

Examples of each research 'type' can be found in this edition of the journal *Music Education Research* (2006).

However, for me, some of Burnard's findings are particularly relevant for the work of music teachers. For example, she urges us to:

■ Create new research methods and norms that will enable us to learn from innovative practitioners;

■ Continue to theorise and study the rapidly changing relationships between music, education, and research, practice and policy, in order to ensure the ability of music education research to respond to changing social, pedagogical, technological, learning and cultural contexts;

■ Work on alternative representations of research;

■ Make the research process more public.

(Burnard 2006, p.150)

Think wider

Finding metaphors for the processes of research can be helpful in finding a way into research as an activity. One metaphor that I have enjoyed over the years, and explored in some detail in my own Ph.D. studies (Savage 2004), is qualitative research as jazz.

Drawing on research that has developed jazz as a metaphor for life itself (Bateson 1990), Oldfather and West suggest that:

Jazz exemplifies artistic activity that is at once individual and communal, performance that is both repetitive and innovative, each participant sometimes providing background support and sometimes flying free.

(Oldfather and West 1994, pp. 2–3)

Within jazz there are numerous paradoxes and dialectics. The jazz group functions and relies on interdependence between participants. At various times, each musician has to play a range of roles. There is a unity in their diversity, but this is a sea of constantly shifting balances and relationships. And underneath this interplay, the deep structure of the music guides the unfolding improvisatory nature of melodic, harmonic and rhythmic expression.

Similarly, in qualitative research there is an improvisatory interplay between the participants and the deep structures of the research methodology. I have found that methodological principles, values, inquiry focuses and findings have all been guided and challenged within the changing and collaborative arena of the classroom. Often I have felt myself to be within the role of a jazz improviser, seeking to play my part within the group in such a way that acknowledges the balance between individual, communal, supportive and extemporaneous research activity.

The process by which I became aware of this reflective role is worth dwelling on for a moment. In the early months of my PhD studies I was looking for a fixed method, a textbook for qualitative research that would tell me all about the how, why and when questions that I considered important. But I quickly realised that such an approach was too formal and reliant on someone else's criteria for research 'success'. Gradually I began to appreciate that such a fixed approach would have failed to capture the very essence and detail of the research field that I wanted to investigate. Oldfather and West express it like this:

> Newcomers may search for the sheet music, or the instructions, and finding none, may be quite uncomfortable until they develop an intuitive sense of the guiding deep structures. [. . .] The trick is to be able to feel the music. This ability comes through both understanding the deep structures and giving oneself to the freedom to let go and apply those deep structures in improvisatory ways.
>
> (ibid, p.23)

And in many senses this ability is one that I continue to strive for in my ongoing research activities. I have learnt to let myself go to the 'freedom' that qualitative research methodologies allow, yet to constantly depend and rely upon my understanding of the 'deep structures' of the methodologies that I have adopted within a particular piece of research. Within this interplay is the acknowledgment that one's experience of the research process in action is as important and valid as one's critical and rational explanation of it (often in hindsight). This blending of effect and cognition is vital if one is to construct vivid and accurate accounts of the research process:

> Experience is the bedrock upon which meaning is constructed, and that experience in significant degrees depends upon our ability to get in touch with the qualitative world we inhabit. This qualitative world is immediate before it is mediated, presentational before it is representational, sensuous before it is symbolic.
>
> (Eisner 1993, p. 5)

Eisner's comment reminds me of Burnard's call to work on alternative representations of research findings. Formal research articles may suit one particular audience, but alternative forms will be required within the field of music education. Although research can be construed as scientific enquiry, for us it needs to be musical as much as it is scientific.

Extract 9.3

Source

Sudnow, D. *Ways of the Hand: The organization of improvised conduct.* Cambridge, Mass., and London, The MIT Press. pp. 146–152.

Introduction

Continuing with the themes of jazz, improvisation and research, Sudnow's extraordinary book explores how he learnt to play jazz piano. Having tried to learn jazz in a 'classical' way (i.e. this scale goes with this chord, etc.) he adopted an alternative approach based on extensive listening and an intricate understanding of the shape of his hands at the piano keyboard. This extract comes towards the end of the book and contains another key piece of advice for any young jazz musician.

Key words and phrases

jazz, improvisation, research

Extract

I learned this language through five years of overhearing it spoken. I had come to learn, overhearing and overseeing this jazz as my instructable hands' ways – in a terrain nexus of hands and keyboard whose respective surfaces had become known as the respective surfaces of my tongue and teeth and palate are known to each other – that this jazz music *is* ways of moving from place to place as singings with my fingers. To *define* jazz (as to define any phenomenon of human action) is to *describe* the body's ways.

Little bits and pieces of jazz-handlings showed themselves to me, revealed as that jazz music in my hands' ways, and I did nudgings to myself, taking an inner course of action to help the outer one out, it may be metaphorically said. I perked up with the assistance of saying to myself: Spring-board — get the beat right – keep the hand loose and flexible — bounce around on a place — go for a long reach — breathe deeply — do interweavings — relax — don't go fast until you're ready — let the hands say where and how to go — be careful — remember Jimmy — go for an opening chord by theory — just get started talking — get those shoulders moving — keep that hand from tripping — they're listening to you — you're playing fast bebop, lots of interwindings in tight quarters, get especially bebopical — play beautifully — get down on it — do it.

Little bits and pieces of jazz-handlings showed themselves to me, and particular nudgings worked especially in the beginning, as I took notice and told myself about ways of moving with an instructional nudge 'translated' as a practice, with a quasi-worded reflexive spark turned right back down into the keyboard, dissipated as an inner saying into a singing.

Without getting the beat right, without establishing those prospectivities for articulational reachings, without assessing the pace-ably available presence of ways for classes of rated traverse, without essentializing command over these paced presences in and of the terrain nexus — jazz-handlings did not and cannot appear. For, and I speak generically here, it don't mean a thing if it ain't got that swing, and the 'swing' of jazz-handlings was shored up by express thinking, at first.

But the instruction's express presence, arising from this history, had become situated in the ways of my hands as: 'Listen carefully to the beats' is in the ways of the piano tuner's arm and shoulders; 'wait for the dial to return,' an instruction the young child must noticeably employ, is in the adult caller's wayful, reconfigurating, sequentially unfolding hoverings with the telephone; 'be careful in a typing test' is in the strongly established upright posture; 'reach ahead' is in every undertaken course of talking – so deeply situated within the ways of my hands had the historically theoretic character of my problematics now become.

And to say 'remember Jimmy' is a way I have of saying get the time into the fingers, which I can translate as: Keep strong forward prospectivities, get especially bebopical, relax, with a big ETC. I can institute jazz-handlings by telling myself — looking at my hand and composing its appearance in and through play with a posing that satisfies a look which asks — let me see jazz hands.

Telling myself, 'let me see jazz hands,' works as a nudge in that it instructs and notices everything else at the same time. And my instructions that work, born of my history as explicitly required and consequential noticings, can best be regarded as a usable compendium of caretaking practices for toning up, separably usable because each speaks of all the rest, each another way of saying the same thing; and now and then doing a 'quick' saying to myself has useful instigating payoffs in my current play.

But for the most part I now follow one piece of advice — heard a long time before from jazz musicians, perhaps their most oft-voiced maxim for newcomers, literally overheard through my years of pursuing those notes on the records, regarded from my standpoint of novice and ethnographer as nothing but the vaguest of vague talk, accessible finally as the very detailed talk it was only when a grasp of the details to which it pointed were themselves accessibly at hand — now my central instruction: SING WHILE YOU ARE PLAYING.

A 'speaking I' is struck by the awesomeness of finding myself singing as I play, singing right along with the movements of my fingers, aiming for next sounds with a synchronous reach of two body 'parts,' an achievement formerly quite impossible. How am I taking my fingers to places, for it makes good sense for this I to speak that way (I reach for a cup just there, ready—set—go, now I move my arm there), and singing in perfect concert? How do I know what the next notes will sound like as a joint knowing of voice and fingers, going there together, not singing along with the fingers, but singing with the fingers? A speaking I is struck by the awesomeness of an altogether new coupling, a new hookup, a new organization between my vocalizations and my fingerings. How is that done—I take my fingers to places so deeply 'mindful' of what they will sound like that I can sing *at the same time*, both on the way down into the terrain, these piano pitches. Are the singings I do merely given to me as some payoff to keep me engrossed, my fingers operating through independent mechanisms beyond my awareness? Am I really singing along behind the sounds at a rapid rate, with a differential lag in timing I do not notice, some split-second 'neurological' delay? Is an overwhelming impression of the jointly aimed singing of a unidirectional and multilaterally influenced body an illusion of ignorance about my real workings? And my sayings themselves—are they too a token of some sort for the real happenings?

I choose places to go, in what this speaking I finds as miraculous ways, miraculous merely against the background of my history with the piano, and a history of other speakings that seem to leave little room for a conception that would not partitionalize 'my' body in some way (This history simultaneously reconstructs doings to render them into a form for close study, contributing to as it derives warrant from such partitionalizing.)

From an upright posture I look down at my hands on the piano keyboard during play, with a look that is hardly a look at all. But standing back I find that I proceed through and in a terrain nexus, doing singings with my fingers, so to speak, a single voice at the tips of the fingers, going for each next note in sayings just now and just then, just this soft and just this hard, just here and just there, with definiteness of aim throughout, taking my fingers to places, so to speak, and being guided, so to speak. I sing with my fingers, so to speak, and only so to speak, for there is a new 'I' that the speaking I gestures toward with a pointing at the music that says: It is a singing body and this I (here, too, so to speak) sings.

Summary

Sudnow's writing exemplifies the metaphor of research as jazz beautifully. He reminds us of the central role of the human body in all our actions – as teachers, writers or musicians. To define jazz (substitute 'teaching' or 'research'), he says, is to define the body's ways. Just as Sudnow could only become a fluent jazz pianist through understanding the way of his hands as an integral part of the jazz expression, so researchers need to hone their understanding about the role of all their senses as they seek to become fluent in the way of their research. We might say the same about teaching.

Questions to consider

1. Sudnow's central instruction to any aspiring young jazz pianist is to 'sing while you are playing'. As musicians, how many times have we heard this maxim before? Translate this into the processes of teaching or research? What might it mean?

Think deeper

Starting out in a new activity, whether it be jazz piano, teaching or research, can be a traumatic time. It takes a while to find one's feet. Sudnow's work reminds us of some key principles. Firstly, listen to those around you. Immerse yourself in their work. Read research papers and journal articles. Gain an appreciation of the various styles and approaches of educational research in the field of music education and other related fields.

Secondly, start playing. However tentative at first, doing research is the best way to learn about research. As with any new venture, mistakes will be made but do not be overly concerned about that. Find a venue to work within (this might be your classroom), develop relationships with others that you trust (your pupils and fellow teachers) and have a go!

Thirdly, find your voice and use it! Your voice is distinctive and unique. Find avenues or pathways through which you can express your voice. Initially this might be in private (perhaps in a research journal) but, increasingly, look for ways to share your voice in public settings (write a piece for a newsletter, subject association bulletin, website, etc.). As you do this, listen out for complementary voices. Learn to value these and work with them where possible. Make sure that your research does not remain a private venture. Collaborations are the key to it remaining a vibrant and fulfilling activity.

Think wider

Metaphors like those developed by Sudnow in relation to learning to play jazz piano, or Oldfather and West in respect of qualitative research as jazz, are helpful in broadening our understanding of what it might mean to be an educational researcher. Ultimately, as we have discussed throughout the chapter, any piece of research begins with a series of choices, whether formally constituted within an advanced degree or externally funded project, or informally adopted within one's own work. Defining the key research question and choosing an appropriate research methodology (and associated methods) are two key decisions that are normally made early on. However, the work presented in the later part of this chapter reminds us that any choices we make as teachers or researchers are, by nature, provisional and that we should be open to a change in path should circumstances develop and alternative opportunities become available.

Conclusion

This chapter has introduced a range of ideas about educational research. It has done so using a range of musical metaphors. It has emphasised that although there are key terms that need to be understood, educational research is a highly creative, and sometimes improvisatory, activity. It requires imagination and responsiveness. Having explored some general ideas about educational research in music education, the following chapter will turn to an explicit research methodology and methods that you may find useful in your own teaching.

References

Bassey, M. (1992) 'Creating Education Through Research'. *British Educational Research Journal* 18:1, 3–16.

Bateson, M. (1990) *Composing a Life*. New York, Penguin.

Burnard, P. (2006) 'Telling Half the Story: Making explicit the significance of methods and methodologies in music education research'. *Music Education Research* 8:2, 143–152.

Eisner, E. (1993) 'Forms of Understanding and the Future of Educational Research'. *Educational Researcher* 22:7, 5–11.

Music Education Research (2006) *Research Methodologies and Methods in the Field of Music Education*. http://www.tandfonline.com/toc/cmue20/8/2 [last accessed 22/05/12].

Oldfather, P. and West, J. (1994) 'Qualitative Research as Jazz'. *Educational Researcher* 23:8, 22–26.

Savage, J. (2004) 'Re-imagining Music Education for the 21st Century: Innovative approaches to teaching, learning and research with ICT'. Unpublished Ph.D. thesis. Available from http://courses.ucan.tv/course/view.php?id=11 [last accessed 22/05/12].

Stenhouse, L. (1975) *An Introduction to Curriculum Research and Development*. London, Heinemann Educational Books.

Stenhouse, L. (1985) *Research as a Basis for Teaching*. London, Heinemann Educational Books.

Teachers as Researchers

Following on from the previous chapter that examined a range of ideas surrounding how one might conduct research in music education, this chapter takes a small detour away from music. It examines one particular approach to educational research that I feel would be of benefit for the majority of readers. If you are currently teaching music, and you have got to this point of the book, then I suspect you may be interested in finding out more about how the knowledge and writing represented here have been produced, as well as the processes of educational research. These may apply to your own work as a teacher.

Action research is:

> the study of a social situation with a view to improving the quality of action within it. It aims to feed practical judgement in concrete situations, and the validity of the 'theories' or hypotheses it generates depends not so much on 'scientific' tests of truth, as on their usefulness in helping people to act more intelligently and skilfully. In action research 'theories' are not validated independently and then applied in practice. They are validated through practice.
>
> (Elliott 1991, p.69)

This is one of the classic definitions for action research. It states, unambiguously, that the action researcher studies the classroom (a 'social situation') with a view to improving the quality of teaching and learning ('action') within it. It is a practical method through which ideas or theories about education are tested out through a teacher's practice. Or, to put it another way:

> Action research happens when people are involved in researching their own practice in order to improve it and to come to a better understanding of their practice situations. It is action they act within the systems that they are trying to improve and understand. It is research because it is systematic, critical inquiry made public.
>
> (Feldman 2007, p.239)

By the end of the chapter we will have introduced action research more thoroughly, read some short examples of it in action, compared it with more general approaches to reflective practice and considered some basic steps to conducting action research within your own work.

Extract 10.1

Source

Phillips, D. and Carr, K. (2010) *Becoming a Teacher Through Action Research.* London, Routledge, pp. 38–40.

Introduction

Our first extract introduces one such approach through telling the story of two student teachers who were beginning to experiment with research through the telling of stories.

Key words and phrases

action research, research, methodology

Extract

In this section, we tell the story of two student teachers as they grapple with the roles of student, teacher, and researcher. Clandinin and Connelly (1994; 1995; 1996; 2000) use a narrative structure to describe the lived experience of teachers. Specifically, they identify three kinds of 'stories,' or narratives teachers use: *secret, cover,* and *sacred.* Secret stories are those the teacher lives out within the safety of the classroom. Cover stories are those a teacher might tell to disguise the secret practices within the classroom.

Sacred stories are those imposed upon teachers via the district office or state or federal governments. The use of this narrative structure to tell the stories of teachers is useful in highlighting the dilemmas, contradictions, and demands teachers live among and around. Such a structure can also be instructive to preservice teachers, who enter the classroom of a mentor-teacher as both a guest and a student.

Phillips (2001) considers the use of narratives in a case study of two preservice teachers' student teaching in two different schools. Both student teachers are asked to conform and to demonstrate competence in teaching, as told by the schools' sacred stories, and both struggled with feeling like the approach to teaching they were asked to assume did not represent the best kind of teaching or teaching that 'fit' their style.

One student teacher, however, was able to observe, listen, and ascertain not only the sacred, but also the cover and secret, stories of her school. Even though visual mathematics, for example, was not encouraged (sacred story), she found a closet full of manipulatives (secret story). And although the school had adopted a scripted reading program, she discovered sets of novels in yet another 'hidden' space. She began careful conversations with her mentor-teacher concerning these 'other' teaching strategies, and soon, by using the language of the sacred story (state standards and federal mandated testing), she was able to participate not only in her mentor-teacher's cover story, satisfying the demand of the sacred story, but also the teacher's secret stories by using such mathematic and reading strategies in her teaching. This student teacher learned to negotiate power systems at her school by using the sacred story to adopt desired teaching strategies.

The second student teacher did not learn these skills of negotiation. She was more direct and adamant about her philosophies of teaching and was more open in her disagreement with the host school's approach to teaching science. She was offended at the expectation that she, as a student teacher, had to teach science in a traditional manner when research supported an inquiry approach. As a student teacher she maintained that she should be able to explore multiple points of pedagogy. However, her directness, in this instance, forced her mentor-teacher to more firmly support the sacred story, perhaps in order to protect her own secret stories.

The experience of these two student teachers cannot be generalized for all student teaching experiences, nor are they told here to say there is a 'right' or 'wrong' way to enter the classroom as a student teacher. They are told to illustrate the kinds of political landscapes that student teachers may be asked to negotiate. Student teachers often have competing demands: teacher-education program competencies, state and/or federal competencies, district and school expectations, and the mentor-teacher's own expectations of what a 'good teacher' might be. These are not always aligned, and often represent different kinds of secret, cover, and sacred stories. Furthermore, student teachers are often asked to demonstrate the more traditional version of the 'good teacher' before being allowed to deviate from this image. In other words, they must demonstrate their ability to tell the sacred story.

While such demands can certainly complicate the process of learning to teach, they also represent the systems at play for many in-service teachers. In this way, learning to teach *is* learning to negotiate the political landscapes of schools.

Applying the Three Stories to Action Research

Being cognizant of sacred, secret, and cover stories when conducting research in another's classroom can be critical. The student teacher may, for example, be excited about a certain approach to teaching and may anticipate 'trying this out' in the mentor-teacher's classroom. If the mentor-teacher is resistant to the idea, the student teacher may too quickly decide that the mentor-teacher is 'traditional.' But many other factors may be at play: the sacred story of the school or district may not support such teaching methods; the mentor-teacher may use such methods as a 'secret story' but does not feel comfortable having such a story be made public. It could be that the mentor-teacher feels threatened by such methodology for a variety of reasons. What we are suggesting is that student teachers may need to become students of stories. They may need to listen hard to what is being said around them. What 'code' language, if any, is used? How are teachers at the school site negotiating government demands? How are they aligning themselves or resisting such demands? What are the differences in what is said publicly and what is done privately?

There are times when student teachers must be compliant in order to gain admission into the 'education club.' This can be painful; sometimes, it results in a temporary loss of idealism and hope.

However, as teacher educators, we have found that action research is a process that student teachers can use in powerful ways to not only support their idealism, but also to learn to teach in an influential manner. Action research, if carefully negotiated, can be an acceptable space in which to try alternative practices. In many instances, this process is shared with a mentor-teacher who equally delights in such learning and supports the student teacher during the difficult times of becoming a teacher.

In your role as student teacher-researchers, we encourage you to enter the classroom as story collectors. Perhaps this is the first critical trait of all excellent teacher-researchers: the ability to hear in multiple layers the stories administrators, teachers, and students tell of their lives. Expect such stories to be contradictory—even as your own stories may be replete with such contradictions. And know that in the retelling of such stories we bring new questions into our lives that keep us intrigued with the teaching/learning process, even as such retellings help us to make sense of our lived experiences.

References

Clandinin, D. J., & Connelly, F. M. (1994). Personal experience methods. In N. K. Denzin & Y. S. Lincoln (Eds.), *Handbook of qualitative research* (pp. 413–427). Thousand Oaks, CA: Sage.

Clandinin, D. J., & Connelly, F. M. (1995). *Teachers' professional knowledge landscapes*. New York: Sage.

Clandinin, D. J., & Connelly, F. M. (1996). Teachers' professional knowledge landscapes: Teachers stories—stories of teachers—school stories—stories of schools. *Educational Researcher, 25* (3), 24–30.

Clandinin, D. J., & Connelly, F. M. (2000). *Narrative inquiry: Experience and story in qualitative research*. San Francisco: Jossey-Bass Publishers.

Phillips, D. K. (2001). Learning to speak the sacred and learning to construct the secret: Two stories of finding space as preservice teachers in professional education. *Teaching Education, 12*(3), 261–278.

Summary

One of the most significant skills for a teacher–researcher is the ability to tell the story of one's teaching. This extract explores how different stories can be told about two young teachers' work. These stories spring from different perspectives (the secret, cover and sacred metaphors) and allow the student teacher in each case to represent and explore their work in alternative ways. The authors encourage us to enter our classrooms as story collectors and suggest that one of the most important traits that an action researcher needs is the ability to hear and represent the multiple layers that exist within the story of a particular lesson or classroom.

Questions to consider

1. Pick a specific lesson or sequence of lessons that you have taught recently. How could you tell the story of your own teaching through the metaphors of the secret, cover and sacred stories?

2. What contradictions does your story contain? What intriguing questions arise from it?

Investigations

If possible, find a like-minded and trusted colleague to work with through the questions and investigations contained within this chapter. Tell them the story of your teaching using the three metaphors. Ask for their feedback. What questions did they ask? What did they find intriguing? How does an alternative perspective help you make sense of your own practice? This process of making your work public is a vital element of action research, but start doing this in a safe place.

Think deeper

'Dunwich Revisited' (Savage and Challis 2001) tells the story of a curriculum-based music project run at Debenham CEVC High School between December 1999 and March 2000. Within it, all pupils in Years 7, 8 and 9, together with a Year 10 GCSE group, participated in the composition of an electro-acoustic piece based on Dunwich (a place with a remarkable history on the east coast of Suffolk). A distinctive feature of the project was the use of a range of technologies to compose, develop and perform musical ideas. The final piece, entitled 'Dunwich Revisited', was performed by 35 pupils at the Celebration of Schools' Music held at Snape Maltings Concert Hall on March 7, 2000.

The published article shares insights from this curriculum project drawn from a range of qualitative data collected by myself, the head of music at the time, and Mike Challis, an electro-acoustic composer who was also a member of the school staff. It drew on a piece of action research that I conducted during the project. This process of research helped me examine my own pedagogy, particularly in the area of musical composition.

The article itself is a representation of the events that occurred but, by nature, is a selective representation that others (see below) can interpret and reinterpret.

As a piece of research, it explored many ways in which digital technologies can be used within the classroom. For example:

> The sound (or signal) processors proved a particularly successful tool. Pupils were able to capture electronically a variety of instrumental or vocally produced sounds, manipulating and changing the sound through a variety of effects. These processors proved to be a simple and effective way of opening up a new world of sounds for the pupils. The processors' analogue-like dials encouraged a free, improvisatory-type approach to the production and manipulation of sounds. In a relatively short amount of time, pupils were able to generate sounds that they felt reflected the initial stimulus which they had chosen.
>
> (Savage and Challis 2001, p. 142)

As a result, it encouraged me to think hard about what the process of composition with digital technologies should really look and sound like within the classroom. This process of thinking and questioning has continued over the last 12 years.

Think wider

The second definition for action research quoted above draws on the Stenhousian notion that research is systematic enquiry *made public*. It is important for teachers to find ways to share their work and invite comment and feedback on it. Writing an academic article, such as that which Mike Challis and I did, as teachers, in 2000 is one formal way that this can be done. However, there are many other more informal approaches too.

Making public the findings of one's action research project invites others to interpret and re-contextualise it in various ways. For example, Martin (2012) has written recently about the 'Dunwich Revisited' project to help advance his argument that the teaching of composition should be more broadly conceived than just being concerned with pitch and duration:

> Although pitches and durations are a central structural feature of many mixed-style approaches based in popular music, much electronic music can be understood as 'organized sound'. Thus the almost exclusive focus on MIDI keyboard entry and notation-based sequencing in most school programmes is unwarranted. Savage and Challis (2001) view the dominance of sequencing and/or notation software in music classrooms as 'unhealthy', not because there is anything wrong with MIDI tools, but because teaching focused in this way is often restricted to 'the controlling of pitch and time parameters, neglecting an understanding of musical composition beyond these traditional elements' (Savage and Challis 2001, pp. 2–3).
>
> It should be clear from the preceding discussion that what Landy (2007) terms 'sound-based music' is practiced by numerous composers using various styles and methods, and is as 'serious' an approach to composing as

that which is based on pitch–duration systems. If this is the case, teaching practice needs to avoid the assumption that composing with sounds is simply an exploratory, novice stage suitable for young learners and beginners.

(Martin 2012, p. 8)

So, whilst action research is an activity that you could carry out within your own teaching, it is important to recognise at this early stage that sharing your work and your emerging research findings with others, however formally or informally, is an important and vital step in utilising action research as a research methodology.

Extract 10.2

Source

McIntosh, P. (2010) *Action Research and Reflective Practice*. London, Routledge, pp. 44–46.

Introduction

Processes of thinking and reflecting on one's professional practice as a teacher are not the sole preserve of action research. For many years prior to the invention of 'action research', models of reflective practice have been encouraged and developed. The work of our next author has examined the relationship between action research, reflection and reflexivity in considerable detail. In this extract, he explores whether reflection is a skill and, if so, is it something that can be learned in a technical way?

Key words and phrases

action research, research, methodology, methods, reflection, reflective practice

Extract

Reflection as a skill? Is reflection something that can be learned in some technical way, as a clinical procedure or an interpersonal interaction may be learned? It is hard to categorise reflection in the same way as these examples, but there are some similarities in how we come to understand how to do these things which are primarily to do with our knowledge of them and the way in which we are guided to practise them. It has for some time been an expectation for learners and indeed researchers in the qualitative domain to reflect upon the experience of learning and researching and what is found through these experiences. And yet often people are not prepared or equipped for these activities;

they are merely advised or required to do it and to provide evidence that they have done it. It is through this expectation that models of reflection have come to be significant in the learning lives of those in health and social care and education. But, arguably, if the foundations of the purposes of reflection, its aims and how it can become accessible to aid learning are not present, then the reflections evidenced are superficial; there for the purposes of assessment and nothing more. As a matter of contention, I argue that reflective practice as it is taught and practised now is failing for these reasons. Reflecting becomes real and works when it is understood, not when it is required as an outcome.

The seminal work of Donald Schon (1983) began to analyse the way in which professionals think in action. Primarily, he saw a model of preparation for professional life as one which supplied technical knowledge relevant to the practice of that discipline, but which failed to provide the capacity to work through complexity associated with any professional activity. It is through Schon's work that the terms of thinking *in action* (i.e. while doing something) and *on action* (i.e. after it has been done) have come to have significance in recent professional education. Schon's argument is that whilst professionals are able to deal with the specifics of their discipline, they are ill equipped to manage the human interactional relationships between that discipline and its impact on social life.

Schon (1983) uses a range of professional activities to describe this, including architecture, town planning and psychotherapy – all grounded in specific knowledge as enclosed disciplines, but when released into the real world of population consultation, such as in town planning, becoming highly charged, with unforeseen layers of complexity to be managed and worked through.

As a result, the concept of critical reflection in adult learning began to permeate into professional education through the work of people such as Jack Mezirow. Mezirow (1990: 14) focused particularly on 'transformative learning', suggesting that:

> Perspective transformation is the process of becoming critically aware of how and why our pre-suppositions have come to constrain the way we perceive, understand, and feel about our world; of reformulating these assumptions to permit a more inclusive, discriminative, permeable, and integrative perspective; and of making decisions or otherwise acting on these new understandings. More inclusive, discriminating, permeable and integrative perspectives that adults choose if they can because they are motivated to better understand the meaning of their experience.

As with Schon's notions of how professionals think, presuppositions based on technical professional knowledge assume that things will just happen as planned because the knowledge suggests it. But, of course, this is not the case. It then becomes important, as Mezirow (1990) indicates, to enter into an act of transformation whereby what we believe we know becomes reformulated as understanding the meaning of an experience which has emerged not as a technical rational puzzle to be solved in the 'high ground' of professional knowledge but in the 'swampy lowlands' of human interaction (Schon, 1983). This has led to a variety of models and principles collectively known as 'reflective practice', which are practised within professional education and practice.

Ghaye and Ghaye (1998: 16–18) suggest ten principles of reflective practice, which I have precised below:

1. It needs to be understood as a set of meanings, statements, stories, etc., which produce a particular version of events. This reflective discourse – or conversation – is at the heart of the improvement process.
2. It is fuelled and energised by experience. Reflecting on something is our experience and all that it comprises. Reflecting on experience is a way of interrogating our actions and thinking in particular ways.
3. It means returning to re-look at our taken-for-granted values, professional understanding and practices. It is not about reflecting on the extraordinary; it is about the ordinary, everyday occurrences of the working day. In this 'reflective turn' we consider the parts played by ourselves and others in these occurrences so that we may deepen our understanding of them.
4. It is about learning to explain and justify the way we go about things.
5. It means considering what we do 'problematically' – by constantly inquiring and questioning what we do systematically so that we may learn continuously from it.
6. It means putting what we know and learn to use, and informing improvement – by doing something positive and constructive through the knowledge we create which is purposeful. Engaging in thinking around what interests will be served through this process is important.
7. It means applying critical thinking to practice by asking probing or challenging questions, both of self and collectively so that transformation can take place.
8. It is a way of decoding the symbolic landscape around us – for example, why an environment is equipped in the way that it is, the way in which human relations occur, what appears significant or worthy within the environment, and the way in which these things are responded to. Symbolism is an important element in the reflective discourse.
9. It is a linkage between theoretical knowledge and practical application, enabling practitioners to create meaningful theories of action that are live and real.
10. It is eclectic, and is comfortable with drawing on different ways of knowing. It is not prejudiced in how knowledge is gained or understood and acts as an intersection between different approaches.

Having an appreciation of these principles and implementing them are, of course, two different things, for in order to act upon them there needs to be some guidance. One way of developing knowledge of reflective principles into the skill of reflection is through a 'reflective conversation' (Ghaye and Ghaye,

1998). Although the Ghayes refer specifically to teaching in this discussion, there is easy transfer into other disciplines, so I refer to 'the practitioner' in more general terms, replacing the Ghayes' 'the teacher'.

References

Ghaye, A. and Ghaye, K. (1998) *Teaching and Learning through Critical Reflective Practice.* David Fulton. London

Mezirow, J. *et al.* (1990) *Fostering Critical Reflection in Adulthood.* Jossey-Bass. San Francisco

Schon, D. (1983) *The Reflective Practitioner: How Professionals Think in Action.* Temple Smith. London

Summary

Starting with the influential work of Donald Schon, McIntosh introduces the notions of thinking in action and thinking on action. These concepts have had a big impact on models of reflective practice within education. These models, advanced by Mezirow (1990), Ghaye and Ghaye (1998) and others, contain a number of common elements that McIntosh summarises in his ten points of reflective practice.

Questions to consider

1. What are the similarities and differences that you can spot between McIntosh's ten points and your emerging understanding of action research?

Investigations

Each of the points that McIntosh presents could be reflected upon for some time! For this investigation, reconsider his ninth point. Reflective practice is a link between 'theoretical knowledge and practical application, enabling practitioners to create meaningful theories of action that are live and real' (McIntosh 2010, p. 46). Spend a few moments flipping back through this book. What key points from our discussion about the music education research literature have struck you? How have you been responding to the various questions and previous investigations? What, if any, links have you been able to draw so far for your own practice as a teacher? As a result of these links, has your teaching improved? How do you know?

Think deeper

Reflective practice of the type that McIntosh explores in his chapter has many resonances with action research. But, whilst one might say that all action research contains elements of reflective practice, it is probably not the case that all reflective practice could be conceptualised as action research. However, there are fine distinctions here and the important thing, for now, is to appreciate that action research, reflective practice and the notion of 'reflexivity' contain varying degrees of conceptual overlap. For McIntosh:

> Action research in broad terms concerns the lived experiences of people and the understanding of the essences of reality. It therefore has two main thrusts: knowledge production through education and socio-political action; and empowerment through the process of people constructing and using their own knowledge. . . . The ideology of action research is one of collaboration and it is likely to sharpen people's capacity to conduct their own research and liberate minds for critical reflection within the existent framework of knowledge, and to uncover that which did not exist within their conscious frame of knowledge that can be used for their own purposes.
>
> (McIntosh 2010, p. 53)

In other words, action research as a process can help you uncover and explore things that you do not know and are probably unable to locate just through a process of critical reflection. It is also a process through which you should aim to collaborate with others and, as we discussed above, make a public statement about your work.

Think wider

McMahon's article (McMahon 1999) confirms that action research contains a number of distinct elements beyond those covered by a general interpretation of reflective practice. Reflective practice, he argues, can be seen as the specific application of experiential learning to activities carried out as part of one's profession or job. This experiential learning, with its emphasis on the improvement of practice through reflection on experience, could involve the teacher in going through a sequence of actions indistinguishable from (at least some of) those of the action research spiral; (we will consider what this spiral looks like below).

But McMahon identifies the key difference between action research and reflective practice as one to do with strategic action:

> Strategic action is a deliberate and planned attempt to solve a particular problem or set of problems using a coherent, systematic and rigorous methodology. Action research, by definition, always involves such strategic action. By contrast, strategic action is not integral to reflective practice. Reflective practice can lead to strategic action, but this is not inevitable. Reflective practice can be a useful precursor to action research. It is not identical to it.
>
> (McMahon 1999, p.163)

Extract 10.3

Source

Altrichter, H. *et al.* (2008) *Teachers Investigate their Work*. London, Routledge, pp. 9–11.

Introduction

In our final extract we turn our attention to the actual process of action research. What does it look like and what would I have to do to follow a process of action research in my own work?

Most writers about action research conceptualise it as a spiral of practical and conceptual activities. Perhaps the simplest way of representing it is as a circle with four principal activities:

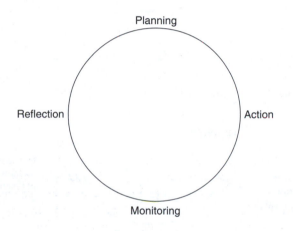

From this, more complex process charts can be drawn. In this example, from the work of a science teacher reported in McNiff (1988, p. 27), you can see the two 'cycles' that the teacher has worked through in his action research.

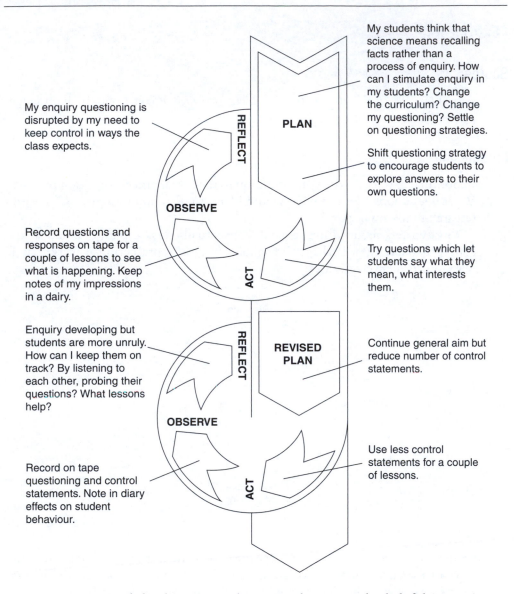

My students think that science means recalling facts rather than a process of enquiry. How can I stimulate enquiry in my students? Change the curriculum? Change my questioning? Settle on questioning strategies.

Shift questioning strategy to encourage students to explore answers to their own questions.

My enquiry questioning is disrupted by my need to keep control in ways the class expects.

PLAN

REFLECT

OBSERVE

Record questions and responses on tape for a couple of lessons to see what is happening. Keep notes of my impressions in a dairy.

ACT

Try questions which let students say what they mean, what interests them.

Enquiry developing but students are more unruly. How can I keep them on track? By listening to each other, probing their questions? What lessons help?

REFLECT

REVISED PLAN

Continue general aim but reduce number of control statements.

OBSERVE

Record on tape questioning and control statements. Note in diary effects on student behaviour.

ACT

Use less control statements for a couple of lessons.

However, whilst diagrams and process charts may be helpful in getting to grips with what action research might entail, it is important to remember that one of the keys of becoming a good researcher is the ability to understand the research process as an art that needs to be continuously perfected rather that a set of procedures that one has to implement in a religious manner. With that key thought in mind, the following extract identifies nine steps that you could take in an action research project.

Key words and phrases

action research, methodology, methods

Extract

As a starter, think of your research as being made up of nine steps that you need to take. These are all interrelated and not necessarily sequential, but it helps to list them separately as a mental checklist:

1. *Identify a research support group*
   If possible you need to establish yourself as part of a group that can share experiences and provide mutual support. Often a research support group is made up of people who are not all from the same workplace. The important thing is for all members of the group to be involved in their own research, and to agree to meet regularly and be good listeners for one another. There are various strategies described in the book, such as analytic discourse (M9), which help groups to provide each other with high-quality support.

2. *Identify your collaborating research partners*
   These are usually people directly involved in the situation you will be researching. They might be colleagues or clients (children if you are a teacher). When you are choosing them, remember that the more closely involved these partners are in your research the more powerful it is likely to be in terms of bringing about change, but the less control you will have over the direction of the change.

3. *Begin keeping a record of your research activities*
   This is often called keeping a 'research journal' and Chapter 2 provides a lot of ideas about different kinds of research diaries, their purposes and how to make them most useful to you. The key idea is to build up a record of all the impressions and ideas that come to you in the course of your professional activities so that you can think back on these over the weeks and months to come. On the day itself and the one or two days following these are vivid and powerful but they are only held in short term memory and will soon be lost if they are not written down. As you are more and more involved in researching your practice, the focus of your research journal will shift to more explicit recording of research activities.

4. *Decide on the starting point for your research and begin investigating it*
   Starting points can be of many different kinds. There may be some aspect of your professional practice that you find problematic and would like to investigate in order to understand it better. You may want to develop a new approach to some aspect of your practice in order to improve it. You may have a very specific question you want to investigate, but more likely you will just have a general area of interest. All of these approaches are fine, because in any case your area of interest is bound to be changed or refined once you start researching.

5. *Clarify your starting point*
   This is the process of progressively refining your area of research through beginning to collect data and analyze it. You may find that your original focus is considerably changed during the early stage of your research. Sometimes

this stage can be frustrating because data analysis is an important skill that you need to develop over time, so you may not immediately see anything very significant in your data. However, this stage can sometimes be very exciting as you begin to see things from new points of view. There are several methods and strategies (Ms) in Chapter 4, some to be carried out alone, and others involving your support group in giving mutual help with this process.

6. *Collect data systematically*

   Data collection has already been an important part of your research in steps 3, 4 and 5 above, but Chapter 5 gives a lot of ideas for different methods of collecting data more systematically. It is important to experiment with different approaches and learn how best to collect rich data. For example, interviewing is a complex process and different approaches to interviewing will result in very different accounts from the same interviewees. Some data is in this sense 'richer' than other data. But what counts as 'rich' will vary and is very much a decision for you to make. Comparing different kinds of data and discussing how they were collected and what makes them more or less 'rich' is always a very useful focus for the research support group.

7. *Analyze data*

   The most fascinating, but also initially the most difficult, part of the research process is data analysis. Typically, new researchers find it difficult to 'see' what is significant in their data, but there are a number of techniques that are very helpful and the methods and strategies (Ms), as well as the more detailed theoretical discussion of the process of analysis, in Chapter 6 should make this stage of becoming a researcher particularly interesting and rewarding. Once again, involvement of your support group and/or research partners will make an enormous difference to how quickly you can acquire the necessary sensitivity to data to become good at analysis.

8. *Developing action strategies and putting them into practice*

   In practice, as soon as you begin recording your impressions and reflections in your research diary you will feel the urge to start taking action. This very immediate feedback from research into practice is one of the great benefits of professionals getting involved in action research. When you are beginning to develop greater competence as a researcher, you will be able to plan action strategies more systematically on the basis of explanatory theories you have developed. When action strategies result in the improvements you predicted this takes your research one further step forward by demonstrating the power (validity) of your explanatory theories. Social situations are very complex, however, and there are always a large number of variables influencing what happens, so you should never expect to find clear and unambiguous proofs.

9. *Make your knowledge public*

   Research was defined by Stenhouse (1983) as 'systematic inquiry made public', and however powerful your research is for your own professional development, it cannot claim to be effective as research until it is shared with others. In Chapter 8 we discuss the many different ways that professionals can make their research knowledge public, and the reasons why this is important for both the status of the professions and the benefit of clients (students, patients, etc.). In practice, action research is never a 'finished' process because each set of 'findings' gives rise to new ideas for action strategies, and another cycle begins. However, it is important to decide on a cut-off point and write up the research and/or present it formally to an interested group (peers, parents . . .). Often written accounts of action research will be in the form of case studies and, when several such accounts are brought together for cross-case analysis, the findings become increasingly stable and capable of informing the action strategies of other professionals working in comparable settings (Somekh 2006).

An important cautionary note is that much of what is written about action research, including this book, may give the impression that it is a step-by-step method that follows a set pattern called the 'action research cycle'. For example, the nine steps in our Quick Start Guide above proceed from data collection to data analysis to the development of action strategies, and finally to the implementation of those strategies. However, while this pattern is a useful way to talk, write and learn about action research, the practice of action research is often more complex because it is research on ongoing practice. That is, even as we collect data, we are immersed in the practice we are studying. The collection of data affects our practice directly and also indirectly because as we collect data we become more knowledgeable about our practice, which changes the way we talk about it and the way we choose to act in our practice situations. The converse also occurs – as we engage in our practice we become aware of new aspects and contingencies that affect our choices of starting points and data collection methods.

References

Somekh, B. (2006) *Action Research: A Methodology for Change and Development*, Maidenhead and New York: Open University Press.

Stenhouse, L. (1983) *Authority, Education and Emancipation,* London: Heinemann Books.

Summary

The extract provides a helpful summary of one action research spiral. By now, I hope, some common themes will be identifiable including the desirability of working collaboratively (point 1) and making your research public (point 9). In between there are a helpful range of other stages and activities that you can apply to a structured piece of research within your teaching.

Questions to consider

1. What are the new elements of action research that are presented here? How could I manage these alongside my role as a teacher?

2. Can my time working as a teacher be counted as my time working as a researcher? Are the two roles complementary in practice as well as in theory?

Investigations

The above extract gives a good introduction to the process of action research. Before embarking on an action research project of your own, you would be well advised to read further chapters from Altrichter *et al.*'s book (Altrichter 2008). It contains a wealth of good practical advice as highlighted within the extract itself.

Think deeper

As a teacher who has conducted action research projects in my own teaching (Savage and Challis 2001; Savage and Challis 2002) and as an academic who has supervised the work of many other teachers engaged in action research projects, clearly I am persuaded about the benefits of adopting such a research method-ology within one's teaching.

Over the last nine chapters we have explored a wide range of ideas about music education drawn from existing research literature. I would like to suggest that action research could be the means by which you are able to take existing ideas, explore them through your own practice, develop new questions for further investigation and report back the findings to the wider educational community. Educational research should not solely be the activity of professional researchers. As I hope I have shown, action research is a process that you can adopt within your wider work. It has many benefits. For example, Wyatt reports that the benefits he noticed from working with teachers on action research projects:

> included their own awareness of their achievements in helping others through doing the research, their sense of their developing research skills, and the rewarding, highly motivating nature of the research experience. . . . Teachers seemed to become more self-confident in different aspects of their work and more autonomous.
>
> (Wyatt 2011, p. 422)

Goodnough's comprehensive review of the research literature in this respect found many further benefits for teachers as they engaged in action research projects within their own teaching:

> In this study teachers reported on the many benefits of engaging in action research including enhancing their confidence in teaching science and increasing their levels of self efficacy in relation to being able to be effective science teachers; viewing learners from a more holistic perspective and becoming more attuned to the learning needs of all students; and enhancing other aspects of their pedagogical content knowledge and classroom practice.
>
> In addition, they developed different views of themselves as critical learners and adopted an inquiry stance to their teaching. The teachers developed new understandings about what it means to be a teacher and hence transformed many aspects of their teacher identities as they made

sense of their data and reflected on the implications for student learning and their own classroom practice. Through establishing particular foci for their action research projects and engaging in the action research process, the teachers were able to compare their current views and beliefs about teaching and learning in relation to new insights that emerged. The concept of teacher identity provides a lens for teachers to understand their own aspirations, beliefs, goals, and practice in relation to teaching, recognizing that teacher identity is constantly changing and under construction.

(Goodnough 2011, p. 83)

Conclusion

My hope is that this brief detour into the world of action research will inspire you to take ideas discussed within this book into the world of your teaching. When you have explored and investigated them for a while, make sure that you tell the world what you have found out! As our final chapter will explore, having a long and happy career as a music educator is something that we would all wish for. Engaging in critical reflective practice and planning and conducting strategic action research can both be central planks in keeping your teaching relevant, powerful and a source of enjoyment for you and your pupils.

References

Elliott, J. (1991) *Action Research for Educational Change*. Philadelphia, PA: Open University Press.

Feldman, A. (2007) 'Teachers, Responsibility and Action Research'. *Educational Action Research* 15:2, 239–252.

Ghaye, A. and Ghaye, K. (1998) *Teaching and Learning Through Critical Reflective Practice*. London, David Fulton.

Goodnough, G. (2011) 'Examining the Long-term Impact of Collaborative Action Research on Teacher Identity and Practice: The perceptions of K–12 teachers'. *Educational Action Research* 19:1, 73–86.

Martin, J. (2012) 'Toward Authentic Electronic Music in the Curriculum: Connecting teaching to current compositional practices'. *International Journal of Music Education* published online (12 April 2012), DOI: 10.1177/0255761412439924.

McMahon, T. (1999) 'Is Reflective Practice Synonymous with Action Research?' *Educational Action Research* 7:1, 163–169.

McNiff, J. (1988) *Action Research: Principles and Practice*. London, Routledge.

Mezirow, J. *et al.* (1990) *Fostering Critical Reflection in Adulthood*. San Francisco, Jossey-Bass.

Savage, J. and Challis, M. (2002) 'A Digital Arts Curriculum? Practical ways forward'. *Music Education Research* 4:1, 7–23.

Savage, J. and Challis, M. (2001) 'Dunwich Revisited: Collaborative composition and performance with new technologies'. *British Journal of Music Education* 18:2, 139–149.

Wyatt, M. (2011) 'Teachers Researching Their Own Practice'. *ELT Journal* 65:4, 417–425.

11

Enjoying Music Education

Whatever stage you are at in your music education career, I trust that you have found this selection of extracts from the research literature, and the associated commentary, helpful. I hope it will inspire you to read the work of the authors represented here further, to reflect deeply on the ideas contained therein and apply them to your work as a music educator.

In this final chapter, I want to present a few extracts that might encourage you further in your music education career. Obviously, the direction of any career pathway is the sole responsibility of the individual concerned, but the extracts included here present some interesting ideas for the decisions you might have to make about your teaching at certain points. More importantly, they contain what I consider to be some key elements that you will need to have a long and happy career as a music teacher.

Extract 11.1

Source

Campbell, M., Thompson, L. and Barrett, J. (2010) *Constructing a Personal Orientation to Music Teaching.* London, Routledge, pp.1–3.

Introduction

This short extract drawn from Campbell's helpful book on constructing a personal approach to music teaching invites the reader to consider their own history as a learner in order to help create positive identity for oneself as a teacher. As part of this process, these opening paragraphs encourage you to reflect on your own musical influences and emphasise the importance of this personal narrative at all stages of our development as teachers.

Key words and phrases

identity, narrative, beginnings, subjectivities

Extract

Each of you has a story to tell about how or why you got interested in teaching or how you became involved in the world of music. Many music teachers are drawn to a life of teaching because they have a genuine love of music, a deep concern for others, and a strong desire to 'pass along' the joy of music to others. In fact, experienced music teachers—those with at least 15 years of teaching—say that being shown how they have affected the life of a student has been a positive and career changing event in their teaching (Cutietta & Thompson, 2000).

Music teachers are hopeful that a new generation of young people will have opportunities to participate in many different kinds of musical offerings and come to appreciate the varied musical activities of those around them. Music teachers are also eager to learn about others—their interests and desires—as well as to teach from a solid base of musical understanding. The majority of music teachers, however, realize that there is more to teaching music than the simple transmission of a teacher's knowledge and musical skills to another less knowledgeable or less skilled other. Rather, to paraphrase Seymour Sarason, music teachers know that the stuff we traditionally call music—the activities, facts, skills and concepts that make up the subject matter—only attains meaning when teaching processes take into account the 'child's curiosity, interests, conceptual level, and need to act on the world' (1993, p. 242). In other words, we not only teach music, we teach people.

Personal Influences

Although these generalities about what music educators value in teaching are important, it is also important to look at the particularities of how you have come to be where you are in your life. What has influenced your decision to be a music teacher? As Eunice Boardman (1992) notes, no mind is a blank slate when it comes to what we believe is good music teaching. That is, each of us comes to teaching with a personal perspective—a stage, so to speak, on which we build our understanding of the way the world is. Whether our beliefs remain unexamined or have been explicitly articulated, our personal perspective forms the basis on which we justify, make sense of, and unify our actions and thoughts. In addition, the beliefs, expectations, ideals, and influences of others also inform our perspective. Collectively, our experiences function as filters in building our images of teaching and learning.

There are many stories that deserve telling and many stories that we can share that will help us make sense of learning to teach, especially if we use a framework that allows us to look at the teaching and learning process as a multidimensional phenomenon. A personal orientation to music teaching and learning looks at all participants in the educational process from a dynamic perspective. That is, as we continue to deepen and extend our knowledge of self and others, it is always in the service of more and better teaching. We are not only present oriented; we are also past and future oriented in our thinking about teaching. Most importantly, a personal orientation framework helps us to understand ourselves; it helps us to understand the music experiences we value, the places and situations that support learning, and the ways we can help others. Think about the influential people in your life who have made an impact on your decision to teach music. Also, think about influential experiences and events that have occurred in your life that may have contributed to your decision to becoming a music teacher.

References

Boardman, E. (1992). New environments for teacher education. *Music Educators Journal, 79*(2), 41–43.

Cutietta, R. A., & Thompson, L. K. (2000). Voices of experience speak on music teaching. *Music Educators Journal, 87*(3), 40–43, 51.

Sarason, S. B. (1993). *The case for change: Rethinking the preparation of educators.* San Francisco, CA: Jossey-Bass.

Summary

Campbell encourages us to consider our own personal story of musical engagement as the foundation of our teaching identity as a music teacher. This is important for music teaching as it is more than just the transmission of knowledge. It is about life itself. Your personal 'orientation' to music teaching and learning is part of a dynamic process that is constantly changing and developing. It is important for us to keep thinking and reflecting on these things. As we do so, we will continue to refine and hone our own view about what music teaching is and why it is important that we do it.

Questions to consider

1. Spend a few moments thinking through the question Campbell raises at the end of the extract. Who are the influential people in your life who have made an impact on your decision to teach music? What influential experiences and events have occurred in your life that have contributed to your decision to become a music teacher?

2. If you have taught music for a while, what events or experiences have you had recently that have challenged you, personally, and made you reconsider why you teach music? (These events may have caused you difficulties but they may also have been life-affirming).

Think deeper

Alan Peshkin's work (Peshkin 1988) highlighted the requirement for any observer of, or participator in, educational events to be 'meaningfully attentive' (p. 17) to their own subjectivity as they conduct and reflect on their teaching or research activities. Peshkin described subjectivity as a 'garment that cannot be removed' which has the capability to 'filter, skew, shape, block, transform, construe, and misconstrue what transpires from the outset of a research project to its culmination in a written statement' (ibid, p. 17). His writing went on to helpfully demonstrate this process through the identification of six subjective 'I's' that he perceived and reflected on during an extended piece of educational research at Riverview High School in California.

Peshkin's 'I's' were drawn from a range of sources, including:

- His own belief and value systems;
- His experiences of a particular environment or place;
- His ongoing experiences of life within the particular school;
- The wider community and the relationships that he, and other members of his family, established within their community.

Peshkin saw these subjectives as falling into two main categories: 'Situational Subjectives' (ibid, p. 18) that changed from place to place and were a subset of the whole array of what might be called 'Intrinsic Subjectives' that made up his reflective 'being'.

Investigations

Peshkin's approach can help you shed new light on your experiences as a teacher and the choices that you make whilst engaged in the activity of teaching. Reflect further on the two questions above. Rather than dismissing your own subjectivity, can you use and embrace it in a positive way to help identify key 'subjective I's' of your own that have shaped your actions as a teacher?

Use the locations that Peshkin describes to help identify these (e.g. your own belief and value system, your understanding of 'music' as a subject area, the school ethos or environment within which you work, etc). Also, remember that some of these 'I's' may be transient (situational) and change from place to place; others will be 'intrinsic', part of you, and will remain with you wherever you work and live.

Later on in this chapter, I will explore briefly with you one of my own subjective I's from a particular point in my career.

Think wider

The Musical Futures initiative has cropped up at several times throughout this book. It is one of the largest and most influential pieces of curriculum and pedagogical development in music education in recent years. Finney's article (Finney 2010) explores how this particular model of curriculum development relates to the emerging identity of three newly qualified teachers in a very thoughtful case study. As Finney writes, uncritical adoption of the pedagogies within the Musical Futures model would be detrimental and achieve little. So, a degree of criticality is required and this extends to one's own sense of identity within a specific teaching context. Finney continues:

> The cases of Anna, Sam and Jon illustrate the complexity of the journey through this hugely significant stage of music teacher identity formation. What they teach us is that, while a full and fair meeting with music curriculum developments such as Musical Futures will have impact, the outcomes will never be easy to intention.

> (ibid, p. 2)

I would encourage you to get hold of this freely available case study and read through the three short accounts drawn from the work of Anna, Sam and Jon. They make fascinating reading and demonstrate very succinctly and clearly how the individually emergent identity of a music teacher is an intricate blend of background, context and pedagogy.

Extract 11.2

Source

Green, L. (2001) *How Popular Musicians Learn: A way ahead for music education.* Aldersot, Ashgate, pp. 214–216.

Introduction

Finney's comments on the formation of music teachers' identities through the Musical Futures project leads us to the work of Lucy Green in our next extract. Here, in the final paragraphs of her influential book *How Popular Musicians Learn*, Green reflects on the roles and responsibilities that music teachers have within an informal music pedagogy.

Key words and phrases

Musical Futures, informal, pedagogy, identity

Extract

But perhaps one of the most needed and most helpful ways to move forwards, for those teachers who believe in the potential of informal popular music learning practices, but who have *not* had personal experience of them, is to put themselves into the position of young popular musicians, and try out some informal learning practices for themselves.

In the case of teachers who are classically trained, this could involve, for example, purposive listening to a recording of music that they like, along with exact copying or looser imitation, either on an instrument that they can already play or one that is new to them. It could also involve attempts to reproduce music known through enculturation, in the absence of a recording to copy. During the time that I was working on the present book I occasionally undertook such tasks, not as a formal part of the research but for my own interest as a classically trained musician. In the process, I experienced a heightening of enjoyment and satisfaction in music-making, as well as significant improvements to my aural and improvisatory abilities. I think the main cause of the improvements was that, although such activities were not completely new to me, the research gave me greater confidence in what I was doing. I became less worried and put off by mistakes, more prepared to explore and less concerned to have a theoretical understanding of the harmonies, modes or other aspects of the music I was playing. With this new confidence and relative lack of inhibition, I found myself persisting with tasks, especially ones I was uncertain about, for longer than previously, and improvements soon began to occur above and beyond what I would have expected. Not only music-making itself, but also listening was enhanced, as such activities are tremendous ear-openers to a range of musical details and increase appreciation of the technique and 'feel' of the musicians being copied. They opened my ears far more than I had anticipated, to nuances, harmonies, voicings, timbre, mix and many subtleties on the original recordings. Björnberg, another classically trained musician and lecturer, made a similar point cited earlier (p. 201) when he wrote that the 'musicness' of even apparently 'poor' music may be discovered through playing the music oneself, adding 'as borne out by my own personal experience' (Björnberg 1993, p. 21).

Not only teachers who are trained musicians, but primary generalists who have little or no background in either informal music learning practices or formal music education, and who feel committed to music in their classrooms, may also benefit from trying out some informal learning practices for themselves. Such practices might include purposive listening, copying, and singing or playing along to records, even if at first this means little more than tapping a rhythm on the furniture. Again, further research is required to ascertain the feasibility and efficacy of this proposal, but it seems at least reasonable to suggest that such practices could enhance the confidence and enjoyment of many generalist teachers regarding music, help them to develop a more relaxed attitude towards music-making with children in their classes, and put them in touch with children's own music-making practices. For those music teachers who are popular musicians and who acquired their own skills and knowledge informally, noticing how they went about their own learning, respecting it and encouraging many aspects of it in their own pupils, alongside the added benefits of formal music education, should perhaps be regarded as a normal part of their teaching methods.

Formal music education and informal music learning have for centuries been sitting side by side, with little communication between them. On one hand, informal music learning practices have missed out on some of the skills and knowledge which formal music education can help learners to develop. As indicated by the musicians in this study, and as several others have told me, many popular musicians feel keenly their lack of formal education. They would like to be able to read music as well as improvise and play by ear; they would like to know a variety of technical terms. On the other hand, formal music education has not always enhanced either the music learning or the enjoyment of those who experience it and has often turned even highly motivated young popular musicians, and undoubtedly other potential musicians, away. By opening out our understanding that there are a multitude of ways in which to acquire musical skills and knowledge, surely we can reach out to more learners and reveal a much higher number of people with the capacity to make music for their own pleasure, a larger proportion of learners who would warrant being 'counted as musical' within formal settings, and a more open attitude towards music-making both on the part of those who specialize in it and on the part of amateur networks of families, friends and others in the community.

Playing music of one's own choice, with which one identifies personally, operating both as a performer and a composer with like-minded friends, and having fun doing it must be high priorities in the quest for increasing numbers of young people to benefit from a music education which makes music not merely available, but meaningful, worthwhile and participatory. Not only do identity, friendship and enjoyment go hand-in-hand with motivation, but they are also intrinsically and unavoidably connected to particular ways of learning: playing by ear, making both close copies and loose imitations of recordings by professional musicians who are respected and admired, transforming what is 'picked up' into a piece of music, improvising, jamming and composing with friends, attempting to create music that both fits in with and is distinct from the sounds one enjoys hearing around, eschewing any necessary concern with regular practice or with technique, and working with peers in the absence of a teacher, lecturer, curriculum, syllabus or system of assessment. The values that accompany such practices emphasize not only cooperation and teamwork, but 'feel', 'spirit' and idiosyncrasy, which are applauded at a level beyond the recognition of 'correct' technique or correspondence with formalized criteria; the development of passion for music; a broad knowledge, understanding and appreciation of a variety of music; commitment and the capacity to gain enjoyment and satisfaction from playing even the simplest music with friends. Surely formal music educators can create a teaching culture which recognizes and rewards such practices and such criteria of success, in the hope of some future day, restoring to people what is already ours: practical musical involvement for the majority.

Summary

Green acknowledges that music teachers have a range of background musical experiences that shape their perspectives and pedagogies as teachers. The informal learning styles explored within her book may be foreign to many teachers who were themselves taught through a formal music education, perhaps in a Western classical tradition. Green's response to these teachers is to ask them to put themselves in the position of young popular musicians and try out some of the informal practices for themselves. This, she argues, can lead to a greater degree of appreciation for a broader range of musical styles and traditions and a greater degree of empathy for the ways in which other musicians learn.

The relationship between formal and informal music education is not 'either/ or'. There are strengths and weaknesses in both approaches; musicians who have learnt under either 'system' can see, and would benefit from, the strengths in the other. The broader aims of a music education (e.g. to understand and appreciate a variety of music, to gain enjoyment and satisfaction from playing with others, etc.) should be the aim for all music educators whatever their pedagogical approach.

Questions to consider

1. Written in 2001, Green closes her book with the assertion that practical musical involvement for the majority needs to be restored. To what extent has this occurred over the last ten years?

2. How can an effective musical pedagogy bridge the perceived gap between formal and informal approaches to music education? What would a musical pedagogy that embraces them as a whole look or sound like?

Investigations

Within the United Kingdom, recent Government policies have stated that every child should have the opportunity to learn a musical instrument and sing. The creation of new music education hubs from September 2012 is designed to support this policy aim. To what extent are these policies successful in your area? What is the role of the individual music teacher within these new arrangements? What role are schools playing?

Think deeper

Moving beyond immediate locality, Green's more recent work (Green 2011) has picked up on these themes of teaching, learning and identity in a global context. In a collection of 20 chapters from authors all over the world, the importance of teacher identity is explored in interesting ways. Green highlights a number of factors in these stories, not least the 'push-and-pull effect of globalisation versus localisation' as mediated through electronic and cultural forces (ibid, p. 13). However, individual family and institutional forces are also considered (ibid, p. 16), along with gender (ibid, p.17) and much more besides. The stories make fascinating reading. But as Green indicates in the final paragraphs of her introduction:

> All the contributors to the book would agree that, as music educators and music-education researchers, we should approach issues connecting musical identity, teaching, and learning tentatively. Among them, the chapters show how different are the *processes* of musical identity formation, and how varied the *contents* of musical identity for individuals and groups in different places; and they illustrate how closely woven musical identity formation is with music-learning and/or music teaching. They point to a need for music educators and researchers to deepen our understanding of the complexity and multiplicity of the influences on children's, teenagers', adult-learners', and our own musical tastes, knowledge, and skills.
>
> (ibid, p. 18).

This reminder about the provisionality in our thinking in this area is an important antidote to an over-zealous approach to navel-gazing! Too much time spent looking inwards at the processes behind how our musical identities have emerged, or their current contents, can have a detrimental effect on our abilities to look outwards. Green's focus in the above extract on placing ourselves in the footsteps of another is as timely and relevant today as the day it was written. Reflecting on the lives and identities of our pupils can be highly productive as the following story shows.

Think wider

Tom's story is unremarkable (Savage 2011). As a young guitarist, he did not enjoy his guitar lessons and became unmotivated, ultimately ceasing to take lessons. The 'failure' (in his words) of his guitar teacher led him to find alternatives, to reject that teacher's pedagogical approach completely, and utilise the potential of the Internet as a social, collaborative learning environment. In previous generations, perhaps, Tom would have given up playing the guitar. Today, he is a highly proficient guitarist. However, would he have learnt more, and perhaps become a more expert guitarist, if he had the benefit of both kinds of teaching?

Arendt, much more eloquently, puts it like this:

> Education is the point at which we decide whether we love the world enough to assume responsibility for it and by the same token save it from ruin which, except for renewal, except for the coming of the new and young, would be inevitable. And education, too, is where we [adults and/or teachers] decide whether we love our children enough not to expel them from our world and leave them to their own devices, nor to strike from their hands their chance of undertaking something new, something unforeseen by us, but to prepare them in advance for the task of renewing a common world.
>
> (Arendt 1961, p.196)

Arendt's words are as relevant today as they were in 1961. Note the responsibility placed on the role of teachers to make decisions on behalf of their pupils and to make these decisions based on their care for them as children. Central to Arendt's thesis is the notion that teachers have access to knowledge and ideas which their pupils do not and that they know something about the best way to introduce these things. But, also notice that she suggests that there are things that are, as yet, unforeseen by children and teachers. Neither group can predict the futures that these children will face, the new jobs and opportunities it might contain, or the types of practical skills or understanding they will need to succeed. However, teachers do know, Arendt says, that we can prepare children for those future tasks through a careful exemplification and study of the world as it is today. She argued that pupils are best prepared for their future lives by teachers who educate them to understand the world that we know. Or, in Furedi's words, 'there is a need to preserve the past for the sake of the new' (Furedi 2009, p. 42).

These ideas are a cautionary note for all teachers. Teachers have a solemn responsibility, and the obligations of such a job require a degree of seriousness that should never be forgotten. Central to these considerations are the development of an appropriate pedagogy (hence our deliberations in Chapters 3, 4 and 5). As this book comes to a close, our final extract will reconsider how your teaching can become a source of constant fascination and a site for genuinely creative activity throughout your whole career.

Extract 11.3

Source

Fautley, M. and Savage, J. (2007) *Creativity in Secondary Education.* Exeter, Learning Matters, pp. 24–28.

Introduction

Teaching can be either a creative or a non-creative activity. My hope is that you will want it to be a creative one! To this end, our final extract is drawn from a practical book that explores what learning to teach creatively is all about. In the following extract nine key points are exemplified.

Key words and phrases

pedagogy, creativity, identity

Extract

We suggest that learning to teach creatively is a life-long task. But it is one that should be started early. Learning to teach creatively includes many elements, including those listed below.

- **being an inspiration;**
- **knowing your subject inside out;**
- **carrying on being a learner;**
- **making connections: how does your subject relate to other subjects?**
- **developing high expectations;**
- **stimulating curiosity;**
- **being an encourager;**
- **balancing lessons and allowing time for students to be creative;**
- **finding your own teaching style.**

1. Being an inspiration

Everyone remembers their good teachers, the ones that inspired them to love a particular subject or the ones that motivated and encouraged them when learning was difficult. What is it about these teachers that make them stick in your mind, even many years after you have left their classes?

Also, perhaps unfortunately, everyone remembers those teachers that didn't inspire, motivate or encourage them! For me, physics was one of those subjects I just didn't understand while at school. Imagine my surprise recently when, while working on an art and science project, I met an astrophysicist called Tim. He works at Jodrell Bank Radio Telescope (part of the University of Manchester) in Cheshire. He inspired me about space, in particular how planets and stars are born, how solar winds blow across the solar system and, of course, the sheer scale of the whole thing. On a recent visit, Tim informed me he had discovered a new star and that he was going to get the chance to name it! I enquired as to the whereabouts of this star.

If the earth were here*

and the sun were here*,

then whereabouts was his star? Approximately 3,000 kilometres away in that ↓ direction!

Now that got my attention! I wish that Tim had been my physics teacher at school. He has a way of presenting the complicated facts of astrophysics in a way that even I can understand and get excited about.

So, the first important point in this section is that we, as 'experts' in our curriculum fields, need to present the knowledge of that field in a way that inspires our students.

2. Knowing your subject inside out

In order to be an inspiration to your students, you must be completely familiar with your own subject area. This will allow you to concentrate fully on the delivery of that knowledge within the classroom. This is as true for teaching at Key Stage 3 as it is for teaching at Key Stage 5. Regardless of curriculum frameworks and modes of delivery that you will be required to work within, the students' initial source of inspiration and knowledge is you. If you are inspiring then your students will be inspired; if you are knowledgeable and can impart that knowledge in an inspirational way they will be encouraged to learn. But as we will go on to see in Chapter 3, while just knowing about your subject is vital, creating opportunities for pupils to be actively involved in the knowledge associated with your subject is equally important. This will involve you in planning carefully and setting appropriate learning objectives that allow for and facilitate opportunities for pupils to be creative learners.

3. Carrying on being a learner

Of course, all of our subjects are in a constant state of change. We never know it all. To teach creatively, it will be important for you to maintain an active interest in your subject area and the current issues and concerns that are being raised within it.

As an example, the QCA's recent consultation (*Futures – meeting the challenge*) has many interesting points of departure and application for teachers. Not least, is the challenge to explore and utilise the potential of new technologies to link subject areas within the curriculum in new ways:

> *In a technology-rich world we need to review and modernise what and how we learn. Imagine how a graphic designer works today compared with 30 years ago. What should a modernised music, art or design curriculum be like? They may use technology as a tool for thinking, making or doing. Technology needs to be used more effectively to help develop learners' enquiry skills, logical reasoning, analytical thinking and creativity. It should support individualised and independent learning, while encouraging wider communication and collaborative learning.*
>
> (QCA, 2005)

The QCA promotes the use of technology as a *force for change* in developing a curriculum fit for the twenty-first century. It is clear from recent QCA statements that such 'joined-up curriculum thinking' should be a priority as teachers not only seek to develop teaching skills but also the more general development of students' creativity, thinking skills, ability to communicate and ability to collaborate. We will return to this work in Chapter 5 when we consider how ICT can help us teach creatively and teach for creativity.

4. Making connections: how does your subject relate to other subjects?

While it is vital that you are able to make constructive links within your own subject area it is imperative that these also extend beyond to other related subjects. Creativity in one subject area does not exist in isolation from creativity in other subject areas. Perhaps this is a strength of much educational practice in the primary sector, where teachers have a little more flexibility to move around and between subject areas? Working within secondary education, the danger is to isolate your own subject from other related, or even non-related, disciplines in such a way that any potential creative spark that students bring with them to your lessons gets extinguished pretty quickly.

You may not feel as comfortable allowing students to develop their knowledge of other subjects within your own lessons. You may also be put under significant pressure to cover so much curriculum content the only practical consequence is that you will think that there is not any time within your lessons to allow for this kind of 'diversion'. Both of these concerns may be legitimate, but try and resist this kind of pressure. Teaching creativity must acknowledge that creativity itself is not limited to specific subject domains. In learning to teach creatively you will have to make connections across the curriculum in such a way that empowers you as a teacher to teach your subject in a new way, perhaps even in ways that you were not taught yourself! Incidentally, this will also create a more inclusive curriculum and educational environment for students, as we will consider in Chapter 6.

5. Developing high expectations

How often do you hear people moaning about today's young people? On occasions it is all too easy to disparage one's own students and put them down in front of other teachers. Try and avoid this at all costs. You have a tremendous opportunity and privilege. An important part of teaching creatively is having a high expectation of your pupils, both individual and collectively.

Spend some time getting inspired about what your pupils might be able to achieve. As a first step, why don't you visit the Creative Partnerships website and read some of the stories of other teachers and students who have worked on a range of different projects (www.creative-partnerships.com) in all curriculum areas. These stories can be a constant source of encouragement and a real inspiration to us as teachers about what young people can achieve given creative teaching and opportunities for developing their own creativity.

6. Stimulating curiosity

Stimulating curiosity is a vital part of teaching creatively. What is it that is particularly interesting about your subject? What might capture a Year 7 student's imagination? Are there any peculiarities or distinctive elements that you could use to engage them early on in their studies with you? Capturing and maintaining a student's interest is a prerequisite for effective teaching and learning. We believe that the majority of children are naturally curious about new things and you should seek to build on this in your teaching.

Additionally, do not fall into the trap of thinking that the only learning a student will do within your subject is within your classroom sessions. As teachers, we are constantly amazed at how students take ideas from our lessons and work through them in their own time, maybe individually or with groups of friends. The increasing availability of high-quality educational materials on the internet has revolutionised how children learn independently. Make links in your lessons to materials online that they will be able to follow up. Get away from issuing only written homework (that you will have to mark!), and encompass a broader range of resources to stimulate your students' curiosity for your subject.

7. Being an encourager

The best teachers are encouragers. There is a direct link here to teaching for creativity. Make sure that through teaching creatively you empower pupils by building them up rather than knocking them down. Communicate a 'can do' attitude in your subject rather than a 'this is difficult or complicated' one. As we will discuss in detail in Chapter 6, Craft's notion of *little c creativity* (Craft, Jeffrey and Leibling, 2001, p56) is built around the notion of *possibility thinking* as a way of life (note that this is not 'impossibility thinking'). We should apply this and state that teaching creatively is built around the notion of celebrating students' positive creative achievements.

8. Balancing lessons and allowing time for students to be creative

All teachers would like more time to teach their subject. Learning to make best use of the time that you have is an important element of teaching. Within your lessons you should seek to include a broad range of activities and opportunities for pupils to work together towards creative outcomes. Students will need the chance to work independently and learn the skills of working in a group with a range of roles. The creative processes that occur during your lessons will be facilitated by this process which we will explore in more detail in following chapters.

9. Finding your own teaching style

Finally, teaching in this way is a highly individual activity. There are many pressures on you as a trainee teacher and you may well feel that you are being told to teach in a particular way. You may even disagree on the advice you are being given! Teacher training is a process of assimilating advice, experimenting with new approaches to teaching and then evaluating the outcomes. The point here is that there is a real danger of you teaching your subject in the way that you were taught. This could be good or bad (or somewhere in between), but either way it is not based on you! Teaching creatively requires you to teach your subject as you – not as some reconstructed memory figure.

There are significant pieces of educational research that explore this issue of teacher identity (Coldron and Smith, 1999; Hargreaves, 1994; Maclure, 1993; Stronach et al., 2002). There is not the time or space to explore these in any detail here. Rather, we will leave this section with the following advice. You may well be the only geographer, artist, musician, mathematician, etc. that your pupils will have direct access to week by week. What a tremendous privilege it is to have a group of young people looking to you for challenges, inspiration and motivation.

Summary

This extract includes some practical advice about how to teach creatively. The key points covered include:

- Being an inspiration;
- Knowing your subject inside-out;
- Carrying on being a learner;
- Making connections with other subjects;
- Developing high expectations of yourself and your pupils;
- Stimulating your pupils' curiosity;
- Making sure you encourage your pupils;
- Balancing lessons and allowing time for pupils to be creative within them;
- Finding your own pedagogical style.

Questions to consider

1. Which of the above nine points caught your attention? Spend a few moments thinking through how they might apply within the context of your music teaching.

Think deeper

As we discussed under Extract 11.1, by adopting Alan Peshkin's approach to the construction of subjective I's, I engaged in a process of reflection on my experiences as a teacher (Savage 2007). I sought to reflect back on a portion of my career and ask myself whether I could identify any 'intrinsic subjective I's' of my own. In doing this, I hoped that I could, like Peshkin, 'create an illuminating, empowering personal statement that attunes me to where self and subject are intertwined' (Peshkin 1988, p. 20).

The five subjective I's that I identified were:

1. The Musically Conservative I
2. The Musically Radical I
3. The Pedagogically Inclusive I
4. The Technological-Enthusiast I
5. The Artistically Appeasing I

Whilst there is not time or space to go into a lot of detail about each of these here, I wanted to close this book by a brief consideration of the final one: the 'Artistically Appeasing I'.

Out of the five subjective I's that I identified, this is the one that I found the most difficult to define. But, contrastingly, I was very clear about where it came from. It came as a result of a seminar given during my PGCE course by Ben Higham, a community musician and founder member of Community Music East, who challenged us with the words of John Cage:

> Art, instead of being an object made by one person, is a process set in motion by a group of people. Art's socialised. It isn't someone saying something but a group of people doing things, giving everyone (including those involved) the opportunity to have experiences they would not otherwise have had.
>
> (Cage 1968, p. 151)

Through his seminar my view of what counted as art or music was challenged at a fundamental level. Rather than being focused solely on artistic objects, he asked us to value the processes by which these objects were formed, as well as the experiences that we had whilst working through these processes. As a classically trained percussionist and pianist, in many ways my career to that point had been about faithfully recreating artistic objects for others to enjoy. I had paid little attention to enjoying the process of making or recreating them, to the extent that practising and making music became a chore that I felt I could live without.

Yet I think that here were the seeds of my belief as a teacher; that engaging pupils in authentic musical processes is as important as creating fine musical products for our children. The process may be even more important than the product, particularly when pupils have enjoyed the experiences contained within the process. This statement cut right against everything that I was taught and valued for many years. My musicality was judged against performance outcomes and I succeeded as a musician because my musical 'products' were considered acceptable by the wider musical community.

This is why I have called this final 'subjective I' Artistically Appeasing. My dictionary gives three definitions for the word 'appease':

1. to bring to a state of peace or quiet;
2. to cause to subside;
3. to pacify or conciliate, especially: to buy off (an aggressor) by concessions usually at the sacrifice of principles.

My Artistically Appeasing I believes deeply in the genuine artistic practice of young people's classroom work at a philosophical, aesthetic and educational level. I still love the music of the Western classical tradition and have sought to pass on that passion to my pupils in various ways. But I believe that the process by which these convictions have been appeased and, in a sense, broadened, has made my approach to teaching more inclusive and tolerant of the various pathways by which pupils can come to know and understand musical knowledge and develop personal ways of expression.

Think wider

Five years have passed since I conducted that process of reflective thinking. In reading through that paper (Savage 2007) I was struck by how many thoughts still ring true today. However, it was a sad indictment of me, and my own music education, that I got to that point, prior to teaching, where music itself became insignificant and, in part, an irrelevance in my life.

As teachers of music, it is vital that our love for music itself is sustained and cherished throughout our careers. Teaching music can be an isolating and draining experience. We need the practical support of other colleagues around us, physically or virtually, to help us through those difficult times.

But we also need the intellectual, artistic and conceptual challenges. Just doing the same old thing is not going to be good enough. I hope that this book has provided you with a series of starting points, springboards, for your own thinking and practice of music education.

Coda

As I wrote in the Introduction, this is a personal selection of authors and ideas that have shaped my career in music education to this point. If I wrote this book again in 25 years' time, it would not include the same set of contents. However, I do believe that there are general principles, ideas and challenges for us all in the various pieces of scholarly work presented here. Please use what you can, ignore what you consider an irrelevance, but whatever you do – keep thinking hard about what it means to teach music musically.

References

Arendt, H. (1961) *Between Past and Future: Six exercises in political thought*. London, Faber & Faber.

Cage, J. (1968) *Silence*. Cambridge, MA, MIT Press.

Finney, J. (2010) 'Musical Futures and Newly Qualified Teachers: A case study'. http://www.musicalfutures.org.uk/media/resources/musicalfutures_live/documents/resource/27542/ITE%20case%20study.pdf [last accessed 12/05/12].

Furedi, F. (2009) *Wasted: Why education isn't educating*. London, Continuum.

Green, L. (ed.) (2011) *Learning, Teaching and Identity: Voices across cultures*. Bloomington, Indiana University Press.

Peshkin, A. (1988) 'In Search of Subjectivity – One's own'. *Educational Researcher* 17:7, 17–22.

Savage, J. (2011) 'Tom's Story: Developing music education with technology'. *Journal of Music, Technology and Education* 4:3, 2 & 3, 217–226.

Savage, J. (2007) 'Reflecting Through Peshkin's I's'. *International Journal of Music Education* 25:3, 193–204.

Index

References to figures are shown in *italics*. References to tables are shown in **bold**.